Cat.

50 YEARS IN TEXAS POLITICS

FORMER GOVERNORS Daniel, Connally, Smith, Governor-elect Clements, and Governor Briscoe attended a reception honoring Author Morehead at his retirement as *Dallas News* Capitol Bureau Chief in Austin in 1978. Former Governor Shivers, out of state, sent congratulations.

— *Author's files*

50 YEARS IN TEXAS POLITICS

— *From Roosevelt to Reagan*
— *From The Fergusons to Clements*

By Richard Morehead

EAKIN PRESS

Illustrations herein were provided largely by *The Dallas Morning News,* including reprints for cartoons by John Knott and Bill DeOre.

TABLE OF CONTENTS

Foreword v
Prologue vii

CHAPTER I

The New Deal. 1
The Allred Years 19
The O'Daniel Era 30
Disenchantment With the New Deal 43
Senator O'Daniel 52

CHAPTER II

Mister Coke 61
Postwar Politics and Government 71
"Landslide Lyndon" Johnson Awarded
            United States Senate Seat 79
The Shivers-Jester Reforms 85
Governor Allan Shivers. 90
Truman As President 96

CHAPTER III

The Tidelands Rebellion and Civil Rights Fight 101
The 1950s—State Government Grows; So Do Taxes 107
Civil Rights Becomes a Dominant Issue. 111
Party Loyalty Becomes a Political Issue. 119
Little Rock, Sputnik, and Trouble in the Schools 129
Ralph Yarborough Keeps His Senate Seat 134

CHAPTER IV

Johnson and Kennedy 143

Tower and the Republicans Emerge 149
The Kennedy Presidency 152
John Bowden Connally Elected Governor 153
1963: Kennedy Assassinated; Johnson Becomes President . . 161
President Johnson 166
The 1964 Elections 175
1965: A Banner Legislative Year 181
The Vietnam War and Great Society 185

CHAPTER V

Republicans Begin a Comeback 191
Reagan Moves to Center Stage 197
1967 — A Poor Year for Johnson and Connally 201
The Emergence of Preston Smith 205
1968 — A Year of Turmoil 214
LBJ Comes Home to Texas 223
Preston Smith, the Governor 226
National Politics: Back Toward the Center 229
Dolph Briscoe Elected 232

CHAPTER VI

Nixon and Watergate 241
Briscoe Takes Over 246
Shake-up in Washington 252
Four-year Terms 256
Political Temperatures Cool in 1975-1976 259
Born-again Jimmy Carter 262
The Political Climate Changes 269
Rising Republicans — Clements and Tower 275
Reagan Wins the Presidency 285

CHAPTER VII

Texas 2000 297
The Government Ahead 308
Index 313

Foreword

This book is dedicated to those who make the American system of government work—the honest and conscientious public officials, public employees, voters and media members. Theirs often is a criticized and thankless task, but their numbers are legion. Special interests, bias, ignorance and downright dishonesty — both financial and intellectual — are the enemies for which those closest to the government must be eternally vigilant.

Research on this book, based on half a century of writing about and observing the government, also has given me a much greater appreciation of libraries and librarians.

I am indebted greatly to my colleagues on *The Dallas Morning News* — its library staff, photographers, cartoonists, and editors for unselfish support. Most of the cartoons are from the late John Knott.

Likewise, help was given cheerfully and professionally by friends at the University of Texas-Austin's Barker History Center, the State Legislative Reference Library, State Archives, Austin-Travis County Collection at the Austin Public Library, and to the audio-visual staff of the Lyndon B. Johnson Presidential Library in Austin.

My special thanks go to Bob Bain, an Austin friend of long writing experience, for expert editorial assistance. Several others contributed to the writing and illustration of this book, whose sole purpose is to improve our understanding of politics and government during the past fifty years.

Richard M. Morehead

JUDGE W. ST. JOHN GARWOOD presents watch to Morehead on behalf of Texas Judicial Council for twenty years service, August 2, 1967, in the Texas House of Representatives. Morehead served 31 years on the Council, longer than anyone in history. — *Author's files*

MOREHEAD RECEIVING State Bar Awards in 1963. Left to right are Morehead, Bar President Leon Jaworski, and Dennis Hoover, also of The Dallas News.

Prologue

The fifty years between the beginning of Franklin D. Roosevelt's Presidency and the second year of Ronald Reagan's administration has seen the political pendulum of America swing from right to left, then back toward the center.

This book attempts to explain these vast changes, both at the state and national levels, and to relate them to Texas and its citizens.

The account begins with the second and final term of Governor Miriam A. Ferguson who with her husband, James E. Ferguson, held the state's highest office four times. The Fergusons were traditional Southern Democrats, products of an agrarian economy.

The history extends through the first term of Governor William P. Clements, the state's first Republican Governor in more than a century. Clements' election represents the state's transition into an urban industrial and petrochemical-based society.

Reflected here are the effects of the Great Depression of the 1930s and smaller economic recessions later; the tragedies of World War II, the Korean and Vietnam Wars; the great civil rights struggle which ended legal segregation of races in the United States but never succeeded in satisfying either the white majority or ethnic minorities anywhere in the nation.

As with all histories, this one has a viewpoint, through the eyes of a newspaper observer who saw much of it happen and knew most of the principals.

Readers will notice this history sometimes varies from the usual chronology of events. This is done so the inception of a program such as school busing for racial integration, and the consequences, can be considered together.

SENATE MAJORITY leader Johnson, former President Truman, and House Speaker Sam Rayburn (left to right) attend John Nance Garner's birthday party at Uvalde, Nov. 22, 1958.

— *Photo from LBJ Library*

1

THE NEW DEAL

On a dark and dreary January day in 1933, Mrs. Miriam A. Ferguson was inaugurated as governor of Texas with this Valentine wish in her address to the joint legislative session:

"If you love me as I love you
Nothing can cut our love in two."

But on the more serious side, the lady governor added, "You and I take up the most serious and desperate task that ever confronted the people of our state.

"On every hand there is want and need and hunger that has already led to despair and desperation. Hope is nearly gone. The burdens of government are falling heavily on the masses. Reduction of taxes must come and come quickly or the government will surely fall. . . ." [1]

The government, of course, did not fall although taxes have risen astronomically in the half-century since Mrs. Ferguson uttered these grim words.

Yet some of the same rhetoric permeated the 1980 elections, particularly on the national level, when conservatives swept into office with the cry for budget-cutting and less government.

Mrs. Ferguson was beginning her second and final term as governor. Her husband, James E. Ferguson, had served one term and part of another, starting in 1915 when the chief executive's salary was $4,000 annually. For the fiscal year 1983, the salary was set at $85,500 a year.

On Saturday, March 4, 1933, less than two months after Mrs. Ferguson became governor of Texas, Franklin D. Roosevelt

1

FDR STARTS to tame the economics monster.

— Cartoon by John Knott in 1933,
reprinted from The Dallas Morning News

was sworn in as president of the United States, with John Nance Garner of Uvalde, Texas, as his vice president.

Since the stock market crash of October 29, 1929, the nation's economy had plunged downward. Dozens of banks had closed. Factories and workers fell idle and thirteen million Americans were unemployed. Farmers could hardly sell their crops and livestock, and the prices were deplorable.

Into this scene of crisis and frustration stepped FDR as a hero figure and a spellbinder on radio broadcasts.

". . . First of all, let me assert my firm belief that the only thing we have to fear is fear itself," [2] President Roosevelt consoled citizens huddled around radio sets, "—nameless, unreasoning and unjustified terror which paralyzes needed effort to convert retreat into advance."[3]

The president pledged to ask Congress, if necessary, for emergency economic authority "as great as that would be given to me if we were in fact invaded by a foreign foe."

With that, President Roosevelt launched a legislative, political, and even judicial offensive that came to be called "The New Deal."

Within the next one hundred days, Roosevelt with Garner's expert legislative help, guided fifteen major economic laws to enactment, and dazzled the formerly-distressed citizenry with radio speeches, press conferences, and other salesmanship.

Forty-eight years later, Republicans occupied the White House and the governor's office in Austin. Ronald Reagan, a seventy-year-old former motion picture actor and two-term governor of California, had succeeded Democrat Jimmy Carter as president, and George Bush of Houston, Texas, was his vice president.

The governor was William P. Clements, Jr. of Dallas, a self-made multimillionaire oil drilling executive, who ended more than one hundred years of Democratic domination of the Texas governorship by upsetting Attorney General John L. Hill in 1978.

The economic times were different, but the public thought its problems with inflation, unemployment, fuel shortages, and a huge federal government deficit posed almost the same hopeless situation as FDR encountered in 1933.

So President Reagan, ably assisted by Vice President Bush, a former Houston congressman, launched his own one hundred-day campaign to clean up the economic mess and set the country on firmer ground.

The *Christian Science Monitor* of May 1, 1981, headlined "100 Days tradition — Napoleon, FDR, and now Reagan."

The comparison with French Emperor Napoleon's escape from exile on Elba, and his one hundred and ten-day thwarted attempt to regain power, was hardly appropriate, however.

In his first one hundred days, President Reagan was to become the first U.S. president ever to survive an attempted assassination. Reagan's assailant was a Colorado youth considered to

3

be mentally ill, who shot the president in one lung and wounded three other men outside a Washington, D.C. hotel.

In Reagan's case, his cheerful endurance of the tragedy helped convince doubters that out of the West had come another hero figure.

Already, the amiable president was winning over his critics with a charismatic mastery of television. Even Reagan's hard-line liberal Democratic foes threw up their hands in their hopeless effort to preserve and defend the massive federal government programs developed during forty-eight years since FDR took office.

By the time Congress recessed its first session of the Reagan administration in August, it had ordered massive cuts in federal spending programs built up during the previous forty-eight years and enacted a three-year twenty-five percent income tax reduction estimated to save taxpayers nearly $748 billion.

This was accomplished over bitter opposition of the leadership in a House of Representatives with a Democratic majority, and with the help of more than forty dissident Southern conservatives led by Texas Representatives Phil Gramm, a Texas A&M economics professor from College Station; Kent Hance, a lawyer from Lubbock; and Charles Stenholm, a cotton farmer from Stamford, all serving second terms. These conservative dissenting Democrats were called "Boll Weevils."

The Reagan program had an easier time in the Senate, where a majority of Republicans had been elected in 1980.

In addition to his achievement of reversing a fifty-year trend toward larger and more expensive government, Reagan nominated the first woman in history to be associate justice of the United States Supreme Court.

She is Sandra Day O'Connor, an Arizona state appeals court judge and former state senator, where she became known as a conservative Republican. The appointment filled a campaign promise by Reagan and was generally applauded by the nation's legal profession, based on Judge O'Connor's qualifications.

As the Reagan administration won its first-year victory in Washington, David Broder, a respected columnist of the *Wash-*

PRESIDENT ROOSEVELT took office in 1933 asking Congress'
assistance in meeting the Great Depression.

— Reprinted from The Dallas Morning News

ington Post, observed that approval of the huge tax cut was an
historic day:

"... almost fifty years of Democratic-dominated economic
and social policy came to an end. The budget and tax victories of
President Reagan on both sides of the Capitol reversed the policies Congress had followed under every President from Franklin
D. Roosevelt to Jimmy Carter."

Further, said Broder, the disarray of the formerly-unbeat-
able Democratic Party was unmistakable, indicating that the
Grand Old Party after decades of defeat had learned again how
to win elections and administer the national government.

"That is an epochal development — and one that is likely to

5

shape, not just this year, but this epoch of American politics."[4]

In his second year, the nation's economy and President Reagan's standing in the popularity polls both declined. In President Roosevelt's case, high unemployment and the economic depression ended when the United States went to war with Germany, Italy, and Japan in 1941.

Reagan's insistence on decentralizing much of the government, reducing taxes, and tightening welfare programs were the opposite of the New Deal program of FDR. Proponents of "Reaganomics" called the president's program for the 1980s the best hope for salvaging the country's overheated and inflated economy.

Joseph C. Harsch, commentator for the *Christian Science Monitor,* made this analysis in 1982:

"It is too early yet to be sure that Mr. Reagan is on the wrong economic track. I have my doubts, and so do a lot of businessmen suffering from high interest rates and the prospect of more recession before the U.S. 'turns the corner' or 'can see the light at the end of the tunnel.'

"But two facts stand out about the American economic scene. One is the continued decline in inflation which is getting down toward a tolerable level. Many economists think that three or four percent inflation is probably good and some would consider five percent acceptable. That goal is in sight.

(Note: during the 1970s and 1980, inflation soared to annual rates in the ten to fifteen percent range.)

"Second, in spite of rising unemployment there are still nearly one hundred million gainfully employed in the U.S. and probably working a little harder today because they hear the hounds of unemployment sounding at their heels.

"Mr. Reagan started out with clear priorities. His goal was to cut the cost and size of the federal government and bring down inflation. He has never lost sight of those priorities. He is having substantial success with both. A lot of Americans, even among those who are being pinched in the process, agree that these two goals are of prime importance."[5]

Despite much criticism of his program from many Democrats and some other citizens, President Reagan remained personally popular and gained the reputation as being a "great communicator" for his ability to present his views on television. Radio was FDR's medium, and he too was able to "go to the people" directly without his statements being sifted first by reporters and commentators.

The Reagan administration's financial problems were magnified by his insistence that the nation rebuild its deteriorating military establishment to discourage the spread of Communism around the world.

In President Reagan, the United States definitely chose a leader of determination.

This 180-degree turn in the course of American politics and government policy coincided with my own career as a reporter of its events. The success of President Reagan's administration exceeded my expectations of what he would be able to accomplish, after nearly four decades of watching the gradual centralization of government, increasing regulation and taxation of the citizens, and a trend which otherwise could have led only to national bankruptcy.

As a country youth from Plainview in 1933, I was awed with my introduction to politics as a committee clerk in the Texas House of Representatives, where I watched Mrs. Ferguson's second inauguration.

Without knowing that thousands had been invited to the Governor's Inaugural Ball that night in Gregory Gymnasium at The University of Texas, I spent my entire first week's legislative salary of twelve dollars renting a tuxedo for the affair, only to find that few of the guests were so formally attired.

Mrs. Ferguson was accompanied everywhere by her husband, former Governor James E. (Farmer Jim) Ferguson, who had been ousted from the office in 1918 through impeachment proceedings largely instigated by University of Texas supporters with whom Ferguson feuded over appropriations and other matters.

Mrs. Ferguson had two distinctions. She was the only Texas governor to serve nonconsecutive terms. After winning a two-year term in 1924, she lost the Democratic nomination in 1926 to Attorney General Dan Moody and in 1930 to oilman Ross Sterling of Houston then defeated Sterling's bid for renomination in 1932.

GOVERNORS MIRAM A. and Jim Ferguson flank famed cowboy humorist Will Rogers on the steps of the Texas Governors' Mansion. Rogers was killed in an Alaskan air crash in 1935.

— *Austin-Travis County Collection*

Mrs. Ferguson, a matronly type, was the first governor I ever saw, as well as the first elected woman governor of any state (1925-1927). Later I came to know Pat M. Neff of Waco and Dan Moody of Austin, who had served during the 1920s.

The 1933 inauguration impressed me mightily.

An honor guard of white-uniformed Ross Volunteers from Texas A&M College led the inaugural march along the north wall of the House of Representatives before Mrs. Ferguson and Lieutenant Governor Edgar A. Witt took their oaths of office on the House rostrum. It was a festive day. But the times were as gloomy as the weather and Mrs. Ferguson's remarks. The previous November, Governor Franklin D. Roosevelt of New York, a Democrat, had ended more than seventy-five years of Republican domination of the United States government by defeating the incumbent president, Herbert Hoover.

The scene had changed dramatically since 1928, when Hoover was elected — with the help of Texas — to the presidency. The first year of the Hoover administration saw a disastrous stock market decline, and during the next three years there was widespread unemployment. Banks and factories closed. In Texas and the Midwest, the disaster was compounded by the worst drought in history which brought the notorious "black blizzards" of dust blowing across, indeed blowing away, the rich soil of farms on the plains.

I was studying journalism at The University of Texas, with my sole income the twelve dollars a week from my half-time job in the Texas House of Representatives, courtesy of State Representative A. B. Tarwater, a family friend from Hale County, and Speaker Coke R. Stevenson. A twelve dollar job in those days was highly prized, and in my case it commenced a lifelong interest in politics and government.

With all its foibles, politics is fascinating and its players are universally interesting if not always admirable.

It is seldom easy to serve in public office, and the 1930s were uniquely difficult. In addition to the fiscal woes of trying to keep the ship of state afloat, holding down taxes on a citizenry littered with bankruptcies, and aiding the impoverished, state officials had a weather problem.

The "black blizzards" blowing dirt and sand from hundreds of miles away permeated even the state capitol. Legislators wore gauze face masks as they went about their duties. Air conditioning and central heating (in those days it was steam-heated radiators, fired by Texas lignite) have made work in the stately old granite capitol infinitely more comfortable. Improved farming practices and irrigation now help hold the topsoil on the Texas plains which once descended over Central Texas as a grimy, choking blanket.

THIS 1936 Knott cartoon on government debt would be just as appropriate in 1982.

— *Reprinted from The Dallas Monring News*

DROUTH AND dust-storms made the 1930s depression worse in Texas.

— *Reprinted from The Dallas Morning News*

My father, E. J. Morehead, kept his sense of humor even after the First National Bank of Plainview, where he had been assistant cashier, went broke early in the Depression. The town's other two banks went broke also. Our family was left with one hundred acres of Hale County land and a few Jersey cows, while my brother Lucian and I were working our way through The University of Texas four hundred miles away in Austin.

"I am sending you my last forty acres by airmail," Pop joked, in one of his infrequent notes. Said another in early March 1933: "If you have got any money in the bank, take it out. Roosevelt is going to close them all."

Indeed, that was just what happened when Franklin D. Roosevelt took his oath as president of the United States March 4, 1933, with John Nance Garner of Uvalde as his vice president.

The new president launched his administration by declaring a bank moratorium. No banking business was transacted. My brother, being wiser, had followed our father's advice and withdrawn his small account from the bank before its doors were locked. He had to finance me and several other students during those eerie days before the federal government authorized the reopening of all the banks that appeared to be solvent.

Eating establishments along the University "drag," as part of Guadalupe Street is called, were generous in extending credit to penniless students, nobody knowing if they would ever be repaid. Grocery stores extended limited credit, and our rooming house on San Gabriel Street was fortunate to include an older student from the North Panhandle who belonged to the Masonic Lodge. Fellow Masons extended credit which he shared with friends lacking such connections.

The Texas legislature had been in session for nearly two months when President Roosevelt and his New Deal administration took over from the hapless Hoover administration in Washington.

Jim Ferguson, the state's co-governor and Vice President Garner, both shrewd small-town Texas bankers, saw the danger of economic chaos from "runs" by depositors on the banks still open in January and February 1933.

Garner urged President Roosevelt to submit federal deposit insurance legislation as an emergency measure to reassure those

FDR TOOK an optimistic view of the nation's outlook.
— *Reprinted from The Dallas Morning News*

who still kept money in the banks. At first, Roosevelt refused, and Garner notified the two banks which he controlled in Texas that he personally would guarantee the depositors' money.

Roosevelt later became a supporter of the idea and the Federal Deposit Insurance Corporation was created with his blessing. The president even took credit for the idea, which Garner had suggested as early as 1908 as a fledgling congressman from Texas. [6]

Meanwhile, Texas bankers — few of whom were Ferguson political supporters — flocked to Austin to urge the governor to "do something" to halt the collapse of the banking system.

Even before Roosevelt and Garner took office, Governor Ferguson acted to close all Texas banks before the depositors exhausted all their cash supply. March 2, Texas Independence Day, a state holiday, came on a Thursday so the banks were closed. Texas banks were also closed on Friday by edict of the governor. On Monday, newly-inaugurated President Roosevelt made the action in Texas official by declaring the nationwide bank holiday. [7]

With the stronger banks open again, national and state leaders attacked the problems of widespread unemployment, sagging prices, and chronic business and agricultural depression. Despite the expenditure of billions of tax dollars, the major problems remained until the 1940s when World War II vastly increased employment and industry. This was a terrible way to end a national economic depression, but the war launched an era of prosperity and inflation which continued into the 1980s with occasional dips. None of these so-called "recessions," however, can be classed with the rigors of the Great Depression of the 1930s.

Six days into his first term, starting March 9, 1933, President Roosevelt launched his recovery program in a 100-day special session of Congress. A keystone was the controversial National Recovery Act (NRA) which gave the federal government unprecedented power over U.S. business and labor. The law provided federal authority to set minimum wages, maximum hours, and to regulate production.

A massive public works program was launched, government workers' salaries reduced up to fifteen percent, gold and silver dollars devalued in relation to paper currency, and the Civilian Conservation Corps created to employ 250,000 unemployed youths in reforestation and related outdoor work programs.

Although loyal to President Roosevelt, the more conservative Vice President Garner questioned the need for the powerful new NRA. Garner also incurred the enmity of John L. Lewis, head of the United Mine Workers, most vocal of the nation's labor leaders.

FDR called Garner "Mr. Commonsense" but Lewis dubbed him "a poker-playing, whiskey-drinking, evil old man," a designation which "Cactus Jack" accepted with amusement.

Back in Texas, even the discovery of the East Texas oil field in 1930 by C. M. (Dad) Joiner failed to halt the inroads of de-

13

EVEN THE holdup men were frustrated when Governor Ferguson and President Roosevelt closed the banks in 1933 to prevent "runs" by depositors. Federal Deposit Insurance was provided to reassure the public.

— *Reprinted from The Dallas Morning News*

pression although it ultimately brought riches to many Texans and millions in taxes to the state treasury. The price of crude oil dropped to as low as ten cents a barrel as East Texas gushers flooded the market.

After martial law was declared to stop lawlessness in the big field, the Texas Railroad Commission was given authority to prorate production to stop wasteful practices and prolong the life of the reservoir. Fifty years later, the success of this effort is shown by the fact that the East Texas field still produced more than 200,000 barrels of oil per day, and the controlled reservoir already had produced about five times the one billion barrels originally estimated it could produce. The world price of oil by 1980 had risen to more than forty dollars a barrel.

In the 1930s Ferguson administration, the legislature was scratching for sums which today seem ridiculously small. The legislature submitted two propositions to the voters in August 1933. The federal government had put the state on notice that unless it helped financially, that welfare funds to Texas would be stopped.

Twenty million dollars in state "bread bonds" for welfare were proposed. With the support of the Fergusons, the legislature had also submitted to the people the question of whether prohibition of alcoholic beverages would be repealed. National prohibition — the fifteen-year-old "noble experiment" — already had been eliminated by Congress with President Roosevelt's support. One plea for returning to legal sales was it would stimulate the economy, create new jobs, and increase state revenues.

With Jim Ferguson campaigning hard for the "bread bonds" and repeal of prohibition, both propositions were approved. Four years earlier, Texans' dislike for legalized beer and liquor had helped carry the state for Republican Herbert Hoover over Democrat Alfred Smith of New York, a "wet" Roman Catholic. At first, Texas legalized sale only of beer of 3.2 percent alcohol content by local option vote. After 1935, package store sales of liquor were permitted, and finally in 1971, sale of mixed drinks became legal.

The Fergusons were instrumental in establishing parimutuel betting on horse races in 1933. The legislation was very con-

15

troversial, and in 1937 a special session called by Governor James V. Allred repealed legalized betting. Parimutuels were pushed primarily by the Waggoner family of Fort Worth and Vernon, wealthy oil and real estate people who had built one of the finest race tracks in the nation, Arlington Downs, between Fort Worth and Dallas in anticipation of legal parimutuels.

The Waggoners drew much support from other ranchers, and debate on the question became furious. The legislation appeared stymied in the 1933 regular legislative session, until the authorization for parimutuels became a last-minute "rider" on the state appropriation bill for the Department of Agriculture. The action was labeled "for improvement of the breed" of horse raising in Texas.

One anecdote shows the mood of the big-city and ranch-country legislators who had supported parimutuels. The day after final passage of the appropriation bill, two pro-parimutuel legislators framed up on a third member, whose principal legislative program seemed to be the so-called "vice" bills for gambling and liquor-drinking. The practical jokers arranged for a fourth member to alert the not-too-bright legislator as the two counted currency in one corner of the House of Representatives.

As the puzzled "vice" backer approached, one member kept counting large bills into the palm of the other.

"What are you guys doing?" he asked.

"It's the payoff on the parimutuel bill," replied the joker, still counting. "Didn't you get yours?"

"Hell, no, I just got fifty dollars!" blurted the newcomer.

Like many accounts of legislative bribery, there's no evidence the above is true, but it does show the mood of the moment. Proponents — and opponents mostly from religious groups — lobbied hard on parimutuels and prohibition repeal, which is usual on such emotional issues.

The Ferguson era ended in 1935 when Miriam A. Ferguson relinquished the governorship to James V. Allred. The Ferguson influence continued for a few years, but never as strongly as when "Farmer Jim" and "Ma" led the faithful in the twenty years spanned by their governorships.

In 1934, one of the losers to Allred was C. C. McDonald, a

STEP RIGHT UP FRIEND! NO CHANCE LIKE THIS AGAIN FOR TWO YEARS!

TWO GOVERNORS FOR THE PRICE OF ONE!

FORMER GOVERNOR Jim Ferguson was truly the right-hand man to his wife, Governor Miriam A. Ferguson.

— *Reprinted from The Dallas Morning News*

Ferguson-backed candidate who ran third behind Tom Hunter. In 1940, Mrs. Ferguson emerged from retirement to run for governor again against the incumbent, W. Lee O'Daniel, but she finished fourth in a Democratic primary where O'Daniel easily won by a majority over the whole field.

James E. Ferguson died in 1944 at the age of seventy-three, and his wife lived quietly in their Austin retirement home until 1961, when she died at age eighty-six.

The Fergusons were always controversial in politics. They campaigned successfully against the Ku Klux Klan in the 1920s and saw the ending of prohibition in the 1930s. They were gen-

GOVERNOR MIRIAM A. FERGUSON

erous in granting pardons to convicted criminals, too generous in the opinion of their detractors. Their daughter, Mrs. Ouida Nalle, quoted her father:

"I have been for something or against something all my life and nobody ever charged me with being a straddler. I would rather be wrong over half the time than to live a life and never be right or wrong any of the time. . . ."

Mrs. Ferguson was described:

"It was not my mother's nature to deceive anyone; she has literally never bothered herself to make a good impression or please 'the right people' . . . Here was a 'tub that stood on its own bottom,' and Texans could sense this when she spoke. The lady wore no man's collar, not even Jim's."[8]

Mrs. Ferguson was the first woman ever elected governor of a state. In Wyoming, Mrs. Nellie Tayloe Ross had been appointed governor in her state a few months earlier in 1924 but was un-elected. In the 1970s, Connecticut and Oregon elected women governors.

The Fergusons had another distinction. Jim Ferguson, dis-barred from seeking state office in 1917, became the first Texan ever to be nominated for president. The American Party chose him as its candidate in 1924 but Ferguson received only 45,000 votes. Yet it did display the maverick quality of Texas Democrats long before ticket-splitting became commonplace in the state.

THE ALLRED YEARS

James V. Allred (he always said the V. stood for nothing) became governor of Texas in 1935, just forty-five days before his thirty-sixth birthday. Four years earlier, the dynamic man from Wichita Falls had become the youngest attorney general in the state's history.

Jaunty Jimmy Allred was the only Texas governor com-mitted fully to the New Deal program of President Franklin D. Roosevelt. He also was the only real liberal among Texas gover-nors since James Stephen Hogg (1891-1895) until the present.

Allred was the first governor that I knew well. When he ran for the Democratic nomination in 1934, I was a novice student

19

GOVERNOR JAMES V. ALLRED (1935-1939) signs a new law. Standing (left to right) Senators E. M. Davis of Brownwood, John Hornsby of Dallas, Attorney General Gerald C. Mann of Dallas, and Rep. W. O. Reed of Dallas.

— Austin-Travis County Collection

reporter for *The Plainview Herald* in my hometown, working during the summer for the experience.

Since I was the only staff member without duties which confined me to the office, I covered the candidates who came to town, most of them speaking from the Hale County courthouse bandstand. After he became governor, Allred credited me with writing a story quoting his runoff opponent, Tom Hunter, a Wichita Falls oilman, that gave Allred the leverage he needed to defeat Hunter. The final vote was close: Allred 497,806 to Hunter 457,785.

In the first primary, Allred led an impressive field of candidates that included C. C. McDonald, the Ferguson candidate, also from Wichita Falls; Lieutenant Governor Edgar Witt, State Senator Clint C. Small, and Maury Hughes, a well-known Dallas attorney.

Only Allred waved the flag of FDR's New Deal. I never did find out what I wrote that gave such a boost to Allred's campaign. I do recall writing stories about the speeches made by both men that hot August (the primaries were later moved from July and August to May-June).

Allred made the more lasting impression, for Hunter was a stocky serious fellow without much flair. Edward C. Clark, the sage of San Augustine who later became Allred's secretary of state and much later President Lyndon B. Johnson's ambassador to Australia, described Allred as the last Texas candidate really to make a statewide courthouse-calling campaign. By the time Allred ran, radio was becoming the most effective medium for reaching the greatest number of voters.

When Allred spoke in Plainview, he made charges and denied countercharges concerning issues in the campaign. From a bulging briefcase, he pulled a handful of papers to prove his veracity and shouted to the audience: "It's all right here if you want to read it!" Then he stuffed the papers back in the briefcase, shook hands with everybody in reach, and got in his car to make the next stop. Nobody had time to accept his invitation to inspect the papers. There was really no opportunity to do so.

My 1934 debut as a "political reporter" for *The Plainview Herald* brought another memorable afternoon.

George Mahon of Colorado City came to town, campaigning for the new Twenty-first Congressional District created by redistricting. Before that Marvin Jones of Amarillo included Hale County in his district.

It was raining at the time scheduled for Mahon's rally. The crowd consisted of the candidate, myself, and one elderly fellow who had come into the bandstand to get out of the rain.

Nevertheless, Mahon made his speech just as if the lawn was crowded with voters. He proved that a candidate does not have to draw crowds everywhere to get elected, for Mahon won.

21

He kept winning for twenty-two more elections, retiring in 1978 after forty-four years as one of the most respected and powerful members of Congress, finally as chairman of the House Appropriations Committee.

While I have never been a hero worshiper, neither am I a cynic as many reporters are. In that first acquaintance, Mahon came across to me like young Abe Lincoln, only better-looking and more polished.

When face-to-face campaigning was the usual way of seeking votes, political rallies provided the best entertainment in town. Frequently, they were accompanied by free barbecue and/or watermelon. Night rallies were the best, for they gave families a reason to enjoy the evening coolness.

Candidates often were humorists as well as strong-voiced speakers. One candidate told of standing in a flatbed wagon addressing a few listeners on the courthouse square. Soon the listeners started drifting away, until only the speaker and one other man remained. Irritated, the candidate stopped.

"Well, you can leave too, if you want to," he said.

"Cain't," said his audience. "I'm the next speaker."

Another version ends:

"Cain't. That's my wagon you're standing on."

Governor Allred brought youth and enthusiasm, as well as a gift for simple expression as in this reference to farmers.

"In times of depression," he remarked in his 1935 inaugural speech "the industrialist can close his plant, lay off his employees, and await better times. Can you imagine a farmer turning his wife and some of his children out to beg while he works part of the farm?" [9]

On his second day in office, Allred began making "fireside chat" statewide radio broadcasts, following the example of President Roosevelt, the greatest master of political radio in history.

Addressing the legislature the same day, Allred gave top priority to issue the last three and one-half million of the twenty-million dollar bread bonds authorized during the previous Ferguson administration.

He also called for a study to set up a state pension program for poor Texans, while in Washington the federal government

ALLRED FACED rough financial problems as governor.

— Reprinted from the Dallas Morning News

was passing the Social Security Act by which workers and employers were to set aside funds for retirement.

Funds for "relief," as the welfare program then was called, continued to be a major problem through Allred's four years as governor. In November 1937, in Allred's second term, the average state welfare payment was fourteen dollars a month, paid to about 140,000 persons. [10] During the same period, the legislature had raised the governor's pay from $4,000 a year to $12,000.

The welfare problem continued to plague Allred and the O'Daniel administration that followed.

In 1935, Allred asked the legislature in special session to increase taxes on natural resources and chain stores to provide more money for the poor, and a sales tax was proposed by some legislators. Neither idea got very far although token taxes were later placed on chain stores and pipelines. The legislature in special session in November 1935 passed the Texas Liquor Control Act, establishing a regulatory board and setting taxes and fees for package store liquor sales. This was estimated to raise about five million dollars a year, three-fourths earmarked for old age pensions and the remainder for public schools.

Allred was reelected governor in 1936, winning the Democratic primary without a runoff against Tom F. Hunter and three others. The second Allred term was highlighted by repeal of the four-year-old law legalizing racetrack betting in the state. Although Texas continued to be one of the nation's major horse raising states and quarterhorse tracks flourished with illegal betting, proponents never succeeded in efforts to restore legal parimutuels. Tracks with legal betting operated in the adjoining states of Louisiana, Arkansas, New Mexico, and in Mexico across the Rio Grande. Opponents claim legal gambling attracts organized crime and is bad for the public.

Some who urged repeal in 1937 pointed to undesirable effects that legal parimutuels had produced in areas where tracks operated. Included were delinquent household bills and an adverse affect on business, although some of this may have resulted from continued economic depression.

Through his second term, Allred built closer ties with the Roosevelt administration in Washington. He visited President Roosevelt and Vice President Garner in Washington but denied he was seeking a federal court appointment. In 1939, the year Allred left the governorship, FDR did name him to be a U.S. district judge in Houston.

Meanwhile in Washington, Roosevelt and Garner had won an overwhelming victory in a campaign for reelection, but a rift developed between the two that was never fully healed.

After the 1936 election and before the second presidential term was launched in 1937, members of the Congress of Industrial Organizations (C.I.O. later merged with the American Federation of Labor) staged sitdown strikes in some automobile plants seeking to implement the workers' demands against management. While the president was sympathetic with the

ALLRED ENLISTED President Roosevelt's help to popularize Texas blackeyed peas.

— *Reprinted from The Dallas Morning News*

workers' cause, Vice President Garner was furious, terming the action an illegal seizure of private property.[11]

The two top national officials also disagreed sharply on Roosevelt's proposal to reorganize federal courts which had been unresponsive to the objectives of the Roosevelt New Deal program. The chief proposal was to add six new justices to the United States Supreme Court, to be appointed by President Roosevelt and thus to create a favorable majority. This effort failed after causing bitter and lasting divisions among conservatives and liberals.

The vice president had even come to dislike the term "New

Deal" when capitalized in reference to the administration's program.

"More and more 'New Deal' annoyed him," wrote Garner's friend and biographer Bascom N. Timmons, a Washington correspondent. "It was exasperating when officeholders, some of them castoffs from other parties, began to refer to the 'New Deal' party. Men in high administration posts for the first time began to say they were 'New Dealers,' not Democrats. These New Dealers admitted to no Democratic party loyalty, and regarded themselves merely as coalitionists with the Democrats. Some of them he (Garner) thought were 'mercenary coalitionists.' "[12]

After retiring as vice president, Garner reflected that President Roosevelt "had the best kind of political mind . . . He was on the crest of a political wave and only two or three times in our history has the other political party been so weak . . . How he would have fared under normal political alignments can only be conjectured. . . ."

While Garner and former President Herbert Hoover, a Republican, were often depicted during the 1930s as irreconcilable antagonists, Timmons said Garner had a high esteem for the man defeated by the Democrats after serving a single term as president.

Garner said Hoover was simply the wrong man for the time. The Texan was Speaker of the House during Hoover's presidency.

After Roosevelt's death in 1945, Garner paid this compliment to Hoover, whose name was equated with failure during the early 1930s:

"I never doubted his probity or his patriotism. In many ways he was superbly equipped for the presidency. If he had become president in 1921 or 1937, he might have ranked with the greatest presidents. These periods were more suited to his talents. I think Herbert Hoover today is the wisest statesman on world affairs in America. He may be on domestic affairs, too."[13]

The rift continued to widen between Southern conservatives, traditional Democrats, and the New Dealers' philosophy expounded from the Roosevelt administration by what Garner called the "coalitionists" of Big Labor, ethnic groups, intellectuals, and others. Probably it started in 1928 with Hoover's elec-

PRESIDENT ROOSEVELT, Governor Allred, and Lyndon Johnson at Galveston in 1937 when LBJ was elected to Congress.

— *Photo from LBJ Library*

PRESIDENT ROOSEVELT, who endorsed young Lyndon B. Johnson of Texas for Congress in 1937.

— *Dallas Morning News Library*

tion, when Texas and some other Southern conservative states turned against Alfred E. Smith, the Democratic presidential nominee, in the South's first defections from the Democratic Party since the War Between the States. The main issues influencing Texas voters in 1928 were not party labels, but the fact that Smith, the governor of New York, was a Roman Catholic, and an exponent of selling liquor legally at a time when Southern Protestants still were quite negative on the issue.

Governor Allred cast his lot with the Roosevelt faction. In 1937, he was joined as a Texas leader of this group by Lyndon Baines Johnson, a former schoolteacher born in the Hill Country at Johnson City who had moved to Austin to serve as state director of the National Youth Administration, a New Deal program designed to provide jobs for needy young people.

For one semester in The University of Texas Journalism School, I was a beneficiary of N.Y.A. I received fifteen dollars a month for typing manuscripts. I needed the money but so far as I could discover my labor for the taxpayers produced nothing of real value except my monthly stipend.

In 1937, Lyndon Johnson was elected congressman from the Tenth District of Texas, backed by President Roosevelt who even came to Texas during the campaign to endorse his new friend's candidacy. LBJ thereafter was on his way, and termed President Roosevelt as being "like a daddy to me."

Allred's and Johnson's careers were related until Allred's death in 1959 at the age of sixty. The two had became even closer after FDR's death in 1945. When news of the president's death came soon after the start of his fourth term, Allred was visiting the state capitol. Together we watched the news wire for verification of FDR's demise. When it came, I walked into the hall comforting Judge Allred, who was crying inconsolably.

In 1939, after Allred decided against seeking a third term as governor (Texas then had a tradition of limiting governors to only two two-year elective terms), President Roosevelt appointed Allred to the federal district judgeship, which Allred resigned in 1942 to run for the U.S. Senate against W. Lee O'Daniel.

Elected governor starting in 1939, O'Daniel quickly became a star of Texas politics. Reelected in 1940, O'Daniel gave up the governorship in 1941 after winning a special election for the U.S. Senate against Lyndon B. Johnson. To retain the office after 1942, O'Daniel won an elective term to the Senate against Allred and others.

After Allred lost his 1942 race, President Roosevelt nominated him to be an associate justice of the U.S. Fifth Circuit Court of Appeals, but the appointment was withdrawn after O'Daniel raised objections as a senator who would be asked to approve the appointment.

In 1949, President Harry Truman appointed Allred a federal district judge in Corpus Christi, where Allred lived until his death from a heart attack.

Jimmy Allred was a great practical joker. Once a middle-aged, pious, woman-chasing state representative from a small North Texas town confronted me irately at the capitol with a demand that I mind my own business. As a young reporter for United Press (International), I was astounded by his charge that I had called the night before and asked who was the woman I saw him with at an Austin hotel. I denied everything. During the day, I learned that the call came from the Governor's Mansion and the caller was Governor Allred, using my name. Allred disliked the legislator anyway, and decided to make the prank telephone call.

Once Allred was the victim of a huge practical joke. On New Year's Day 1936, he attended the Rose Bowl festivities and football game in California where Southern Methodist University was playing Stanford University.

At halftime of the game, a telegram delivered to Allred in his box seat advised that Lieutenant Governor Walter F. Woodul, with whom Allred had differences, had called the Texas legislature into special session. In the governor's absence from the state, the lieutenant governor acts as governor.

Allred was horrified at the message. With Executive Assistant Patrick Moreland, the Texas governor raced down the stadium steps. Unable to find a taxi, he and Moreland persuaded two motorcycle patrolmen to carry them back to the hotel, with the governor of Texas riding as passenger behind one officer and Moreland behind the other. They tried vainly to reach somebody on the governor's staff in Austin to find out what was going on.

Unable to find out by phone what was going on back in Texas, the two men caught the first plane home. On arrival, they discovered the whole affair was a prank, which Governor Allred would have appreciated had he not been the butt of the joke. Aides said the governor never found out the source of the telegram, although he had several suspects around the statehouse. He did learn that Stanford won the football game, 7 to 0.

My recollections of Jimmy Allred and his staff remain warm, although we disagreed frequently on politics.

In September 1959 I was Allred's guest at a memorable farewell party where nobody present, including the host, knew it was his farewell.

Judge Allred invited about one hundred old friends, men and women, to lunch at the Driskill Hotel's Crystal Ballroom in Austin, the scene of so many historic social-political affairs. "The black-haired, fast-talking Allred was in rare form," I wrote in the *Dallas News*. "He introduced every guest present and gave personal reminiscences of many of them. Some of the friendships dated back to his youth. Nearly all had been Allred's friends during his thirty years of public life."

Three weeks later, Allred died unexpectedly in Corpus Christi. If he had any premonition in arranging this farewell party, none of us realized it.

THE O'DANIEL ERA

Radio produced a governor of Texas by the name of Wilbert Lee O'Daniel. He was a master of the medium, as was President Roosevelt. Beyond that, the two men had very little in common except they both ran under the Democratic label.

O'Daniel was more salesman than politician. He knew practically nothing about state government when he announced for the state's highest office May 1, 1938, on his weekly flour-selling radio program. Listeners learned that O'Daniel's platform would be the Ten Commandments and his motto the Golden Rule.

GOVERNOR W. LEE O'DANIEL.
— *Austin-Travis County Collection*

Few outsiders took O'Daniel's candidacy seriously. A relative newcomer to Texas, the Ohio-born son of a Union army soldier came here from Kansas where he sold flour for a milling company.

When O'Daniel announced for office, I was a reporter for United Press stationed at Fort Worth, where O'Daniel lived and made his radio sales pitch for Burrus Mill and Elevator Company before forming his own Hillbilly Flour Company in 1935.

Originally, the program featured the Light Crust Doughboys, a singing instrumental country music group which became popular within the Fort Worth broadcast area. O'Daniel later became the announcer, then a performer, producer, poet, songwriter, and singer.

While the political writers knew little about O'Daniel when he announced, the crowds at his campaign appearances quickly warmed up to the candidate.

Still, he was regarded as only a remote threat to the candidacies of such well-known political personalities as Ernest O. Thompson, Railroad Commission member, former Amarillo mayor, and World War I hero; Attorney General William Mc-Craw of Dallas; Tom Hunter, the Wichita Falls candidate running for a fourth time; and nine others.

When the votes were counted for the first Democratic primary in July, O'Daniel beat all twelve with 573,166 votes of 1,114,885 cast. Thompson was runner-up with 231,630 votes. O'Daniel easily defeated the Republican candidate in November.

As hometown reporter of O'Daniel, in the beginning I did not think he was serious about his candidacy nor do I believe he really expected to get elected. Running for governor was part of his radio show. When he announced on the air in May, O'Daniel asked fans to write if they wanted him to run. An astonishing response of 55,000 writers convinced O'Daniel that he could be more than a publicity-seeking candidate.

The feeling increased in June when O'Daniel put his show on the political road, accompanied by his hillbilly band, singers Texas Rose and Leon, and the three attractive O'Daniel children. Huge crowds greeted the O'Daniel campaign in Texas communities, large and small.

The Sunday morning after the election in July, I was among the reporters covering the O'Daniel weekly radio broadcast from Fort Worth.

"I feel equal to my task and qualified," O'Daniel said. ". . . I humbly bow to the will of the people, accept their mandate, and with the help of God and the cooperation of my good friends and the citizens of Texas, we shall march onward and upward to happier days." [14]

Asked for a statement after attending services at the Magnolia Avenue Christian Church, O'Daniel commented: "This election has been different from anything ever known in Texas

W. LEE O'DANIEL, who won elections both as governor and to the U.S. Senate, on one of his later campaigns.
— *Dallas Morning News Staff Photo*

SIXTY THOUSAND WITNESS the inauguration of Governor W. Lee O'Daniel at the University of Texas football stadium, January 17, 1939.
— *Ellison Photo from Austin-Travis County Collection*

or any other state. So far as I know, it is the first time that a candidate has used the Ten Commandments for his platform and the Golden Rule for his motto. It was a victory for good, Christian people. . . .''[15]

It was not, of course, the first nor the last time that political campaigns have been run successfully on a religious motif. O'Daniel used it well.

The runner-up, Ernest Thompson, commented wryly on the election: "I didn't even see him. The first thing I knew he had passed all of us and left me with a cloud of flour dust in my eyes. I congratulate a fellow who really knows how to run. . . .''[16]

Despite rather contradictory political views, neither President Roosevelt nor Governor O'Daniel had difficulty winning reelection in 1940. Roosevelt took for his vice presidential running mate, replacing John Nance Garner, a liberal U.S. senator, Henry A. Wallace. The Democrats won 81.3 percent of the Texas presidential vote. [17]

In the Democratic primary, O'Daniel won with nearly fifty-four percent of the total vote but had several opponents in the race. In the general election, O'Daniel's margin exceeded FDR's in Texas, with the governor receiving about ninty-five percent of the vote against a Republican and a Communist candidate, neither of whom campaigned significantly.

In contrast with Roosevelt's increasing liberalism, the state Democratic platform on which O'Daniel ran was quite conservative. It called for putting the state on a cash basis as quickly as possible (it had been deficit-financing for years); streamlining state government to increase efficiency and economy; faster industrialization of the state; and full cooperation with the national defense policy as World War II spread across western Europe. The United States entered the war in December 1941 after the Japanese bombed Pearl Harbor in Hawaii and attacked U.S. installations in the western Pacific.

O'Daniel became a folk hero to his supporters, including many older citizens attracted by his promises of getting them a thirty-dollars-per-month state pension. A highway patrol captain who accompanied the O'Daniel motorcade from Fort Worth to Austin for the inauguration January 17, 1939, estimated that 250,000 onlookers lined the route which included stops at cities and towns along the highway.[18]

The inaugural ceremony itself was unprecedented. O'Daniel had urged his followers to come to Austin for the celebration, and they did.

By newspaper estimates 60,000 people jammed The University of Texas' Memorial Stadium for the noontime event. The program included music by O'Daniel's hillbilly band, bands from the state university, Texas A&M, and many others. Ten thousand school children sang, and even a busload of old Confederate veterans was on hand.[19] It was a great day for the former Yankee who had become famous in Texas as "Pass-the-Biscuits, Pappy, O'Daniel."

The new governor quickly proved he was no ordinary Populist by calling for a "transactions tax" to replace ad valorem property taxes. The 1.6 percent levy would apply to all manufacturing, wholesale and retail transactions except charities, salaries, wages, professional fees, and first sales of agricultural products.

The proposed tax created one of O'Daniel's first big confrontations with the Texas legislature, and he abandoned the idea finally in favor of a retail sales tax.

The transactions tax proposal shocked many Texans, as detractors called it a multiplying sales tax which would hit hardest the poor to whom O'Daniel had appealed for campaign support. O'Daniel was an anomaly. Critics called him a demagogue who appealed to both rich and poor under the guise of protecting one against the other.

Despite the new governor's basic ignorance of politics and government, some of his ideas could be described as ahead of their time but were opposed by those he scorned as "professional politicians." The transactions tax proposed both in 1939 and 1941 failed. But it was the predecessor of the general sales tax initiated in 1961 which quickly became the state government's main financial source.

In 1980, the state received more than $2.5 billion from a tax of four percent, excluding food, prescription drugs, and certain other items. Nearly one thousand cities and towns by local option added a one percent sales tax, which netted them $560

"Hallelujah!"

VOTE

GOVERNOR, LATER Senator, W. Lee (Pappy) O'Daniel was a favorite Knott character because of O'Daniel's musical, religion-based campaigns.

— *Reprinted from The Dallas Morning News*

million. Cities and counties, plus some school officials, began advocating additional sales taxes as a substitute or addition to the traditional property tax.

Ironically, by 1980 the principal single source of state government revenue came from federal funds totaling $2.6 billion, almost one-fourth of all the money spent by the state. This occurred despite the fact that the federal government for years had run increasingly into debt and the state government had balanced its budget annually since 1945, with surpluses to invest.

In 1980 the state collected more than one billion dollars in interest on its bank accounts and investments. Much of this represented earnings on trust funds created by the 1876 Texas Constitution for The University of Texas-Texas A&M systems and for public schools.

Originally, this endowment of land—including coastal waters—was of little value. But the discovery of oil created a legacy whose earnings are spent for education, and invested for the future. At the end of 1980, the Permanent School Fund (invested for public schools) totaled more than $2.6 billion and the Permanent University Fund (Texas and A&M) totaled almost $1.4 billion.

In addition, huge trust funds have been established for retirement of teachers and state employees, partly contributed by workers in these two groups. At the end of 1980, the Teachers Retirement Fund had invested $5.6 billion; the State Employees Retirement System, $1.6 billion.

While Governor O'Daniel was not the main mover of the proposition, his second term saw the origin of a constitutional limit on legislative spending that has become the envy of debt-ridden governments everywhere.

Lieutenant Governor Coke R. Stevenson and Representative W. O. Reed of Dallas sponsored the constitutional amendment which was adopted by the legislature in 1941 with O'Daniel's backing. However, a governor has no action to take concerning constitutional amendments which the legislature by two-thirds majority submits to a statewide vote.

The voting date was set for November 1942, by which time O'Daniel had left the executive office to become a United States senator. Stevenson was finishing O'Daniel's unexpired term.

The proposition won voter approval and on January 1, 1945, Article III, Section 49a, became part of the Texas Constitution. It prohibits any legislature from spending more than the state comptroller (tax collector) certifies will be on hand when the bills become due.

An emergency deficit appropriation could be made by approval of four-fifths of the Texas Senate and House of Representatives, but no such emergency situation has ever been declared.

Thus Texas is unique in limiting elected officials to spend only as much as they are willing to levy in taxes for the same period.

This serves as an effective restraint on spendthrift government.

Another foresighted recommendation by Governor O'Daniel was to import water from spring floods on the Rocky Mountains eastern slope to arid West Texas. The suggestion drew little attention at the time, but the 1980s seemed certain to see a serious effort to finance and implement water imports from the Mississippi River basin or tributaries which are fed from the Rocky Mountains.

On much of his program, O'Daniel met hostility in the legislature. He regularly found trouble in the Senate over confirmation of his appointees to state boards and commissions. Some were accused of being nonresidents of Texas; others of being anti-New Dealers or even Republicans. This was deplored by the all-Democratic Senate.

O'Daniel belabored his opponents in folksy weekly radio broadcasts each Sunday from the Governor's Mansion. Debate grew brisk over his efforts to get the transactions tax passed.

Union labor leaders complained loudly over proposed sales taxes and were joined by some business men in objecting to the transactions tax which would apply even to real estate sales. Only first sales of agricultural products, professional fees, salaries, and charitable transactions would have been exempt. One group of legislators sought to substitute higher taxes on oil and gas production for funds to support higher old age pensions and public schools.

The governor's broadcasts generated much mail to legislators asking them to vote for the transactions tax, and later for a sales tax when O'Daniel changed to this recommendation.

The principal vehicle for the sales tax was Senate Joint Resolution 12, which would have — by popular statewide vote — levied a two percent state sales tax and higher natural resource taxes. SJR 12 was passed by the Senate but snagged in the House when fifty-six representatives refused to support it. The resolution never received the one hundred representative votes needed from the one hundred fifty total membeship.

One opponent was Representative Price Daniel, Sr. of Liberty — later speaker of the House, attorney general, United States senator, governor, and Supreme Court justice.

While Daniel was governor in 1961, Texas' first sales tax became law, despite his continued opposition. Convinced there was no other viable alternative to the new tax coming from the legislature at that session, and the state needing the money, Daniel let the measure take effect without his signature.

In 1962, Daniel ran for a fourth term as governor and was soundly defeated by John Connally. One reason apparently was that Daniel received unwarranted public blame for the new sales tax, which he had opposed. Storekeepers sarcastically called the new tax "Pennies for Price."

The State Democratic party platform also urged financing for an old age assistance pension program (by then called "social security" but different from the federal program financed by worker-employer contributions).

This was the main promise on which O'Daniel had been elected both in 1938 and 1940. By August 1940, the 41,565 recipients received checks averaging $32.59 per month. In September 1937, the rolls numbered 26,913 but the checks, divided among fewer people, averaged $40.09 a month. [20]

Despite the growth of federal Social Security, private pension plans, and other aid to the needy by fiscal year 1980, the State of Texas was spending more than $1.6 billion annually on welfare, not counting special expenditures through public schools and eleemosynary institutions operated by the state. The direct welfare cost represented 15.7 percent of the total state spending of $10.221 billion for the year. [21]

Both welfare and Social Security rolls continued to grow in Texas after the return of prosperity during World War II and later. By 1980, Texans receiving Social Security benefits numbered 1.8 million with checks totaling six billion dollars annually. The first deductions from payrolls for Social Security began in 1936 and the first retired persons received benefits in 1940.

In March 1941, Texas had more than 125,000 citizens receiving state-federal old age assistance (welfare), costing nearly eighteen million dollars anually from a state budget totaling $202 million—less than nine percent of the budget. The state's population totaled 6,400,000.

O'DANIEL RODE to victory on the old folks votes.

— Reprinted from The Dallas Morning News

Forty years later, in 1981, the state government dispensed financial aid (separate from Social Security programs) totaling about two billion dollars a year to nearly ten percent of the state's 14,200,000 residents about fifteen percent of the state's total budget.

Medical services for the poor, called Medicaid (separate from Social Security's Medicare program) went to about 650,000 Texans at a cost of $837 million. Keeping 90,000 persons in nursing homes took more than half of this sum.

Nearly one-quarter million children in needy families received direct payments of nearly thirty-four dollars per month each. The governor's budget office estimated a typical family of three children and one adult in the Aid For Dependent Children programs received $566 per month from various government funds—direct aid, food stamps, and medical care. An increase to about $600 per family was included in 1981-1982 budgets by Governor William P. Clements, Jr. and the Legislative Budget Board. [22]

The largest welfare program numerically in 1980 was federally-financed food stamps, which went to 1,150,000 Texans at a cost of $507 million.

At the outset of his second term as governor in 1941, O'Daniel requested forty million dollars additional for social security and renewed his request for a transactions tax to pay the cost.

As usual, O'Daniel lambasted the "Austin bureaucrats" with a theme that sounds more familiar in the 1980s from critics of the federal government.

"Some of the vital functions of our state government have been taken away from the people of Texas and put in the hands of that willful, powerful, smart, and influential handful of people who make it their business to control much of the Texas State Government for their own benefit," O'Daniel asserted.

"Today we have four divisions of government, and the fourth division (overlapping bureaus) in many instances performs all three functions of government—legislative, executive, and judicial. In fact, this fourth division transacts most of the business of the state . . . established through the influence of a relatively small group of selfish individuals, operating through a cunning central organization of powerful lobbyists, generally referred to by some as the third house of the Texas Legislature (composed of Senate and House of Representatives).

"I consider this combination of the third house and the fourth division the basic cause of most of our state governmental ills, and it should be dealt with sternly and promptly." [23]

Himself a businessman, O'Daniel became the most avid business supporter the state ever had, despite his following of Populist-like voters. O'Daniel was indeed an anomoly. When his tax and welfare program met stiff legislative resistance during the governor's first term, he vowed to take the fight to the voters and ask them to elect legislators who would support the undoubtedly-popular governor.

The governor had a few devoted legislative followers, as well as outspoken critics. One story relates how one of O'Daniel's staunch friends in the House of Representatives introduced the governor at an East Texas rally during the 1940 reelection campaign for both officials.

"—What we need is a new legislature," O'Daniel urged the audience, without mentioning his legislator-friend. O'Daniel won reelection but the friend who supported him lost, according to this account.

A senator from Lufkin weathered O'Daniel's opposition in the election by failing to mention on his campaign cards that he was an incumbent, seeking reelection to the legislature. Once the senator stopped at a farmhouse, where he found the owner milking a cow.

"—I want to be your senator," he introduced himself, thrusting out the card. The milker paused, studying the card.

"Well, I think I can vote for you," he replied. "That s.o.b. we got down in Austin now ain't no good."

O'Daniel's second term was highlighted by the passage of an "omnibus" tax bill which gave the governor less than he wanted for old age assistance payments and ignored the transactions and general sales taxes favored by O'Daniel.

The new tax program would raise an estimated twenty-two million dollars a year, an insignificant sum by 1980s standards but a considerable accomplishment in the time of tight money and much smaller state budgets. The bill placed new taxes on motor vehicle sales, stock transfers, cosmetics, and radios. It increased existing levies on oil, natural gas, utilities, insurance company premiums, and a few other items.

More than eleven million dollars of the additional revenue was allocated to help the elderly, bringing the average monthly allotment to thirty dollars. More than five million dollars went to reducing the deficit in the state general revenue fund, then twenty-eight million dollars in the red.

Before the legislature adjourned, the death of United States Senator Morris Sheppard, a Democrat from Texarkana, author of the Eighteenth Amendment to the U.S. Constitution, turned

42

the attention of the governor and Texans to a special race to fill the vacancy.

It also brought to statewide attention the rising political star of Lyndon B. Johnson, congressman from the Tenth District.

DISENCHANTMENT WITH THE NEW DEAL

The disenchantment of conservative Democrats with President Roosevelt's New Deal program started with the Supreme Court-packing scheme of his second term and widened as long as FDR lived.

Many Texas conservatives declined because of party loyalty and tradition to join the Republicans although growing numbers supported other presidential candidates. This started with the "Texas Regulars" of 1944 who favored casting the state's electoral vote to Senator Strom Thurmond of South Carolina, nominee of a Southern States Rights party.

The strictly-loyal but unhappy Democrats, so far as the president was concerned, included Vice President John Nance Garner of Texas and many members of Congress.

While Roosevelt and the Congress ended his first four years in office "with each having great affection for the other," the change after Roosevelt's reelection in 1936 was sudden and long lasting. [24]

In the 1936 election, the Roosevelt-Garner ticket carried every state except Maine and Vermont, leading the president to quip, "As Maine goes, so goes Vermont." Traditionally, the early-voting citizens of Maine proved to be bellwether voters, creating the saying that "As Maine goes, so goes the nation" in politics.

The Democrats not only won the White House again, they polled overwhelming victories in the U.S. Senate and House of Representatives, leading to speculation that the two-party political system was dying, or was dead. That theory has been disproved repeatedly as the pendulum of politics swings in America.

Emboldened by his huge popular and electoral college vote, President Roosevelt set forth to compel better support for his New Deal program.

SOME AMERICANS dragged their feet about supporting FDR's New Deal.

— Reprinted from The Dallas Morning News

His first effort was to pass a law enlarging the Supreme Court so he could appoint six more justices and provide for a majority of judges to uphold the Roosevelt philosophy. This failed. So did the next step of Roosevelt's new thrust — an effort to "purge" at the polls in 1938 the representatives and senators who opposed his legislative program the most vigorously.

"The somber first two years of the second Roosevelt term . . . saw party disagreements over such issues as the sitdown strike, the Supreme Court enlargement fiasco, and the unsuccessful efforts to go along with his entire program. From these Roosevelt and Garner emerged with less warmth than in their previous relations," Timmons wrote.

"The last two years saw them in almost constant disagreement. . . . From Garner's standpoint the reasons were: bigger-than-ever spending proposals; use of relief funds for political

44

purposes; what Garner thought was Roosevelt's complete left-wing swing and the direction he was taking the party; Roosevelt's ever greater ambition for personal power; what Garner regarded as the coddling of Communists and fellow-travelers and their infiltration into the government; and disagreements over executive nominations."[25]

So a Garner-for-President movement evolved, looking to the 1940 election, led by conservative Democrats of Texas.

Meantime, a new political figure had appeared in the state: Lyndon Baines Johnson, congressman from the Tenth (Austin area) District, elected at a special election in 1937 with President Roosevelt's blessing.

Roosevelt came to Texas fairly often during his early presidential years. A son, Elliott, married a wealthy Fort Worth woman and established a chain of radio stations headquartered in the city. As the Fort Worth correspondent for United Press in 1936-40, it was my assignment to cover the president's visits which he made to Fort Worth by special train. Each was a major news event, with massive security arrangements and other special arrangements for the president who had been stricken with poliomyelitis years earlier and required assistance in walking. A wheel chair was part of the president's regular equipment, but his personality far outshone his physical affliction and it was a pleasure to be around him and especially to hear him speak.

Roosevelt also made several trips to Port Aransas for deep-sea fishing. Despite his infirmity, he was an avid angler and loved to fish for tarpon and other game fish along the Texas coast, always with a retinue of family and political intimates.

By 1940, the Roosevelt-New Deal Democrats had virtually taken charge of the Democratic Party at the state as well as national level.

While Garner and Roosevelt competed for the presidential nomination in 1940, W. Lee O'Daniel was running rather independently for a second term as governor, seeking the Democratic nomination.

Again, O'Daniel won over several well-known candidates without the necessity for a runoff. O'Daniel received 645,646 of 1,189,290 votes cast in the July primary. Ernest O. Thompson

FORMER VICE PRESIDENT John Nance Garner in retirement at
Uvalde.   — *Author's files*

again was the runner-up, trailed by Harry Hines of Wichita Falls,
former Governor Miriam A. Ferguson, Jerry Sadler of Longview,
Cyclone Davis of Dallas, and R. P. Condron of La Feria. [26]

Normally, the State Democratic convention in September,
after party nominees are chosen, is "the governor's convention"
to develop plans for enacting the governor's and party's legislative program at the session starting the following January.

But Governor O'Daniel cared little for President Roosevelt
and the New Deal, and FDR's backers in Texas paid little attention to the governor's wishes.

— Reprinted from The Dallas Morning News

FDR AND New Dealers found the Supreme Court blocking some of their program and proposed reorganization to obtain more favorable decisions.

— Reprinted from The Dallas Morning News

WHEN MANY conservative Democrats, particularly Southerners, spurned FDR's program, he sought help from young Democrats.

— Reprinted from The Dallas Morning News

State Democratic Chairman E. B. Germany of Dallas was O'Daniel's friend but the governor's electoral support was so diverse that many O'Daniel leaders lacked identifiable party labels.

Elliott Roosevelt was State Democratic vice chairman. Hal Collins of Dallas, temporary chairman of the September 1940 state convention, criticized New Deal policies in his keynote speech, pointing to the increasing size and cost of federal government.

"... The best governed people are the least governed," Collins insisted. "But we are getting expensive overdoses of government from an endless chain of government employees that infest the homes; the farms, and business establishments throughout this great land of ours." [27]

The *Dallas Morning News* reported the response of Elliott Roosevelt almost turned the State Democratic Convention into a third-term-for-Roosevelt rally, as the speech brought delegates cheering to their feet.

"There is no room in Texas for hyphenated Democrats," FDR's son said, "any more than there are hyphenated Americans. There are no Willkie Democrats—only a renegade Democrat heading the Republican ticket." [28]

The reference was to Wendell Willkie, a New York lawyer and former Democrat nominated for president by the Republican Party. By the time of the State Democratic convention in September, John N. Garner of Texas had lost his bid for the presidency in favor of FDR's unprecedented third term. Thousands of anti-New Deal Texas conservatives sought a way to express their disappointment over the national leadership. Many looked for a new political outlet.

Although Willkie was once a Democrat, changing parties is hardly a political phenomenon in the United States. Southerners were so bitter after the War Between The States that many became so-called "brass collar" or "yellow dog" Democrats, who would "vote for a yellow dog before they would vote for a Republican." It took a century for this war-born prejudice to disappear, and in parts of Texas and the Old Confederacy anti-Republicanism continued even longer. It was a situation Franklin Roosevelt exploited skillfully in forming a coalition of "solid South" conservative Democrats with union labor, ethnic groups, and city political machines of the North and East.

Interestingly, successful political candidates often have departed from their party.

"At a Jackson Day dinner January 8, 1938, which both Garner and Roosevelt attended, Roosevelt said he had bolted his party on its presidential candidate on his first vote, casting it for Theodore Roosevelt instead of Alton B. Parker. That wasn't the Garner kind of Democrat," biographer Timmons wrote. [29]

More recent is the example of Ronald Reagan, the Republican who became president in 1981. Reagan was a supporter of

49

VICE PRESIDENT Garner's bid for presidential nomination in 1940 failed when FDR sought an unprecedented third term.

— Reprinted from The Dallas Morning News

FDR in 1933, but over the years his loyalty waned as he observed the results of the New Deal and programs put into effect by presidents and congresses after World War II.

Meantime, Texans displayed their political independence regularly by voting for liberal Democrats for president and electing conservative Democrats as governors, members of Congress, and other state and local officials.

A definition of "liberal" and "conservative" is pertinent here.

Before FDR, Southern conservatism was equated with states' rights as opposed to centralization of government power in Washington. Conservatives favored keeping taxes and expenses low, and for many years Southerners espoused white supremacy and mostly favored separation of races.

Liberals recommended generous spending for welfare and other public programs, racial integration and "affirmative action" to promote ethnic minorities and women as a civil right, and government subsidy for the "little man," be he a farmer plagued with bad weather and short crops or a laborer organized into a union to obtain good wages and working conditions.

After military government of the South ended in the 1870s following the bitter Reconstruction period, many of the "liberal" goals were pursued by the Populist Party which was organized in a log schoolhouse at Pleasant Valley, nine miles west of Lampasas in Central Texas in 1877. It helped spark an agrarian and labor movement that became the Populist Party.

From this modest beginning grew a strong political movement, mostly from the Middle West and South, that elected some Populist candidates to state and local offices and backed such presidential candidates as William Jennings Bryan before the movement faded toward the end of the nineteenth century. The controversy continues over what is a true "liberal" or "conservative."

Lynn Landrum, a popular *Dallas Morning News* columnist of the mid-twentieth century, always insisted that he was a genuine liberal although critics termed him a reactionary. Landrum urged that government stay out of individual lives as much as possible and leave the citizen free to make his own choices.

With the disenchantment of the 1970s over what incoming President Reagan termed an economic "calamity" brought about by government, conservatism came back into style. Even some former backers of "liberal" ideas questioned the direction which government had traveled in the previous fifty years.

One development was a call by state governors to return more authority to the states, including greater control over taxes and spending. As in the early 1930s, taxpayers' revolts took place across the United States manifested by the adoption of Proposition 13 by California voters and a similar restriction placed by voters in Massachusetts on the taxing of property by state and local government.

51

SENATOR O'DANIEL

Some of Governor O'Daniel's friends—and some others who wanted Lieutenant Governor Coke R. Stevenson promoted to governor—urged O'Daniel to resign as chief executive and let Stevenson appoint him as United States senator, succeeding Sheppard.

This would give O'Daniel, as an incumbent senator, an advantage in being elected senator later.

Instead, O'Daniel confounded predictions by giving the appointment to Andrew Jackson Houston, eighty-seven, the only surviving son of Texas hero General Sam Houston. The announcement was made by O'Daniel on April 21, anniversary of the battle of San Jacinto, on the battleground where Sam Houston rose to lasting fame.

The elderly son, a sometimes painter and writer, was barely known in political circles. Because of his age, one thing was certain: Houston would not run for the Senate seat after serving his appointed time.

Instead, the race attracted a powerful field of Texas political names: Governor O'Daniel, Attorney General Gerald C. Mann, Congressman Martin E. Dies of Lufkin, and Congressman Johnson.

During his student days at Southern Methodist University, Mann first became widely known as "the Little Red Arrow" quarterback for the university's famed football teams. He was four times elected attorney general before announcing for the Senate position in the 1941 special election which Governor O'Daniel set for June 28.

Dies had attracted national attention as chairman of the House un-American Activities Committee, and appeared to be the favorite of the most fervent anti-New Deal conservatives.

Lyndon B. Johnson, thirty-three years old and with four years in Congress, was the clear choice of President Roosevelt and his New Deal followers in Texas.

Johnson's announcement for senator was made from the White House steps, and he claimed the president's endorsement. "Of all the members of the Texas delegation in Congress,

Johnson was considered closest to the president and his policies," wrote historian S. S. McKay in describing the period.

While the president, probably realizing that a direct endorsement of Johnson might adversely affect the candidate's chances in Texas, commented: ". . . All I can say is Lyndon Johnson is a very old, old friend of mine." [30]

When O'Daniel announced for the Senate on May 19, 1941, in a statewide radio broadcast from the Governor's Mansion, "O'Daniel referred to Roosevelt as 'my old, old friend, the president.'

"Laughs, giggling, and handclapping from the crowd of several hundred assembled in the mansion living room to hear the broadcast showed their full appreciation of the governor's sally at the expense of Congressman Johnson." [31]

O'Daniel again adopted the Ten Commandments and the Golden Rule as his platform and asserted he would take to Washington if elected "an inbred and inerasable common touch with the common man."

Twenty-nine candidates announced in the special Senate election, which required only a plurality for victory. Later, the legislature changed the law to require runoffs in special elections.

O'Daniel won with 175,590 votes of 575,879 cast — less than one-third of the total. The runner-up was Johnson with 174,270, only 1,311 votes behind O'Daniel. Mann ran third with 140,807 and Dies fourth with 80,655. Dies carried every county in his congressional district, while Johnson lost two counties in the east end of his Tenth District to O'Daniel.

Several rural counties, mostly in East Texas, were slow certifying election totals and for three days it appeared Johnson might be the winner, although the candidate never claimed victory. As the country votes put O'Daniel ahead, there was much bitterness in the Johnson camp, leading to muttering of irregularity in the late returns which gave O'Daniel the decision.

Both the Texas Election Bureau, a highly-accurate operation conducted by Texas newspapers and broadcasters, and the State Canvassing Board declared O'Daniel the winner.

A Texas Senate committee investigated the election, but took no action to change the results.

A few Johnson partisans still contended the election had been stolen from their candidate, and later used this to excuse actions on Johnson's behalf in the even more controversial United States Senate election where Johnson was declared the winner in 1948 over Governor Coke Stevenson.

In the days before the Republican Party became an important factor in Texas politics, starting in the 1960s, all of these controversies were among fellow Democrats. Policing of the elections was a party matter, although in special elections Republican candidates sometimes announced without serious expectation of victory.

The growth of a two-party system provides an adversary setting that is more conducive to honest election-watching and vote-tallying, although complaints of irregularities persist and some doubtless still occur.

After winning the special Senate election in June, O'Daniel took his time about going to Washington to accept the new office. One big event remaining was the marriage of the O'Daniels' attractive daughter, Molly, to Jack E. Wrather, Jr. of Tyler, an East Texas oil man.

The wedding was certainly different. The governor had invited all Texans listening to his radio broadcasts to attend the wedding at the Governor's Mansion, and thousands did. Most never got inside the house, and slices of wedding cake were even flipped to guests packed outside on the lawn by members of the official honor guard. O'Daniel arrived in Washington by train and took his oath as senator on August 4, 1941, where he promptly introduced a bill making strikes unlawful.

On the same day, in Austin, Coke R. Stevenson took the oath as governor in the Supreme Court chamber, then located on the state capitol third floor. Senator H. L. Winfield of Fort Stockton, who had been elected president pro tempore by other senators, became the acting lieutenant governor, with authority to serve as governor in Stevenson's absence.

Governor Stevenson's wife, Fay, a very popular member of the state's official family during his years as state representative, Speaker, and lieutenant governor, was critically ill by the time her husband became governor. A few months after moving into

PRESIDENT FRANKLIN D. ROOSEVELT and Prime Minister Winston Churchill of Great Britain during World War II.

— *Dallas News Library*

the Governor's Mansion, Mrs. Stevenson died of cancer.

The O'Daniel era in Texas politics continued until 1948, when he finished a six-year Senate term after he was reelected in 1942.

But O'Daniel as senator fell far short of generating the controversies and attention that had occurred during his two years and seven months as governor. In a state and a period known for colorful politicians and strange politics, O'Daniel was a star attraction. His impact on the national scene was never great.

By the time of the 1942 election, the United States had gone to war against Germany and Japan, after the Japanese made a surprising and devastating attack on the U.S. fleet at Pearl Harbor in the Hawaiian Islands December 7, 1941, and moved to take over U.S. forces in the Philippines in the Far East.

The war and this nation's effort to arm itself and assist its allies overshadowed all else.

During O'Daniel's first term in Washington he attempted without success to get Congress to appropriate funds to develop the "Schoch process" for making synthetic rubber from natural gas, of which Texas then had a large surplus.

The process was named for Dr. E. P. Schoch, a foresighted University of Texas at Austin professor of chemical engineering. Dr. Schoch contended his method would make artificial rubber for about half the cost of producing it from crude oil, or from guayule, a plant grown in the southwestern United States and used experimentally as a rubber substitute.

The war cut off the nation's usual supply of natural rubber from the Far East, and America badly needed a replacement to supply its millions of motor vehicles and military machines. [32]

After the war, Dr. Schoch campaigned against building natural gas pipelines from Texas to industrial states of the North and East, much of it intended to replace coal as fuel for industrial boilers. Using natural gas as boiler fuel, Dr. Schoch once told a legislative hearing, would be "like shooting the buffalo for its hide."

But, the pipeline builders prevailed and many large lines were built to export Texas gas at wellhead prices of a few cents per thousand cubic feet. Producers often joined the pipeline developers because they wanted a larger market for the gas which was considered almost a nuisance in the production of oil. Huge quantities of gas were burned in flares in the field to remove the potentially-dangerous by-product of oil production.

As natural gas became more popular for fuel all over the country and the state's huge petrochemical industry developed, gas became much more valuable and often scarce. Newly-found gas was selling for as much as six and seven thousand dollars by 1981.

Although the economics of the era defeated Dr. Schoch's effort to save Texas' gas resources for chemical usage, future events proved him to be correct about the value of gas.

When an oil and gas shortage struck the nation in the 1970s, government and industry leaders launched efforts to replace natural gas with coal for generating electricity. Although

FEDERAL CONTROL has been a problem for oil and gas producers since the 1930's.

— Reprinted from The Dallas Morning News

Texas has more gas than any other state, it was the first to prohibit selling natural gas for additional boilers and for a phase-out of existing gas-fired boilers.

This was done by order of the Texas Railroad Commission. Electric utility operators in Texas already saw early the need for curbing this use of natural gas. All new generating plants built in Texas after the mid-1970s were designed to burn lignite, abundant in East Texas, or were planned for nuclear energy. Construction of nuclear plants, however, was handicapped by environmental objections and mechanical problems.

W. Lee O'Daniel announced for reelection as senator in 1942. His main opponents were James V. Allred, the former governor-attorney general, who resigned as a U.S. district judge to make the race; and Dan Moody, another former governor-attorney general, who had established a successful law practice in Austin during more than a decade of absence from public life.

O'Daniel remained a political maverick; Allred, the choice of President Roosevelt's New Deal supporters; and Moody, the candidate of conservative traditional Texas Democrats who disliked both O'Daniel and Allred.

Still supported loyally by rural voters and the old folks, O'Daniel won more than forty-eight percent of all votes in the first Democratic primary, while Allred was runner-up with over thirty-two percent.

The second primary held in August 1942, a month after the first primary, was a bitterly-fought contest with Allred on the attack. He charged O'Daniel with being an isolationist who failed to support the war effort fully.

Despite early indications of opposition to the war as well as President Roosevelt's policies, O'Daniel convinced most Texas voters that he was not really an isolationist.

He won the runoff election with fifty-one percent of the Democrats' votes to forty-nine percent for Allred. O'Daniel had no difficulty in the general election.

For the remainder of his political life, "Pappy" O'Daniel made few waves in Washington.

"O'Daniel was ineffective in the Senate and it was reported that no proposal he ever made there received move than four votes. After dealing in real estate in Washington for a short time, he moved to Dallas and formed an insurance company, which he headed. In 1956 and again in 1958 he sought the Democratic nomination for governor but ran a poor third in each race."[33] O'Daniel died May 11, 1969, and was buried in Dallas. He was seventy-nine years old.

[1] *The Dallas Morning News,* January 18, 1933.
[2] Quoted by Richard L. Strout, *Christian Science Monitor,* May 1, 1981.
[3] *Op. cit.*
[4] *Albuquerque Journal,* August 2, 1981.
[5] The *Christian Science Monitor,* March 2, 1982
[6] *Garner of Texas,* by Bascom N. Timmons, page 179

[7] *The Fergusons of Texas: Two Governors for the Price of One,* by Ouida Ferguson Nalle, page 178

[8] Nalle, *Op.cit.*, page 225

[9] United Press, *Kaufman Daily Herald,* from an Allred scrapbook.

[10] *Dallas Morning News, Op.cit.*

[11] Timmons, *Op.cit.*, page 205

[12] *Op.cit.*, page 279

[13] *Ibid.*

[14] *Fort Worth Star-Telegram,* July 25, 1938, quoted by S. S. McKay in *W. Lee O'Daniel and Texas Politics 1938-1942.*

[15] *Ibid.*

[16] The *Austin American-Statesman,* July 26, 1938, quoted by McKay.

[17] *W. Lee O'Daniel and Texas Politics 1938-1942,* McKay, page 327

[18] McKay, *Op.cit.* page 132

[19] *Op.cit.*, page 134

[20] *Op.cit.*, page 338

[21] Texas Comptroller's Fiscal Notes, October-November 1980.

[22] Governor's Budget Office and Department of Human Resources.

[23] *Senate Journal,* 47th Legislature Regular Session, 1941, page 22-35 (from McKay book)

[24] Timmons, *Op.cit.*, page 216-218

[25] *Op.cit.*, page 240-241

[26] *Texas Almanac,* 1980-1981, page 540

[27] *Dallas Morning News,* September 11, 1940

[28] *Ibid.*

[29] Timmons, *Op.cit.*, page 231

[30] McKay, *Op.cit.*, page 429

[31] *Op.cit.*, page 422.

[32] *Ibid.*

[33] *Handbook of Texas,* Volume III, written by Wayne Gard.

COKE R. STEVENSON, leaving the governorship in January 1947 after five and a half years in the office.

— Dallas Morning News Staff Photo

2

MISTER COKE

Coke R. Stevenson was the governor of Texas with whom I formed the closest acquaintance. Whether he was the best governor of all depends on one's philosophy. A self-educated lawyer-banker-rancher from Junction, Kimble County, Stevenson was an unabashed conservative who truly considered public office to be a public trust not to be exploited for selfish or personal gain. I admired him greatly.

The warm feeling began, no doubt, when Stevenson appointed me to a half-time job as committee clerk in the House of Representatives when he was Speaker in 1933 when I had arrived newly in Austin to attend The University of Texas. Without the twelve dollars a week which the position paid, I could never have attended the university in those depressed times because my father, who had been employed in a Plainview bank which closed, lacked the money to support me and a brother attending The University of Texas Law School.

After I graduated from journalism school in 1935 and took a twenty-five dollars per week job with United Press (later United Press International) at the state capitol, I became well acquainted with Governor Allred, a very personable and kind man who treated this young reporter with utmost respect. It was appreciated and I remained a friend of Allred as long as he lived, despite differences in political philosophy. His differed greatly from the old-style conservatism of Coke Stevenson.

From 1936 until 1940, I worked for United Press as a one-man bureau at the old *Fort Worth Press* in that city. A colleague just thirty miles away in Dallas' UP office was Walter Cronkite, later to become the most famous television news personality in the world.

Cronkite also became a lifelong friend, who laughed about his first broadcasting job with an Austin radio station. It paid three dollars fifty cents a week, for part-time sports announcing. The position held by Cronkite didn't last, however, and the station manager advised Walter to "stick to writing, because you will never make it in broadcasting," Walter told me years later.

When he was in the big time and famous in later years, Cronkite once complained jokingly that while I made thirty dollars a week as a UP "bureau chief" his pay was only fifteen dollars weekly.

While I had good training in state government reporting as an office boy for UP's state capitol bureau headed by Gordon K. Shearer, my career in statehouse reporting really started with my return to Austin in 1940, still with United Press. In December 1942, I accepted higher pay with the *Dallas Morning News* staff in Austin.

O'Daniel was governor when I returned to the capitol, and he made little effort to make friends with the press, whose writers generally gave low rating to the chief executive and his ability as a public official. However, reporters in those days seldom reflected personal bias in their news coverage, as some of their successors did.

Governor O'Daniel seldom held a press conference. He communicated with his constituents mainly by radio, and his audience remained large. O'Daniel moved the governor's private office to a former reception room on the second floor of the capitol, where he sat behind a large desk, a reclusive and inaccessible figure to all except a few close friends and political advisers. Even some of his staff members complained of lack of access to their chief.

Coke Stevenson as governor was just the opposite. He moved back into a smaller private office on the capitol second floor and used the reception room for ceremonial occasions.

Stevenson's relationship with most reporters was the closest of any governor. He held press conferences almost daily and discussed state problems with reporters. While many of the sessions produced little news, they gave us a deep insight into Governor Stevenson and we kept his confidence.

The reporters and governor were friends in those years, rather than adversaries like some later newspeople considered their role to be. Stevenson invited the male members of the capitol press to his ranch every summer for two or three days of outdoor living, fishing, and storytelling along with some of his close friends from the area. It was an exciting experience for this young reporter to be included.

On one occasion, the governor — arising as usual before dawn — invited me to go with him on an inspection trip around the ranch. After coffee, I sat beside the state's chief executive as he drove a battered Ford coupe around rough ranch roads, pointing out the sights including deer and wild turkey. As the sun rose brilliantly, we stopped at Seven Hundred Springs, a famous watering hole near his ranch.

"Dick, I believe an occasion like this calls for a celebration," the governor said. I agreed, hardly realizing that he was pulling a bottle of Ten High Bourbon from beneath the driver's seat.

Stevenson wiped the dusty bottle with his khaki sleeve and handed it to me. I hardly knew what to say, being a novice in such situations.

But I took the bottle, drank a mouthful, and handed it back to the governor. My eyes watered and my hair rose as I swallowed the stuff. Stevenson calmly took a drink also, then we drank from the springs, a welcome chaser to the hot bourbon. The governor was moderate in all things, but believed socializing was best done during the daytime, and the nights reserved for sleeping.

After Stevenson, until the 1970s caused a changed relationship — really a strained relationship — all governors and the capitol press enjoyed friendly relationship and met rather frequently on social occasions and trips.

Stevenson held county offices before coming to Austin, and asserted that he never deliberately intended to become a public official but each time ran "for the purpose of getting a particular job done."

In contrast with some others, including his predecessor O'Daniel, Stevenson eschewed showmanship in the political arena and "steadfastly refused to be cast in the role of entertainer." [1]

Of all Texas governors, Stevenson most truly could be considered a cowboy, although Dolph Briscoe, Jr., who served 1973-1979, also was a rancher. Stevenson often wore low-quarter shoes instead of cowboy boots along with a conservative western hat with business suits and neckties.

"He was born in a log cabin and he went to work for a living when he was a boy, but he never allowed the story of his life to be presented in Algeresque trappings. He was a true son of the Hill Country, but he has never set himself up to be a hillbilly. He is a ranchman, born and bred, but no man has ever been able to get him to be picturesque for political purposes." [2]

Another description by Edmunds Travis, a reporter of the era:

"Coke Stevenson is neither a sight to see nor a sound to hear. He castigates no element of the people for the enjoyment of others, sings no hymns of hate, makes no appeal to group prejudice. Indeed, he can keep quiet longer and use fewer words in breaking his silence than anyone who has loomed large in Southern politics in many years." [3]

The above quotations come from a book published after Stevenson left the governorship and one year before a race for the United States Senate ended his political career.

Stevenson's close friends called him "Coke" unless it was a public affair where "Governor" is the customary address. Often he was respectfully called "Mister Coke" even by those well-acquainted with the governor.

A "Mister Texas" title was affixed by cartoonists depicting the governor as typical of the state's background. Unless told, nobody around Coke Stevenson in public life would ever suspect his formal schooling lasted only twenty-two months. But he was an avid reader of books and newspapers.

More than once, he complained jokingly of his *Dallas News* newspaper being thrown "late" at the Governor's Mansion after he was drinking coffee.

"What time did it get there, governor?"

"It was after five o'clock," he replied.

AFTER FORMER Governor Stevenson lost the disputed 1948
Democratic primary race for U.S. senator to Lyndon Johnson,
Stevenson and *The Dallas News* urged Democrats to support
Republican candidate Jack Porter in the general election.

— Reprinted from The Dallas Morning News

Of course delivery in Austin of a newspaper from Dallas before 5 a.m. is unlikely, but the governor usually fetched the paper just as soon as it arrived each morning.

For relaxation, Stevenson returned to his ranch on the
South Llano River and chopped cedar. He also loved music and
dancing, country style.

Leaving the governorship in 1947 after winning two elective
terms and serving sixteen months of O'Daniel's second term,
Stevenson summarized his administration to the legislature:

"It is easy to follow the pattern of my public service.

"First of all, I resolved that whatever I did should be done
within the framework of the Constitution.

"Second, I would be a good steward of the state's finances.

"Third, I would be of all assistance possible in promoting
the agricultural interests of the state.

"Fourth, I would give every consideration to a proper solution of the problems of labor.

"Fifth, I would assist in every possible way in the development of a great highway system and regulating the transportation of the highways.

"Sixth, I would liberally support those schools, colleges, and universities which continue to teach the fundamental concepts of our democratic system. [4]

As governor during the entire period of World War II, Stevenson presided over a state government whose expansion was temporarily restricted by the fact that building material and the nation's energy were devoted to winning the war.

But Stevenson did take the reins of a pre-war government whose general revenue fund was more than thirty million dollars in the red and see the treasury build a thirty-five million dollar surplus before he left office. While these figures seem puny in the light of later multi-billion-dollar state budgets, the financial accomplishments of the Stevenson administration were major.

Stevenson was governor throughout World War II, and all differences that he held politically with the national administration in Washington disappeared when the Japanese attacked Pearl Harbor. At Christmas 1941, the governor's message to Texans was:

"This hour is too solemn for ordinary Christmas greetings. Once again our nation is plunged into cruel war. Trials and tribulations stare us in the face. But we are a brave people. Christian endeavor fortifies us. We will win the victory of the forces within us. Let us therefore lift our eyes to the star of Bethlehem, external symbol of love and peace, and pray earnestly for the triumph of right and justice, and for the relief of distressed peoples in every land. Peace on earth, good will toward men." [5]

Texas contributed more than any other state to the war effort in terms of men, energy, training, and manufacturing facilities.

The Texas National Guard was summoned to train under federal direction a year before the United States entered the war. Trained at Camp Bowie, near Brownwood, the 36th Division went to North Africa early in 1942 and its citizen-soldiers performed heroically, suffering heavy casualties in the invasion of Italy and on the western front.

The Second Battalion, 131st Field Artillery, was en route to the Western Pacific when Pearl Harbor and the Philippines were attacked by the Japanese. The Texas unit was diverted to Java, where the U.S. was attempting to establish a beachhead in a Japanese-controlled area. Most battalion members who survived the fighting were taken prisoner and endured almost four years of maltreatment by their captors.

A few of the battalion joined the army air corps (predecessor to the air force) after reaching Java and escaped with airmen who managed to evade the Japanese.

Major General Willie Scott, the Texas National Guard's commanding general in 1981, recalled the days before World War II. Scott was a student at Wayland College in Plainview, and played basketball. All of his teammates were enlisted as "weekend soldiers" in the local Guard outfit, partly because it was a patriotic thing for many young men to do, and because the pay for attending Guard drills helped supplement the students' meager incomes.

"When our unit was called up before the war," said Scott, "it wiped out Wayland's basketball team. As National Guard men at Camp Bowie, we won the division basketball championship."

About three-quarters of a million Texas men and women served in the military during World War II. More than one and one-quarter million trained in the state, including twenty combat army divisions and more than two hundred thousand airmen.[6]

Situated in Texas were fifteen army posts, more than forty military air training and defense installations, twenty-one prisoner-of-war camps, and numerous war manufacturing enterprises.

Two of the war's greatest commanders were born in Texas: General of the Army Dwight D. Eisenhower at Denison and Fleet Admiral Chester W. Nimitz at Fredericksburg.

Infantryman Audie Murphy of Farmersville was the war's most decorated hero. Oveta Culp Hobby of Houston was appointed to head the new Womens' Army Corps (WAC).

Many Texas legislators and several congressmen joined the armed forces. Navy Lieutenant Paul Eubank of Matador and Air

Force Lieutenant Duncan Hughes of Georgetown were killed in action. Both were state representatives.

Texas' contribution in manpower and training facilities was enormous, yet one of the state's most important contributions was oil. ''The Allies floated to victory on a sea of Texas oil,'' asserted Ernest O. Thompson, who served both as an army general officer and as Texas Railroad Commission member, one of the nation's top advisers on supplying the armed forces with gasoline, oil, and other products needed to deliver and move the huge mechanized military machine that achieved the victory over the Japanese and Germans.

The Petroleum Administration for War, staffed by knowledgeable industry experts mostly from Texas, was established to keep petroleum supplies flowing. Production was sufficient, largely because of Texas' big oil output, but delivery was difficult. Enemy submarines lurked in shipping lanes of the Gulf of Mexico as well as along the Atlantic and Pacific coasts.

Many American tanker ships and German submarines were sunk.

Through tremendous effort, a ''Big Inch'' pipeline was constructed to carry oil and products to the New York area without the hazard of shipping by sea.

Thirty years later, when an oil shortage resulted in the United States from efforts of the Organization of Petroleum Exporting Countries (OPEC), national leaders failed to heed the experience of the Petroleum Administration for War in developing domestic supplies. Instead, consumer-oriented groups in Washington backed the creation of a cabinet-level U.S. Department of Energy to deal with the shortage but excluded industry energy production experts from the planning and management until the 1980s.

OPEC nations still control world oil prices, however, because the United States had become dependent on the Middle-East, African, and South American nations for more than one-third of its oil.

Efforts were under way in the 1980s to make the nation energy-independent again by conserving petroleum, increasing coal, lignite, nuclear, synthetic and other substitutes for oil and

STEVENSON makes a point.

gas. Energy independence could be expected again after the year 2000, by most estimates if development is not impeded.

State government under Coke Stevenson during the war was maintained in status quo.

The most significant achievement was adoption in the November 1942 election, effective in 1945, of the constitutional amendment (Article III, Section 49a) to put the state government on a pay-as-you-go basis. Voters adopted this by a 96,418 to 72,816 majority.

In normal times, the proposition probably would have failed because of opposition from spending groups seeking state funds. But the conservative mood of wartime provided a different climate.

Also adopted during Stevenson's administration, with his strong support, was the so-called "Good Roads" amendment to the State Constitution (Article VIII, Section 7-a). It declares that three-fourths of all motor fuel and other "road user" taxes shall be spent building and maintaining roads. The other one-fourth goes to public schools.

With this provision, Texas dedicated tax revenue to provide the nation's best highway system. The "road user" financing was enough to keep up with the state's mounting highway needs until the late 1970s when the use of more fuel-efficient vehicles ended a long period of highway tax revenue rising along with increased use of automobiles and trucks. In the 1970s, the legislature, with Governor Briscoe's urging, provided that additional general revenue shall be spent on highways.

Texas managed to provide the nation's best highways and the lowest gasoline tax at the same time, however, and without incurring debt through issuing bonds for highway improvement.

One of Governor Stevenson's wartime responsibilities was to maintain good relations with Mexico, our neighbor across the Rio Grande who frequently disagrees with policies of the United States and state governments.

In September 1943, Governor Stevenson traveled to Mexico City on a goodwill trip at President Roosevelt's suggestion. Chief of Staff General George C. Marshall and Nelson Rockefeller, then involved in economic aid to Latin America, also attended festivities hosted by President Manuel Avila Camacho in the Mexican capital.

I went along with Stevenson as a reporter. We traveled in two Texas highway patrol cars driven by state troopers in plain clothes.

We drove through West Texas to El Paso, and lavish official functions were held by the Mexicans in Juarez, Chihuahua City, Torreon, Parras, Saltillo, Monterrey and Victoria as well as Mexico City.

Nobody produces such fiestas with more gusto than the

Mexicans. We were wined, dined, and entertained at every stop, and the governor enjoyed it all.

Our diplomatic escort for the trip was Luis Duplan, Mexico's consul general at Austin with whom Stevenson had formed a close friendship. The party included several Austin newsmen.

Despite the exhaustion of covering all this territory in two weeks by motorcar, when the festivities ended in Mexico City, Governor Stevenson chose to return home nonstop — one thousand miles to Austin. One patrol car blew out a tire, leaving it without a spare, but the two cars pushed ahead with the governor relieving the highway patrolmen as driver.

I was staggering-tired when we reached Austin after twenty-four hours of steady riding. Stevenson didn't even go to bed. He stopped briefly to check at his capitol office, then drove another one hundred seventy miles to his ranch south of Junction, where he rested by chopping cedar trees.

Stevenson won a second elective term as governor in 1944 against a dozen Democrats without a runoff, and against a nominal Republican candidate.

President Roosevelt won a fourth term at the same time, but was seriously ill and died the following year, elevating Vice President Harry S Truman to the presidency.

Politics took a back seat until the horrors of World War II ended with the Japanese surrender aboard the battleship USS Missouri in Tokyo Bay September 2, 1945, after President Truman authorized the dropping of atomic bombs on Hiroshima and Nagasaki.

With the end of war, political activity resumed in full force.

POSTWAR POLITICS AND GOVERNMENT

Domestic disputes that had been laid aside during the war quickly surfaced after the hostility ended.

Divisions widened between conservative and liberal factions. Even before the war, some conservatives professed to see a threat of Communism and subversion to undermine the United States. Some of these complaints were branded as witch-hunting

71

but the controversy was real. Turmoil on The University of Texas-Austin campus symbolized the situation.

Dr. Homer Price Rainey had been elected president by the Board of Regents in 1939 but quickly developed philosophical disputes with the governing board and other state officials. The faculty generally supported Rainey's position, while students demonstrated in his behalf and even walked out of classes.

The differences were numerous. Some critics claimed subversive activities were countenanced by President Rainey. Once the regents fired three economics staff members over Rainey's protest because of a commotion caused when they were refused permission to address an anti-labor mass meeting.

The squabble was investigated by the legislature. In 1944, the Board of Regents fired President Rainey after he accused them publicly of overstepping the board's authority.

Liberal Democrats urged Rainey to run for governor in 1946 on a vindication platform, which he did. It was a bitter campaign, which Rainey lost in a second primary runoff with Beauford H. Jester, a Corsicana attorney then serving on the Texas Railroad Commission.

Jester led thirteen candidates in the first primary, followed by Rainey and former Attorney General Grover Sellers of Sulphur Springs. Jester took a rather high road in discussions during the campaign, so far as the Rainey dispute was concerned. Sellers lambasted the ousted educator relentlessly.

Jester easily won the runoff by 701,018 votes to Rainey's 355,654, and had only nominal opposition from Republican Eugene Nolte, Jr. in the general election.

Because construction and expansion of most state programs had been postponed during World War II, the Jester administration faced both a challenge and an opportunity.

During the months between his inauguration January 21, 1947, and his death aboard a train en route to Houston from Austin July 11, 1949, Beauford Jester was perhaps the most effective governor Texas ever had.

This was accomplished despite Jester's reputation as a playboy-type. He was a cheerful, outgoing individual, who loved people, including the rigors of political campaigning.

GOV. BEAUFORD H. JESTER and son at a Christmas tree in the Governors' Mansion.

— *Austin-Travis County Collection*

In 1946, while Jester pursued his "People's Path" campaign theme, I traveled with him in East Texas. It was a delightful trip, although physically tiring. Jester visited places where statewide candidates seldom trod.

At Coldspring, county seat of San Jacinto County, Jester shook hands with almost the town's whole six hundred population as he toured the courthouse square.

"Every candidate for governor who visited Coldspring got elected," a local citizen informed Jester. History indicated that the last gubernatorial candidate to campaign in the piney-woods area town was James Stephen Hogg in 1890.

Jester staff members credited me with a suggestion which helped him win the nomination and election. As recalled years later by James Egan, then a Jester staff member, the campaign entourage stopped one night at a Huntsville hotel. I was invited, as the only reporter on the trip, to Jester's room for a social hour with the candidate and his staff. The talk turned to issues of the race.

"You asked Jester 'why don't you come out against new taxes'?" said Egan. "Beauford said he would do it, and the next day you sent a story about his no-new-taxes position after he had stated it publicly."

The offhand suggestion seemed a rather obvious idea. The state treasury was in excellent condition in 1946, partly because of the new "pay-as-we-go" provision of the state constitution and partly because the state had spent relatively little on expansion and construction during World War II. Most government services were restricted during the war. After the war, the demands for greater spending on government services grew rapidly.

Jester's first term saw legislation passed creating Texas State University for Negroes located in Houston, and offered a constitutional amendment adopted later that year by voters to allocate ten cents per one hundred dollars valuation of the state property tax to four-year state institutions of higher education not receiving building funds from the Permament University Fund, an endowment shared by The University of Texas and Texas A&M systems.

April 16, 1947, brought one of the state's greatest disasters when a ship loaded with explosive nitrate blew up in the harbor at Texas City. Five hundred fifty persons were killed, hundreds more injured, and an estimated thirty-five million dollars in property damage inflicted.

The legislature in 1947 took steps to improve the state's public education system. It created the so-called Gilmer-Aikin Committee composed of legislators, educators, and others to recommend improvements to the 1949 legislative session. These were later adopted, and gave the state an educational system considered among the best in the nation at that time.

Creation of the committee resulted from efforts by State Representative Claud H. Gilmer of Rocksprings and Senator

74

James E. Taylor who opposed continuation of the "rural aid" financial system which the state had been following.

The two legislators incurred the wrath of the Texas State Teachers Association, mostly represented by school administrators, who demanded more money for the schools without waiting for any study. Creation of the committee was a compromise to allow time for setting up a better program in Texas. Senator A. M. Aikin, Jr. of Paris was named co-sponsor because of his long friendship with the education group.

The bill to establish Texas State University for Negroes also ventilated a pent-up controversy. In 1885, the first students enrolled at Prairie View Agricultural and Mechanical College (later named university), according to a mandate in the state constitution to provide higher education for black residents.

In 1946, the National Association for Advancement of Colored People filed suit against The University of Texas at Austin with Heman Sweatt, a black Houston postman, as the plaintiff. Sweatt sought admission to the all-white law school on the ground that Texas provided no equal opportunity for Negroes to study law. At the time, the state law and constitution prohibited coeducation of whites and Negroes. After an earlier lawsuit, Mexican-Americans had been legally classified as Caucasians.

Seeking to defuse Sweatt's lawsuit against the university, then-President T. S. Painter, the legislature appropriated $3,350,000 to establish Texas Southern University in Houston. Included was $350,000 to operate a temporary (segregated) law school for Sweatt and other black applicants in Austin located in a house near the state Capitol and taught by University of Texas law school faculty members. In 1950, the United States Supreme Court decided in favor of Sweatt.

"It was clear from the opinion that a good faith effort to supply equality of treatment without integration was insufficient; rather, it must be equality in fact," explained W. Page Keeton, dean of the University Law School. [7]

The highest court declared in the case that separate facilities likely would produce among black students a feeling of "inferiority . . . that may affect their hearts and minds in a way likely ever to be undone."

75

A law school was established at Texas Southern University after it got into operation. The University of Houston, a former community college taken into the state system in 1947, also operates a law school about a quarter-mile from the TSU campus.

The controversy over equality of educational opportunity continued unabated in the 1980s although legal segregation was dead and schools at all levels were open to all races.

Black leaders and educators continued to argue for the improvement, not just the survival, of universities operated particularly for members of that race. They contended that black students have special needs requiring special educational treatment.

The United States Department of Health, Education and Welfare by 1981 had ordered the state to provide fully equal educational facilities at the historically-black universities under penalty of losing hundreds of millions of dollars in federal funds for Texas schools.

One West Texas legislator sought to solve the question by terminating Prairie View and Texas Southern, but this idea was opposed by Governor William P. Clements, legislative leaders, and the Coordinating Board, Texas College and University System.

The Coordinating Board in a survey of the state's educational needs for the 1980s, termed the two institutions "essential to Texas because they serve vital needs. They will continue to do so for the foreseeable future. The presidents of both schools have taken a strong position that without the availability of their universities, many young black students could never attend college."

In 1980-1981, Texas Southern had more than eight hundred students enrolled and Prairie View had more than 5,500. About forty percent of all blacks attending public institutions of higher education in Texas enrolled at the two mostly-black universities, and the others were scattered among numerous community colleges and universities.

Nearly one-third of TSU's enrollment came from aliens, mostly from the Middle East, and approximately two-thirds were black. A few white students were enrolled at the Houston school.

At Prairie View A&M, a branch of Texas A&M, located forty-five miles northwest of Houston in a rural setting near Hempstead, sixty miles northwest of Houston, blacks still represented eighty-eight percent of the enrollment thirty years after the Supreme Court prohibited segregation in the Sweatt case ruling. The other Prairie View students were whites and Hispanics.

"The participation of blacks and Hispanics in Texas public higher education has increased significantly — in some respects dramatically — during the past decade in terms of enrollment, degrees received, employment, and representation on governing boards," the Coordinating Board reported in 1981.

The number of these ethnic minorities, however, still did not attend colleges and universities in proportion to the percentage of the general population.

Blacks comprise about twelve percent and Mexican-Americans twenty-one percent of all Texans. In 1978, the board found 8.8 percent blacks and 12.2 percent Hispanics among students enrolled in public higher education in Texas. In 1970, the enrollment was 6.6 percent blacks and 7.8 percent Hispanics.

Projections indicate increasing percentages of minority-group students will be attending colleges and universities in the state. In 1979, almost one-half of the first-graders in Texas public schools came from these groups. Included were 31.6 percent blacks, 15.4 percent Hispanics, 1.1 percent Asian, and 51.9 percent whites. The first-graders also included 322 American Indians among the 231,598 total enrollment.

The above figures mean that higher education can expect rising percentages of racial minorities and relatively smaller percentages of white students during the 1980s and later. [8]

The legislature in 1947 enacted several labor laws, all over the protest of the leaders of organized labor.

These prohibit any employee action which disrupts the service of an electric, gas, or water utility; a so-called "right to work" bill outlawing contracts requiring workers to join a union; forbid strikes by public employees; outlaw secondary strikes and boycotts; require written consent by a worker before union dues can be deducted from his paycheck; make unions responsible for damages caused by their members in the case of breach of labor contracts; and place unions under both civil and criminal anti-trust laws. [9]

The above laws continue to be opposed generally by labor leaders but remain on the statute books despite efforts to revoke them.

A huge postwar higher education building program likewise was launched after voters approved a constitutional amendment in August 1947. The University of Texas was allowed to issue ten million dollars in bonds—and Texas A&M five million dollars for building bonds to be financed by the Permanent University (endowment) Fund, a practice formerly prohibited.

Schools outside the state university and Texas A&M systems were allocated shares in a new building fund to be financed by ad valorem property taxes.

The first year of Governor Jester's administration also saw the beginning of the legal battle with the United States government over ownership of the offshore "tidelands," whose prospective worth for producing oil, gas, and other minerals was coming to be realized.

The United States Supreme Court held that California tidewater areas belong to the federal government. Texas had a much larger stake in the outcome of this dispute because it had claimed a continental and state boundary three leagues (10.35 miles) from its shoreline under the agreement by which it joined the United States February 19, 1846, after ten years as a republic.

More than four million acres of the state's 176,266,000 total acres were involved. Oil and gas production already had started offshore. Submerged areas of the state, including lakes and riverbeds are property whose income is held in trust as an endowment for public schools of Texas.

"If they try to apply it (the California decision) to Texas, I'm in favor of seceding before giving our property to the federal government," commented Bascom Giles, commissioner of the General Land Office. [10]

Attorney General Price Daniel advised the School Land Board to continue leasing Texas offshore tracts to oil and gas developers. Governor Jester, Commissioner Giles, and Attorney General Daniel were the lease board members.

The battle over the tidelands had just begun. Before Texas officials fought it to a successful conclusion, it had figured prominently in political as well as judicial history, and caused Texas voters to turn against the Democratic presidential candidate Adlai Stevenson in 1952 in favor of Republican Dwight D. Eisenhower. Eisenhower promised to help defend Texas' right to this valuable property, and he did.

"LANDSLIDE LYNDON" JOHNSON
AWARDED UNITED STATES SENATE SEAT

A controversial election for the United States Senate held in 1948, in Texas, literally changed the course of American history.

Awarding the questionable victory to then-Congressman Lyndon B. Johnson allowed him to become president of the United States, as a result of events which followed.

As a reporter involved in covering some aspects of that election, I have always believed that an honest, fair count would have given the Senate seat to former Governor Coke R. Stevenson.

The official results showed Johnson a winner by eighty-seven votes over Stevenson in the Democratic runoff primary held August 28, 1948.

My view that Johnson "won" the election on stolen votes in South Texas is supported by Robert W. Calvert, retired chief justice of the Texas Supreme Court who was chairman of the State Democratic Executive Committee when the county voting returns were certified.

"I was fully convinced that an election fraud had been perpetrated in Jim Wells County by which two hundred one votes had been mysteriously added to Johnson's total and one had been added to Stevenson's total," wrote Calvert. [11]

This was greater than the eighty-seven-vote margin by which the State Democratic Executive Committee certified Johnson as winner, and by counting the questioned votes.

In a preface written after the Calvert book was finished, the jurist noted new evidence in 1977 that the 1948 election was stolen from Stevenson.

". . . Now fortuitously, just before publication," wrote Calvert," my conclusion that election fraud was committed in

U.S. SENATE nominee Lyndon Johnson, President Harry Truman, and Mayor Pro Tem Homer Thornberry of Austin (later congressman and federal judge) on Truman's campaign train in fall of 1948.

— *Photo from LBJ Library*

the 1948 Senate race in Box 13, Jim Wells County, has been confirmed by the election judge.''

If the Duval County election judge had been willing to tell the truth in 1948, Texas and American history would have been different.

Nevertheless, Calvert said he would have voted — if necessary — to certify the nomination for Johnson because of a legal precedent set in 1932 in a contest for governor between Mrs. Miriam A. Ferguson and Ross Sterling, won by Mrs. Ferguson. In that race, the Texas Supreme Court declared that the state political party executive committee must certify the vote totals submitted by the party's county chairmen regardless of any other circumstances.

In the Johnson-Stevenson race, the state committee voted twenty-nine to twenty-eight to certify the returns showing Johnson received 494,191 votes to 494,104 for Stevenson. So it was unnecessary for Chairman Calvert to cast any tie-breaking vote.

The stormy election was accompanied by numerous court actions, including one appeal to the United States Supreme Court which, in effect, decided not to consider the merits of Stevenson's complaint that a United States Senate seat had been stolen from him.

Central in the dispute were two hundred three votes — which proved to be decisive — reported several days after the election from Box 13, Jim Wells County, in the South Texas bailiwick of political boss George Parr. Until this report added two hundred two votes for Johnson and one vote for Stevenson, it appeared that Stevenson had won in an unexpectedly-close statewide ballot.

Efforts to conduct a meaningful investigation of what happened in Box 13's case were thwarted by Johnson and Parr forces, although Stevenson produced testimony that the late votes were added alphabetically, tallied in different-colored ink from the original list, and included names of dead persons and others who said they had not voted in the election.

T. Kellis Dibrell and James Gardner, young lawyers who had been Federal Bureau of Investigation agents, helped Stevenson's effort to prove the voting fraud. Once, they got to see the Box 13 tally sheet with the questionable votes, at a bank. But the list was taken away from them before they could finish reading the names or make any notes.

They did recall enough names to know the alphabetical tally and were able to show later that the additional "votes" came from names in graveyards and persons who asserted they had not voted in the runoff election.

Candidate Johnson stopped Stevenson's attempt to see the tally sheet and question fully those claimed to be voting. A friendly state district judge in Austin gave Johnson an emergency restraining order, without notice to Stevenson, which stopped the Stevenson investigation.

The State Democratic Executive Committee's legalistic decision to award the nomination to Johnson, ignoring the fraud claims, left Texas Democrats more divided than usual. The event forever placed a stigma on Lyndon Johnson's political career.

In the first primary Stevenson had received 477,077 votes to 405,617 for Johnson and 237,195 for George E. B. Peddy, a well-known Houston lawyer. Because Johnson was regarded as the "liberal" candidate in the Democratic campaign, Stevenson's ultimate victory appeared to be almost certain.

In the party runoff primary, Stevenson made a campaign mistake that has been disastrous to other front-running political candidates.

"Stevenson's runoff campaign was as inept as any major political campaign waged in Texas in my time," recalled Judge Calvert. "It was the type of inoffensive, no-issue, don't-rock-the-boat, fence-straddling campaign by which most candidates with long leads seek to nurse a candidacy to eventual victory. It was the same kind of campaign waged by Dewey in losing to Truman in the same year." [13]

The Johnson campaign, managed by John B. Connally, by contrast was a "tireless, dynamic, whirlwind campaign in a helicopter and caught the imagination of enough voters to pull up even on election day. And even if it was, I voted for Johnson, not because I loved him more but because I believed over the long haul his election would prove of greater value to this country's future." [14]

Although Calvert maintained amicable relations with Stevenson as lieutenant governor and governor, early in his state political career, Calvert — a representative from Hillsboro — had lost a hard-fought race for speakership of the Texas House of Representatives. Conservatives elected Stevenson, while the so-called "liberals" and less conservative legislators supported Calvert, who later won another race for Speaker.

The 1948 race for the Senate nomination was Stevenson's last. He endorsed, but did not campaign for, the Republican candidate Jack Porter, a Houston oilman and former Democrat.

Johnson won the general election by a margin of two to one, but Porter's total was better than usual for a Republican candidate in Texas during that period.

Coke Stevenson retired to his beloved ranch on the South Llano River and practiced law in Junction for another twenty-seven years until his death June 28, 1975. In 1954, thirty-two years after the death of his first wife in 1941 while they lived in the Governor's Mansion, Stevenson married Marguerite Heap, a widow of World War II, and became the father of one daughter. A son by his first wife, Coke, Jr., became Stevenson's law partner at Junction.

During retirement, Stevenson occasionally endorsed candidates, sometimes Republican candidates but always conservatives.

But the bitter defeat in 1948 on the results of Jim Wells County Box 13 ended his political career.

The presidential contest, to which Calvert referred as a parallel to the Johnson-Stevenson campaign, brought a victory to Harry S Truman, Democrat, who ascended to the presidency in 1945 on the death of Franklin D. Roosevelt, and Republican Thomas E. Dewey, former governor of New York.

Early polls indicated Dewey would win, but Truman conducted a hard-hitting personal campaign that brought him victory for a four-year elective term.

A third candidate was Governor J. Strom Thurmond of South Carolina, nominated on a States' Rights (Dixiecrat) Party ticket by conservative Southern Democrats who couldn't bring themselves to vote for Truman or Dewey. Thurmond carried only Alabama, Louisiana, Mississippi, and South Carolina.

Truman won Texas easily: Truman 750,700, Dewey 282,240, Thurmond 106,909. Three minor party candidates received about 7,000 votes.[15] In 1948, Texas ballots carried only the names of party electoral college delegates on the ballot, not the name of actual candidates.

Interestingly, some Texas Democrats joined a movement to draft Dwight D. (Ike) Eisenhower, a five-star general who led Allied forces to victory in World War II, as the Democratic candidate for president in 1948. Eisenhower had no political party affiliation during his life spent in the army. Conservative Demo-

TWO 1948 cartoons reprinted from *The Dallas Morning News* editions reflect Truman, who won despite adverse polls, and the Republican convention which nominated Tom Dewey, where delegates considered him a certainty to become president.

— *Reprinted from The Dallas Morning News*

crats opposed nominating Harry S Truman, and joined the campaign to nominate Eisenhower at the Democratic National convention. Governor Jester and Wright Morrow, a Houston lawyer and Democratic National committeeman-elect, led the draft-Ike effort in Texas.

"Ike could win on any ticket," commented Governor Jester. "He could pull Democratic factions together as nobody else could." [16]

But Eisenhower already had made known that he would neither seek nor accept the presidential nomination in 1948. So the boom collapsed. Four years later, as a Republican candidate, General Eisenhower won the presidential nomination, with help from Texans of both Democratic and Republican persuasion.

THE SHIVERS-JESTER REFORMS

The regular biennial session of the Texas legislature in 1949 lasted from January 11 to July 6, the longest in Texas history. It also was the final session for Governor Beauford H. Jester, and perhaps the most productive in Texas history. Later, a 140-day limit was put on regular sessions.

On July 11, five days after the session ended, the governor was found dead in his Pullman berth on the Southern Pacific Railroad train after it arrived in Houston. Death came from a heart attack. Earlier in the day, he enjoyed an outing with his staff.

Within hours. Lieutenant Governor Allan Shivers, forty-one, took the oath as governor of Texas at Magnolia Hills, the family farm near Woodville, where the Shivers family was vacationing following the long legislative session.

In 1946 Shivers had been elected lieutenant governor after serving as a state senator from Jefferson County.

Although the session under Jester's direction had been one of the most progressive in Texas history, performing tasks which had been postponed by the restraints of World War II and the immediate postwar period, part of the implementation was left to the Shivers administration.

Foremost of the 1949 regular sessions' accomplishments was passage of the Gilmer-Aikin laws which changed the Texas

85

public school system from one of outmoded policies left over from the state's earlier days as a rural economy to a system which was generally regarded as one of the best in the United States.

Other accomplishments of that legislative session included:

• Created a Legislative Budget Board to plan and oversee spending of the state's money.

• Established a Legislative Council to do research for the lawmaking branch, replacing piecemeal special study committees.

• Reorganized the Texas prison system with the result that within a few years it changed from being criticized as one of the worst in the United States to being the very best. Under a new prison board and director, lawmakers provided for better-trained and better-paid prison employees, improved facilities, and additional training and educational opportunities for inmates. By 1980, however, overcrowding became a serious problem.

• Created a State Board of Hospitals and Special Schools to modernize treatment for mentally and physically-ill citizens requiring public facilities.

• Repealed the poll tax as a requirement for voting. The fee had been collected in Texas for nearly a century, and was attacked in Congress and the federal courts as resulting in disfranchisement of the poor and racial minorities. The tax, however, was only $1.75 a year including administration charges and served mainly as a voter-registration system.

• Established the Youth Development Council with a citizens' governing board to oversee the handling of juvenile delinquents.

"During its first regular session, January 11-July 6, 1949, the Fifty-first Legislature of Texas enacted into law three bills which effected a complete reorganization of the Texas public school system," wrote Representative Rae Files Still of Waxahachie in her book *The Gilmer-Aikin Bills.*

As one active in this effort, Mrs. Still, a former public school teacher-turned legislator, knew whereof she spoke.

"These laws made sweeping changes in the administration of the system and in methods of school finance, beginning at the highest state level and continuing through the smallest local unit. This reform by legislation was done in accordance with na-

GOVERNOR JESTER'S administration faced huge problems concerning state institutions in 1947, which he helped overcome with the assistance of Allen Shivers who became governor in 1949 at Jester's death.

— Reprinted from The Dallas Morning News

tionally-accepted standards of excellence for public school administration and advanced thinking in public school finance.

"The fact that such drastic changes were consummated in a field so close to the general public during one regular session of a state legislature amazed those who were familiar with similar efforts in other states. The enactment of any one of the three bills would have been considered a legislative accomplishment of some magnitude. The passage of all three at one regular session could have resulted only from intensive effort by those interested in the program." [17]

"Those interested in the program" included business interests as well as educators, and public officials ranging from liberals to conservatives. It was the most nonpartisan effort the state had ever seen to solve a complex and complicated problem, close to the heart of nearly every citizen and community.

Mrs. Still described the politically-powerful Texas State Teachers Association as "distrustful" when the Gilmer-Aikin Committee launched its study in 1947 created by a legislative resolution sponsored by two conservatives, Senator James E. Taylor of Kerens, Navarro County, and Representative Claud H. Gilmer of Rocksprings. Taylor was a country newspaper editor recently returned from service in World War II. Gilmer was an attorney and rancher. Both disliked the political manner in which state funds had been dispensed to public schools in the past, and they proposed the two-year study with the reluctant approval of public school officials who were having increasing difficulty at every legislative session in getting the funds they claimed were needed from the state.

Politically-powerful Dr. L. A. Woods, State Superintendent of Public Instruction, and public school administrators and boards around the state led opposition to the changes in 1949.

One new law provided for appointment of a State Education commissioner as chief administrator of the department. Formerly, the state superintendent was elected statewide, and the governor appointed a nine-member governing board.

The Gilmer-Aikin laws established a new board, elected by congressional districts. The first elected board took office in January 1950.

The quality of the new State Board of Education was typified by its first chairman, Robert B. Anderson, a former state legislator who had become manager of the huge Waggoner oil and ranch interests headquartered at Vernon. Anderson gave much time to the new office, as did other board members. They chose as the first commissioner of education to establish the program Dr. J. W. Edgar, who had been superintendent of schools at Austin and Orange. Edgar also served on the Gilmer-Aikin Committee which formulated the program and who understood its objectives.

Chairman Anderson later served as Secretary of the Navy and Secretary of the Treasury under President Eisenhower.

The quick success of the Gilmer-Aikin program stemmed largely from the high caliber of those chosen to put it into effect.

Other parts of the program dealt with organization of schools at the local level, resulting in consolidations of many very small and expensive schools, state financing of public schools, and such details as maintenance, selecting textbooks and curriculum, and building standards. The standard was to provide state assistance, offering every student an opportunity to obtain a good, basic education.

State funds were distributed according to "average daily attendance," which furnished an inducement for school authorities to keep the students in class.

Previously, state funds were distributed on an enrollment basis described as "rural aid" because country schools had the worst financial problems and smallest offerings to students.

Discrimination against blacks and Hispanics occurred frequently under the old fund allotment. The laws until 1954 required separation of black and white students in public schools. Hispanics were classed as "Caucasian" by court order which allowed this group to be segregated only in the first grade while the youngsters learned English.

The Gilmer-Aikin laws provided equal treatment financially in educating all races, and equal standards for schools, although achieving these goals then and still is elusive. The new laws did stop the practice of some school boards taking state money intended for educating blacks and / or Hispanics and spending it on white schools, while making little effort to educate racial minorities.

The Gilmer-Aikin plan worked well, although perhaps with diminishing effectiveness because of such unforeseen factors as court-ordered busing for racial balance among students at extreme expense to districts. Dilution of educational quality also was blamed on various special programs to assist less-able students, "progressive promotion" for low achievers, diminished teacher morale, and a "white flight" from the social and financial problems of inner-city schools such as Dallas and Houston to suburbs where education quality is considered higher and the problems fewer.

The same period has witnessed a decline in influence of the Texas State Teachers Association, particularly after many Texas teachers and administrators objected to seeing the state organization join the union-like National Education Association.

Several school groups formed organizations separate from T.S.T.A. Classroom teachers particularly seek a stronger voice in the operation of schools, rather than leaving the decision-making totally to administrators and school boards.

GOVERNOR ALLAN SHIVERS

Allan Shivers, who held office from July 11, 1949, until January 15, 1957, served longer as governor than anyone in Texas history. Three others tried for longer tenure later — Price Daniel, Dolph Briscoe, Jr., and Preston Smith — but all were retired by the voters after six years in office.

Besides his durability as a candidate, Allan Shivers may have been — all things considered — the best governor of his time.

Shivers had the qualifications of a leader: an outgoing personality, toughness, commanding presence (six feet two inches tall), and a sound education that didn't spring from a rich upbringing although later he became wealthy. While attending The University of Texas at Austin, Shivers worked as a state capitol elevator operator. He was president of The University of Texas student body before graduating to become a lawyer at Port Arthur.

In 1935, at twenty-eight years of age, Shivers became "the boy senator" by winning his first election. He never lost an election, serving successively as lieutenant governor and governor before leaving public office in 1957 to become active in business and banking. He also served on The University of Texas Board of Regents, during part of those years.

Shivers never gave up his political personality even after he quit running for office.

An example of this:

During Governor Briscoe's administration, Shivers and his wife Marialice paid a call on Briscoe. While they waited in the reception room for Briscoe, I visited with these two longtime friends. A group of tourists came into the reception room, which is on the official capitol tour.

90

GOVERNOR ALLAN SHIVERS rolls his own at the Stamford Rodeo.
— *State Archives Photo*

Like an old hunting dog sniffing a quail, Shivers instinctively rose and started shaking hands with the astonished tourists, introducing "I'm Allan Shivers."

A few moments later, Briscoe emerged, greeting the Shiverses warmly. A more reserved man, Briscoe didn't introduce himself to the sightseers, even though he was running for reelection.

The incident illustrates the difference in style. Shivers was the consummate candidate even when he wasn't running for anything. He had a good memory for faces and names, beyond what one learns from books on salesmanship. With Shivers, it was native talent.

Shivers also was a formidable adversary. His political battles with leaders of organized labor were classics, and the animosity never ended. Shivers broke with the Democratic party's national leadership in 1952 and 1956 when as governor he led a Democrats-for-Eisenhower movement that carried the state into the Republican presidential column.

He was a sometimes-adversary also of Lyndon B. Johnson, in the 1950s and 1960s.

The long 1949 regular session of the legislature adjourned after Governor Jester vetoed the second year of the biennial appropriation to operate state hospitals for the mentally ill, tuberculars, and the eleemosynary institutions.

The state comptroller reported there was insufficient income in sight to pay that portion of the state's budget, so the legislature faced the task of increasing taxes immediately or postponing the responsibility until the governor called a special session.

After Jester's death, the new governor quickly pledged to carry out the appointments which Jester promised to make, except two for judgeships in South Texas.

"In an effort to get Senator Rogers Kelley of Edinburg to approve Paul Brown for Fire Insurance Commissioner, Jester had promised to name Judge Harry Carroll of Corpus Christi to the Fourth Court of Civil Appeals, and to appoint Luther Jones of Corpus Christi as District Judge, replacing Carroll," wrote capitol correspondents Sam Kinch and Stuart Long in their biography of Shivers.

"It turned out that George Parr, the 'boss' of Duval County with influence in other counties of the area, wanted these two appointments and no second choices. Carroll withdrew when it came into controversy, and Shivers named two judges closer to Parr than Carroll and Jones — geographically at least — District Judge Lorenz Broeter of Alice to the Fourth Court, and Sam Reams of Alice as District Judge. (Senator) Kelley agreed to these two, but Parr was not mollified. In his typical hot-headed fashion, he pledged to support Caso March (a Waco lawyer who had announced for the 1950 Democratic nomination) for governor, and Duval County came through in the Democratic primary the next July with 4,239 votes to 108 for Shivers."[18]

It was the only county Shivers lost in his bid for an elective term in 1950. Parr again proved he could deliver his votes where he wanted them to go.

In January 1950, Shivers called a thirty-day special session of the legislature to raise the money needed to keep state hospitals operating during the year starting September 1, 1950.

The new governor demonstrated his political skill by getting an agreement, before the legislature met, for a ten to fourteen percent increase in existing taxes on oil, natural gas, sulphur, insurance premiums, and several other business operations, plus a one-cent increase in the cigarette tax to four cents per package.

The increases were designated to be temporary, which they weren't, as is usually the case. But Shivers did get pledges from lobbyists for the prospective taxpayers that they wouldn't oppose the proposal, estimated to net more than twenty million dollars per year. Before introducing his tax program, Shivers called on the legislature to appropriate more money for the 1950-1951 year than the undernourished hospital system had been getting.

Failure to make the needed improvements, Shivers told the legislature, "would mean turning our backs on those less fortunate citizens in crowded mental hospitals, on children who are physically and mentally handicapped and need a helping hand, on thousands of fellow Texans who are dying of tuberculosis.

"Texas, the proud Lone Star State — first in oil — forty-eighth in mental hospitals, (there were only forty-eight states at the time),

"First in cotton — worst in tuberculosis,

"First in raising goats — last in caring for state wards."[19]

Little wonder that Shivers passed his legislative program easily. The groundwork had been laid with the assistance of newspapers and broadcasters around the state, as well as a campaign by Claud H. Gilmer, chairman, and the State Board of Hospitals and Special Schools.

GOVEROR SHIVERS SPEAKS to President Eisenhower on the White House steps. Governor James Byrnes of South Carolina (center) and Mrs. Oveta Culp Hobby, Houston publisher who became Eisenhower's Secretary of Health, Education, and Welfare in 1953, in the background.
— *Shivers Collection AP Wirephoto*

ALLAN SHIVERS "gives 'em hell" in a speech supporting Eisenhower for president, Harlingen, Texas, October 1952.
— *From Shivers Collection*

As an officer of the Austin Professional Chapter of Sigma Delta Chi, I helped the organization put together a statewide publicity program to help the new administration achieve what was unquestionably a worthy goal. This is unusual for newspaper reporters, and it was the only such effort that I ever saw involving the media, much less one participated in.

But Allan Shivers was a persuasive person, popular with the press, as was his press secretary, Weldon Hart. Sigma Delta Chi worked with Hart in getting news people from all over Texas to inspect conditions in the state hospitals and write about them. The reporters told readers the horrors at what they saw of human misery and neglect.

The program was enthusastically approved by the legislature and dramatic improvement resulted just as rapidly as new hospitals could be built, medical personnel employed, and treatment modernized. An unexpected result was that with better medical treatment and nutrition, mentally-ill and sick patients began living considerably longer than before. Tuberculosis was virtually wiped out.

After the special session, it was politics as usual in Texas. The Democratic race for governor became a six-man race, but Shivers received more than eighty percent of the party vote, with Caso March of Waco a distant second. Also it was a non-contest at the general election where Shivers easily defeated Republican Ralph W. Currie of Dallas in a small turnout.

The election was livelier in the state race for commissioner of agriculture and on the national front.

John C. White of Wichita Falls defeated J. E. McDonald, who had served twenty years as commissioner of agriculture. McDonald ran as a Democrat but in recent years had openly espoused Republican candidates for national office. White charged McDonald had been in office too long. Ironically, White served as commissioner for twenty-five years before resigning to become Democratic national chairman during President Jimmy Carter's administration.

TRUMAN AS PRESIDENT

After winning his own term in 1948, President Harry Truman proved to be different from the expectations of both his supporters and his opponents. Truman was more conservative than many of his backers preferred. He unexpectedly pleased some of his former conservative critics, especially in foreign affairs.

Perhaps the most successful program of the Truman administration was the so-called "Marshall Plan" of economic aid to countries devastated by World War II. It was accompanied by establishing the North Atlantic Treaty Organization, designed to furnish military protection against the spread of Communism from the Middle East to West Germany.

The program was named for General George C. Marshall, U.S. chief of staff during World War II, who served as Truman's secretary of state during the war.

I had interesting experiences involving both Truman and Marshall, at widely-separated times and places. While accompanying Governor Coke Stevenson to Mexico City on a good will mission during the war, I was invited to a reception at the United States Embassy, where General Marshall was also a guest.

The lawn swarmed with military brass as well as civil officials from both countries. The tables where drinks were served were crowded. While standing in a line which moved very little toward the serving table, I noticed majors and colonels in U.S. military uniforms constantly broke our ranks to tell the bartenders they wanted "a drink for General Marshall."

While I stood there thirsty, probably a dozen drinks were ordered "for General Marshall" by these linebreakers. Of course, the general probably got one or two of them, but if Marshall had drunk everything served in his name, our chief of staff would have been drunk for a week, which he wasn't.

My experience with Truman, except while he was running for office, came after his retirement when he was at Baylor University to receive an honorary degree.

At a press conference, I introduced myself to Truman as a reporter for *The Dallas Morning News*. "What for?" he snorted,

PRESIDENT TRUMAN had trouble holding down prices and raising wage simultaneously after World War II.

— *Reprinted from The Dallas Morning News*

showing his irritation that the newspaper hadn't supported him or many of his appointees.

One Truman appointment criticized by *The News* was that of Tom C. Clark, a Dallas attorney chosen to be attorney general of the United States. Later, Clark was appointed to the U.S. Supreme Court but *The News* never gave him very high marks.

As attorney general, Clark filed suit in 1948 seeking to apply federal ownership to the offshore tidelands of Texas and Louisiana, as had already been done in California. It was a highly unpopular action in Texas, which was fighting for its land rights bestowed in the annexation agreement with the United States in 1845.

Once Congress passed a law which would have recognized Texas' special claim to a 10.35-mile (three-league) offshore boundary. President Truman vetoed it. The issue remained alive, helped elect Attorney General Price Daniel of Texas to the U.S. Senate in 1952, and put Texas into the Republican presidential column behind Dwight D. Eisenhower the same year. Eisenhower, a native Texan, promised to support the state's tidelands claim. His opponent, Democrat Adlai E. Stevenson of Illinois, said he would not approve the Texas position.

The success of President Truman's administration, in terms of taking a middle course, resulted partly from the fact the political parties in Congress were more evenly divided by 1950.

Truman's upset victory over Dewey in 1948 gave Democrats working majorities in both the U.S. Senate and House of Representatives as well as giving Democrats dominance in governorships around the country.

The pendulum swung toward the Republicans in 1950 without any president election. Republicans won a forty-nine to forty-seven margin in the Senate, and the House showed a two hundred thirty-five to one hundred ninty-nine Democratic majority after losing twenty-eight Democratic seats. [20] Because conservative Democrats, particularly from the South, often vote with Republicans, the president and congressional leaders needed consensus politics to obtain results.

The country was further unified by a war. In June 1950, North Korean and Chinese Communist troops attacked South Korea, a U.S. ally. The president ordered U.S. troops under General Douglas MacArthur to repel the invaders. As in the later war in Vietnam, political restraints were placed on military prosecution of the war, and the Korean conflict became a battle of frustration.

General MacArthur wanted permission, which Truman refused, to pursue Chinese Communist troops into Manchuria to destroy air bases supporting the North Koreans.

The controversy became intense in the United States with the result that President Truman removed General MacArthur from command in the Far East. [21]

April 19, 1951, MacArthur delivered his famous farewell address to Congress.

"War's very object is victory — not prolonged indecision," he told the national leaders and public. But the lesson was forgotten again when United States forces were sent to South Vietnam in the 1960s for the purpose of halting another Communist invasion from the North.

Fear of Communist encroachment ran strong after World War II, even within the United States. It became an issue in many political races around the nation, where persons suspected of pro-Communist sympathies were criticized as disloyal Americans. Laws were passed requiring public officials and public employees to swear they did not belong to any subversive organization. U.S. Senator Joe McCarthy, a Republican from Wisconsin, became controversial with his investigating committee seeking to discredit those of pro-Communist leanings.

In 1950, California voters elected Richard M. Nixon to the United States Senate, over Representative Helen Gahagan Douglas, a prominent liberal Democrat in a campaign where candidate Douglas was accused of favoring the spread of Communism in the United States. Nixon won and later became president. During the 1950 Senate campaign, Mrs. Douglas "established the image of Nixon as a ruthless campaigner, an image that would harm him in future races." [22]

[1] *Mister Texas: the Story of Coke R. Stevenson,* by Booth Mooney, 1947, Texas Printing House, Inc., page 2.

[2] *Ibid.*

[3] *Ibid.*

[4] *Ibid.*, page 3

[5] *Coke R. Stevenson,* Frederica Burt Wyatt and Hooper Shelton, page 64

[6] *Ibid.*

[7] *Handbook of Texas,* supplement.

[8] A Plan for Higher Education in the Eighties, Coordinating Board, Texas College and University System, pages 50-51.

[9] *Dallas Morning News,* August 31, 1947

[10] *Op.cit.*, June 24, 1947

[11] *Here Comes The Judge,* Robert W. Calvert, page 128.

[12] *Dallas Morning News,* September 12 and 23; *Fort Worth Star-Telegram,* September 21 and 28, cited by J. Evetts Haley in *A Texan Looks at Lyndon,* 1964.

[13] Calvert, *Op. cit.,* page 124.

[14] *Ibid.*

[15] *Texas Almanac,* 1949-1950, page 474

[16] *Dallas News,* July 2, 1948

[17] *The Gilmer-Aikin Bills,* by Rae Files Still, page 1

[18] *Allan Shivers, The Pied Piper of Texas Politics,* Kinch and Long, page 63

[19] *Op. cit.,* page 74

[20] *Politics in American 1964,* Congressional Quarterly Service, page 10

[21] *Op. cit.,* page 12

[22] *Op. cit.,* page 11

3

THE TIDELANDS REBELLION AND CIVIL RIGHTS FIGHT

Democrats dominated both the national and state governments in the early 1950s, but rebellion brewed in Texas. Texas supported Truman for president in 1948 and the state had political clout in Washington with Tom Clark as attorney general, Sam Rayburn as Speaker of the House of Representatives, and Lyndon B. Johnson emerging as a majority leader in the Senate, as a colleague of longtime Senator Tom Connally of Marlin.

Early in 1952, Truman eliminated himself from consideration for another term. He was sixty-eight years old, and saw the Southern rebellion forming. Truman always was an astute politician.

Texas proved to be the key to the Republican nomination of Eisenhower for president in 1952, and it also could take much credit for the November election defeat of the Democratic nominee, Governor Stevenson of Illinois. Southerners generally were unhappy with the Democrats' choice, partly because civil rights had emerged as a strong political issue starting with Franklin D. Roosevelt and remained highly controversial.

"Civil rights" per se could hardly be considered an issue, but the controversy arose over how best to address the problem, especially in the South where racial segregation in public facilities long had been required by law. Southerners relied on an 1896 United States Supreme Court ruling that "separate but equal" facilities met the Constitution's requirements, although many citizens knew well the racially separate facilities frequently were unequal.

Most Texans held the Southern viewpoint on racial segregation. They considered Northern apologists for "de facto" segre-

AFTER YEARS of litigation and wrangling with Washington, Texas finally won its tidelands claim in the Eisenhower administration as Senator Price Daniel as a main mover.

— *Reprinted from The Dallas Morning News*

gation (in fact, rather than by law outside the South) to be hypocrites who often patronized blacks for political purposes.

In 1952, however, the tidelands dispute was more important in the presidential race. Attorney General Price Daniel announced for election to the United States Senate, to succeed the retiring veteran Tom Connally. Daniel emphasized that he could more effectively fight the state's tidelands battle in Washington than in Austin.

When Daniel told me he intended to offer tidelands as his main campaign theme, I expressed doubt it could be developed into a vote-getting proposition. Daniel proved me to be wrong. He was elected to the Senate, helped pass a law recognizing state ownership to the three-league boundary, then came back to Texas to win the governorship on his reputation gained largely as a tidelands champion.

Texas played a major role in both the Democratic and Republican national conventions held in Chicago in July. Dwight Eisenhower was commander of the North Atlantic Treaty Organization as 1952 started. While he no longer openly rejected suggestions that he run for president, he did nothing visibly to seek the office.

But admirers of the famous general placed his name on New Hampshire's primary ballot in March against Senator Robert A. Taft of Ohio, a respected conservative who was campaigning hard for the presidency. Eisenhower won in New Hampshire and other preferential primaries, and a campaign proceeded on his behalf in Texas, although the Republican state machinery was controlled by old-line party regulars who considered Eisenhower a political question mark. Despite a close vote at the Republican national convention, Eisenhower won over Taft on the first ballot. Conservatives were disappointed, but drew consolation from the nomination of Senator Nixon of California for vice president.

The Democratic convention was badly split, with Senator Estes Kefauver of Tennessee leading on the first ballot and Governor Adlai E. Stevenson of Illinois playing the reluctant candidate, who was "drafted" during the convention as a consensus. Senator John Sparkman of Alabama, who was considered liberal on most issues except civil rights, became Stevenson's running mate.

The result in November was a landslide for the Republicans. They easily elected Eisenhower-Nixon, gained control of both Houses in Congress for the first time in more than twenty years and elected governors in thirty of the forty-eight states. [1]

Governor Shivers, who was running for reelection in Texas against Ralph Yarborough and others, went to Springfield, Illinois, in August after Stevenson's nomination and presented Texas' tidelands claim to the candidate.

"I went back late in the afternoon," Shivers recalled, "and he told me he would veto a bill restoring Texas' title — just as

President Truman had done on two occasions. I asked him to put that in writing, and he did, in a handwritten note."[2]

Afterward, Shivers informed reporters he had advised Stevenson he couldn't support the Democratic nominee for president "because of his stand" on the tidelands question. While the "Democrats for Eisenhower" campaign got under way in Texas, actively led by Claud Gilmer and Tom Sealy of Midland, Shivers helped orchestrate the program without officially heading it.

In anticipation of the coming crisis facing Democrats in Texas over the tidelands issue, the legislature (one hundred eighty-one Democrats) had passed a law in 1951 permitting cross-filing of candidates so more than one party could back the same nominee.

In October 1952, three articles which I wrote showed the intensity of the battle. A month before the election, Governor Shivers announced he intended to vote for Eisenhower, although by then nobody expected him to do otherwise. "I will vote for Texas-born Dwight D. Eisenhower for president of the United States. I fear Stevensonism will be Trumanism with a Harvard accent."[3]

To his differences with Stevenson over tidelands ownership, Shivers added doubt that the Democratic nominee could "clean up that mess in Washington" resulting from the Truman administration and also would accelerate "the trend to the left that is carrying us swiftly toward socialism in many forms and guises."[4]

In later years, Shivers sometimes supported other Republicans, but contended he remained an independent Democrat with no thought of joining the Republican Party.

At Houston on October 18, candidate Stevenson pointed out the election's importance to Texas. "No wonder Texans say 'the New Deal' wears a Texas brand,' " said Stevenson. "for twenty years, Texans in the Democratic Party have helped to shape the destiny of this nation. It would be ironic if now, at the zenith of her economic power, Texas should lose her political influence in the life of this country."[5]

Speaker Rayburn, as state chairman of the Stevenson-Sparkman campaign, and Senator Tom Connally tried to hold Texas Democrats in line. The state Republican party already had cross-filed on their November ticket all the Democratic nominees for statewide office except Agriculture Commissioner White, who rejected the GOP nomination.

Attorney General Daniel, running for senator on both party tickets, said he had been threatened by national Democratic officials with loss of his patronage in Washington if he was elected senator.

"I care not what political reprisals you might threaten against me for supporting Dwight D. Eisenhower for president," Daniel wired Stephen A. Mitchell, chairman of the Democratic National Committee.

Nearly two million Texans voted in the 1952 presidential election and Eisenhower received 53.1 percent of their votes. Nationally, the Republican candidate did better, with a 55.1 percent majority of nearly sixty-one million votes cast. [6]

One can say the coastal states, including Texas, won at the ballot box a territorial claim denied them by the federal government. The 1952 election with its Texas and Southern rebellion from the Democrats paved the way for ultimate victory.

Aided by Democrats representing Texas in Congress, a new submerged Lands Act was passed and signed by President Eisenhower in 1953, recognizing the historic boundaries of tidelands states, including three leagues — more than four million acres — offshore Texas in the Gulf of Mexico. The area has grown steadily in oil, gas, and sulphur production and development is projected for many years.

Enacting the new law didn't end the controversy. Some federal officials attacked the act in court. A final favorable decision from the United States Supreme Court upheld the states' claims in May 1960. (United States versus Louisiana, Texas, Mississippi, Alabama, and Florida).

While the unlikely topic of offshore territorial rights dominated the state government's efforts on the national scene, the decade of the 1950s brought a more personal and intense domestic struggle over civil rights, and the United States' Supreme Court's 1954 decision outlawing separation by law of black and white students in the public schools.

— *Reprinted from The Dallas Morning News The Evening News, Cartoonist Knott.*

THIS KNOTT cartoon appearing in 1932 depicts the permanent problem of financing public education.

— *Reprinted from The Dallas Morning News*

THE 1950s — STATE GOVERNMENT GROWS;
SO DO TAXES

The expansion of state government in the 1950s brought the threat of the first deficit in eight years. Deficit-spending had been the rule until voters adopted the pay-as-you-go amendment to the state constitution effective January 1, 1945. But the war-imposed restrictions on nonmilitary spending ended the state treasury's long deficit by November 2, 1944, except for brief intervals later.

Early in 1952, State Comptroller Robert S. Calvert warned that the rate of state spending compared to income would mean a temporary deficit in 1952 during a slack tax-collecting period. Part of this was attributed to the fact that a new natural gas "gathering" tax passed by the legislature had been tied up in lawsuits contending that the tax was unconstitutional.

The Supreme Court ultimately decided the law was an unconstitutional burden on interstate commerce, since it applied almost entirely to gas sold to "long line" pipelines for delivery outside Texas. Millions of dollars in taxes paid under protest had to be refunded.

This was the first of three attempts by the legislature to tax the pipeline gas leaving Texas. About half of the state's big natural gas production was sold to customers beyond Texas borders, and Texas gas was eagerly purchased at relatively low prices (compared to later years) by users from New England to California.

Most gas producers and many purchasers in Texas also opposed the tax efforts, arguing that it would hurt the state's economy as well as increase energy costs generally.

Natural gas originally was considered a nuisance by drillers seeking oil, because it is dangerously flammable. For years, hardly any market existed for gas, which requires pipelines for transportation unless liquefied by freezing under pressure. Sellers agreed to twenty-year contracts at prices often below ten cents per thousand cubic feet. By the 1980s, newly-discovered gas sold for four to six dollars per thousand.

Texas has taxed oil and gas production for half a century, and the state's revenue has been large even though the amount in retrospect seems modest because the tax is based on a percentage of the price paid at the well.

Meantime, the price of oil increased from less than a dollar on a forty-two-gallon barrel to $35-$40 on the world market in 1981.

In fiscal year 1980, state revenue from the natural gas production tax totaled more than $734 million and on crude oil nearly $786 million despite declining production of both.

After the federal government imposed price controls on natural gas sold interstate in the 1970s (earlier in some cases by Federal Power Commission regulations), more Texas-produced gas was developed and sold for higher prices within the state. The petrochemical industry expanded rapidly in Texas and purchased the gas which producers were unwilling to sell interstate pipelines because of low prices enforced from Washington. The interstate lines continued to buy large amounts of Texas gas, however, because of long-term contracts made years earlier when gas was cheap.

A result was to create an appetite for cheap gas that could not be satisfied after the worldwide energy crisis of the 1970s. Higher prices forced conservation, and some industries which had converted from coal to cleaner, cheaper natural gas in the 1950s converted back to coal in the 1980s.

In Texas by 1980 new electric generating plants all were designed to use abundant lignite coal mined over much of East Texas, or nuclear energy. Environmental, political, and mechanical problems, however, left the future of additional nuclear energy for electricity in doubt.

Governor Shivers and other Texas supporters maintained good relations with President Eisenhower's administration from 1953 through 1960. Eisenhower appointed Robert B. Anderson, chairman of the State Board of Education, to be his secretary of the navy in 1953.

A severe drought during the first six years of the decade severely crippled Texas' farming and ranching industry, and brought demands for more water development. Most of the rain which fell ultimately ran down riverbeds into the Gulf of Mexico as floodwater.

The spring of 1953 also was notorious for tornadoes in Texas. On May 11, one tornado hit downtown Waco killing one hundred fourteen persons and injuring nearly six hundred, while causing more than forty million dollars property damage. Earlier the same day, another twister struck San Angelo in West Texas taking eleven lives and injuring one hundred fifty-nine.

Other concerns of the period were illustrated during a Mutual Broadcasting System radio interview on December 1, 1953, with Governor Shivers.

The interviewers were Sam Kinch, Sr. of the *Fort Worth Star-Telegram* Austin bureau; Dan Smoot of "Facts Forum," a Dallas-based organization; and myself, a capitol reporter for *The Dallas Morning News*.

Shivers' responses indicated:

• Communists had infiltrated the leadership of some Texas labor unions in Port Arthur and other places.

• President Eisenhower's popularity in Texas had suffered during the year partly because of frustration over the drought and sagging economy, but citizens were happy that Eisenhower halted the Korean War.

• Importation of oil "is doing great harm to the discovery of additional reserves" in the United States.

Shivers proved to be less than a prophet concerning racial segregation in public schools.

"If segregation should be ended by the United States Supreme Court, what would it mean in terms of money to the state government of Texas?" I asked.

"The Supreme Court can't end segregation," replied the governor. "It can't pass a law to end moral issues of that type . . . (if so) ultimately it would mean a building cost and an outlay of many millions of dollars over a very short period of time." [7]

Integration, Shivers continued, would mean a loss of jobs for Negro teachers. He didn't expect to see black teachers in racially-mixed classes "in my or your generation."

The governor also warned of accepting federal funds for public schools.

"If there is anything in the world that is local and ought to be governed locally, it should be the public schools of the na-

THIS KNOTT cartoon appearing in 1932 depicts the permanent problem of
financing public education.

— Reprinted from The Dallas Morning News

tion,'' Shivers commented. ''We don't need (federal aid) and
the federal money ought not to be taken into the school system
because control follows the tax dollar.'' [8]

In 1953, Texas received very little federal funds for state
spending. But by fiscal year 1980, almost one-fourth of the total
state budget represented revenue from Washington. The federal
''aid'' amounted to $2.6 billion dollars. Along with it came, as
Governor Shivers predicted, problems related to efforts to regulate the state's expenditures from Washington. [9]

One of the largest headaches proved to be federal interference in the operation of public schools, often ordered by United
States judges seeking to enforce racial integration. Threat of
withdrawing federal funds, which school boards and administra-

tors had come to expect and included in school budgets, was the penalty most often invoked to force compliance with federal orders. For that reason, a very few, small districts declined to accept federal money.

In 1980, the federal outlay for education through the state budget totaled $555 million, more than one-tenth of the total five billion dollars spent on public education by the state. Education represented nearly half of the state's $10.2 billion for the year.[10]

CIVIL RIGHTS BECOMES A DOMINANT ISSUE

The question of civil rights and racial desegregation-integration intensified after World War II in 1945 and erupted into the greatest domestic news story of the century when the United States Supreme Court declared compulsory segregation of whites and blacks to be unconstitutional. (Brown versus Board of Education of Topeka, Kansas, May 17, 1954)

In Texas and other Southern states, compulsory *integration* was unthinkable for most white residents at the time, and there were dark predictions of violence.

In the historic decision, Chief Justice Earl Warren and the unanimous court did not declare races must be *integrated*, only that compulsory *segregation* could not be enforced by law or local ordinance.

Hundreds of other civil rights cases in the ensuing quarter-century left the full impact of the court decision still in doubt. Federal courts later applied the doctrine to "de facto" situations outside the South where blacks have been largely segregated by circumstances other than legal requirements. White resistance to these rulings often was great.

The controversy continues and may require further amendment of the U.S. Constitution to clarify the full extent of "civil rights" for all races, not just blacks and Hispanics. An example is an effort to give preferential treatment to racial minorities on admission to professional training and job promotions over whites who are admittedly better qualified.

Also unresolved are questions of rights of citizens to privacy, such as "white flight" to city suburbs resulting from court-ordered busing for integration in central city schools, or "private" clubs and business establishments catering to invited clientele.

Into the 1980s, it became evident that court-ordered busing for racial balance in schools was failing.

April 21, 1981, the *Wall Street Journal* editorialized "End of the Bus Line?" concerning a federal judge's decision that Los Angeles public schools could stop racial busing, notwithstanding previous decisions from other sources.

On appeal, the federal judge's decision was upheld by the Supreme Court.

The *Wall Street Journal* editorial noted:

". . . By the time the disengagement (busing in Los Angeles schools) the case had shown in microcosm how you could take a morally impeccable cause like school desegregation and turn it into a political disaster and ethical morass.

"The campaign for school busing based itself on at least three major kinds of arguments: The first was moral and constitutional: It pointed to the self-evident obnoxiousness of behavior of local authorities who had for reasons of race denied equal protection of the law to some of the children under their care. The second . . . minority children needed to be educated together with white classmates in order to achieve. The third was political: Busing would improve our climate of racial, and ethnic relations.

"Over the past twenty years we have seen the constitutional argument lose its compelling character. Partly this came about simply because more people had to endure the costs of busing. But partly it was because the early plea that no child be excluded from a school on account of race was a far cry from the later demand for statistical balance. . . .

"The second argument, that this was the way to get minority children to do better, has also been collapsing. For various reasons, busing programs have not in fact been able to make a significant overall impact on minority children's achievement. The latest . . . report suggests that schools do indeed make a difference in what children achieve academically — but that the difference comes from factors like a stress on academic learning and discipline.

"The argument for group relations has also been dying. For one thing, the futility of busing in many places is becoming apparent. Suburbanization continues to take white children out of city schools. In Los Angeles there are not really enough whites left to spread around for purposes of racial balance, and the case reached a low point when the judge took up the question of whether for this purpose he could count some Hispanic kids as white. Moreover, in many cities—Los Angeles among them—minority communities are much divided over busing. Of the 7,000 Los Angeles children who elected to return to their neighborhood schools this week, less than half were white.

"On top of this come the large intangibles. Busing proponents still claim that this is the route to minority achievement and group harmony. Maybe. It is just as likely that the whole fight has made its contribution to a loss of faith in public school systems. . . ."

The above is a fair and accurate summary of the results of racial school busing, in my opinion.

Many Texas blacks also became disenchanted with the idea of requiring racial integration to equalize educational opportunities.

In a hearing on court-ordered busing of children in the Dallas Independent School District in May 1981, Mrs. Kathlyn Gilliam, the first black president of the school board, testified she had changed her opinion about the value of busing children for racial balance. [11]

Originally, Mrs. Gilliam had supported the effort of the National Association for Advancement of Colored People to require racial busing.

After five years under the program, Mrs. Gilliam testified it had been a "negative experience" for the black community of Dallas.

"It never turned out to be what black parents envisioned it would be or wanted it to be," she said. "It has been such a negative experience for black parents that the whole thing has blown up."

Mrs. Gilliam asserted that the real issue is "whether we are going to educate our children. A bus won't teach you one thing."

Mrs. Gilliam added that she "don't buy the idea that a black child can't be educated where he lives" instead of being bused to another school which includes more white students.

Not all blacks, nor whites either, agreed with Mrs. Gilliam that court-ordered busing had failed to accomplish its purpose. U.S. District Judge H. Barefoot Sanders later issued an order for the school district to keep moving toward equalizing the proportions of whites, blacks, and Hispanics in the schools and on the faculties, according to the numbers living in the district.

He explained these were "goals" rather than a judicial mandate, and there was prospect that the district's long legal battle had ended after more than a decade in the courts.

In Houston, Federal Judge Robert O'Conor decided in 1981 that forced integration had gone far enough in that city's school district. The question had been in litigation since 1956 under scrutiny of four federal judges and with eight different plans intended to meet the courts' idea of how desegregation should be accomplished. [12]

Judge O'Conor declared that the district had attempted to establish a fair system, and that no better solution to its racial divisions was in sight. In addition to Houston's integrated schools, the court allowed continued operation of one hundred four single-race schools which Judge O'Conor said were "the product of its majority of black and Hispanic pupils rather than a vestige of past discrimination."

The decision was subject to appeal to higher courts.

A quarter-century after court-ordered desegregation was applied specifically in Texas, forty-six districts were still operating under the supervision of federal judges. More than a thousand Texas districts taught both white and black children separately before the system was declared unconstitutional. Many of these desegregated voluntarily and quickly to remove the added expense of dual school systems as well as from legal orders.

Most of the court orders required busing of students in an attempt to balance racial mixtures, although the flight of Anglo families to other districts sometimes left large majorities of black or Hispanic students.

The long-pending court battles involved all of the state's large school districts.

After the Brown decision, I was assigned to cover many civil rights controversies in Texas and outside, including admission of the first black student to the University of Mississippi in Oxford in 1962, accompanied by much violence and the death of one French correspondent; the use of U.S. paratroopers to carry out a federal judge's order for officials at Little Rock, Arkansas, to admit nine black students in September 1957 to the previously all-white Central High School; desegregation of public schools in Dallas, New Orleans, and many other cities; plus an Atlantic Ocean "wade-in" at St. Augustine, Florida, where a group of blacks accompanied by white sympathizers commenced using a beach previously restricted to whites. An adjoining stretch of beach of comparable size and quality had been used exclusively by blacks for years.

Racial barriers fell quickly in many places after the Supreme Court decision. Some communities in the South found segregation laws burdensome, such as school systems with so few black students it made a quality offering impossible as well as expensive.

A most satisfying writing assignment was an association with the Southern Education Reporting Service, financed by the Ford Foundation and headquartered at George Peabody University in Nashville, Tennessee.

Immediately after the Brown decision, a group of concerned Southern newsmen approached the Foundation with a proposal to establish a reliable center of information on the progress of school desegregation in the region. A grant was made and a small central staff employed, headed by C. A. (Pete) McKnight of North Carolina, later one of the South's most distinguished newspaper editors, for the *Charlotte Observer*.

S.E.R.S. employed me as its part-time Texas correspondent to report monthly on developments in response to the court decision.

One experienced working reporter from each state was employed to report monthly to the information service on progress of desegregation in eleven states which once formed the Confederacy.

We were directed to write only unembellished facts, without adjectives, so anyone seeking reliable information on the South's response to the Brown decision could find it at one source in Nashville. The S.E.R.S. staff also researched special requests for information.

Most of the nation's editors respected the Southern Educational Reporting Service's reports, although a few took liberties with the facts they received. The main result, however, was to make available full facts of the situation, and to minimize the distribution of incorrect and inflammatory rumors.

The worst reporting of the South's civil rights controversy came from reporters and broadcasters making occasional forays to places where emotions ran high, such as Little Rock, when President Eisenhower followed Attorney General Herbert Brownell's advice to use federal paratroops to prevent violence during court-ordered integration of Central High School.

The outside press frequently painted the situation much worse than it was. Violence was practically nonexistent although Little Rock white citizens deeply resented the intrusion of federal force, especially the army, into their school system.

Little Rock came to be viewed, because of these hyped-up reports, as a city of violence, which it wasn't. I was in Little Rock as a reporter for three school-opening sessions. Emotions ran high, but the injuries — except psychological — were minimal. The nation really owes Little Rock an apology, in my opinion.

The experience of Little Rock in the quarter-century after forced integration of Central High is worth noting because it typifies the problems that court-ordered racial mixing brought to other cities.

The continued scenario of the Little Rock story is reported as follows:

LITTLE ROCK, Ark. — In the 1957-58 school year, nine black students attended Little Rock Central High School in a student body of almost 1,900.

During the next 24 years, the Little Rock School District changed dramatically. The federal troops sent by President Dwight D. Eisenhower to enforce desegregation of Central High are long since gone, and the school has become a model of integration.

But many school officials and parents are concerned that before too long, segregation will return to the district, because the number of white students is declining steadily.

The 1980 census showed that about a third of Little Rock's population is black, but this year, the school district has about 65 percent black students. The first three grades are 75 percent black.

At Williams Primary School, even though it is in a predominantly white area of western Little Rock, seven white children are among the 108 1st-graders enrolled.

Four days before the fall term began, the school board voted 4-3 to group white students together in the primary grades (1st, 2nd and 3rd) so that at least 35 percent white students would be in any class that had whites. The plan would have created several all-black classes.

The plan was challenged immediately by John W. Walder, attorney for the plaintiffs in the district's long-standing federal desegregation suit. U.S. Dist. Judge William R. Overton struck down the plan.

The Little Rock School District is surrounded by the Pulaski County School District, which has a 21 percent black enrollment this year. Until the 1960s, the boundaries of the Little Rock district were the same as those of the city of Little Rock. Since then, the city has expanded, while the school district has not.

As a result, the city's newer, mostly white neighborhoods have sprung up in the Pulaski County district.

"Whites are more affluent and more mobile. They've moved to the perimeters of the city but the district boundaries have not followed them," Walder said.

"Black people are filling the vacant houses that the whites have left behind. Also, the birth rate of blacks is slightly higher than that of whites, so there has been an increase in the number of blacks in the school system," he said.

School Supt. Paul Masem said any "white flight" to private schools is not significant. "The actual fleeing is minimal."

The erosion of whites from the school district began about 10 years ago and has been continuing steadily ever since, Masem said.

In 1970, the district had 58 percent white students. A busing plan was implemented under federal court order in

1973, and a year later the student population became a majority black.

Black enrollment has increased by about two to three percentage points a year since 1970, Masem said. [13]

More violence marked the integration of public schools in New Orleans than had occurred in Little Rock, but the publicity was less. Local officials and police had learned better how to handle the situation, including the press.

Once Mayor deLesseps Morrison of New Orleans called reporters into his office to urge them to avoid faking stories. He reported seeing one television camera crew arranging a demonstration by Negro children. Most news coverage, however, was done responsibly and the efforts of a few to make matters appear worse was resented by other reporters. The situation was bad enough without embellishment.

Although the Supreme Court made its principal decision in 1954, desegregation really got under way following the court's implementation decree of 1955. Resistance continued for years in some places but others complied rapidly.

The 1955 directive called for "all deliberate speed" to abolish compulsory segregation. This was taken to mean local federal judges had leeway to decide the best course individual school districts must follow to end discrimination.

Some federal judges later expanded the doctrine of "desegregation" to mean court-ordered busing to achieve racial balance within districts and individual schools. Mostly, the Supreme Court let lower courts decide civil rights controversies without interference from the highest court.

Negroes attained full legal and political rights in the meantime and became a political force almost exceeding their numbers. Hispanics, by contrast, made less political impact. In 1981, San Antonio elected the first Hispanic mayor of any large U.S. city—Henry G. Cisneros, a Harvard-educated university professor and urban affairs specialist. Hispanics are San Antonio's principal population group.

Many U.S. cities, including several in the South, elected Negro mayors, and blacks have been elected to Congress, city councils, schoolboards, and legislatures all over the country.

One must look backward a quarter-century to see just how far the United States, and especially the South, has come in shedding the stigma of slavery, discrimination, and racial intolerance. It is one of the great movements of our history.

World War II attracted many Southern blacks as well as rural whites to industries in the North and West for war industry jobs. After the war, thousands of poorly-educated blacks and their families remained in northern cities, frustrated and unemployed.

By the 1970s, the population movement was from North to South, especially younger people with job skills needed by the Sunbelt's booming economy.

Often, social barriers persisted between whites, blacks, and Hispanics, and emphasis increased on recognizing black culture and Hispanic culture as well as the traditional white-oriented society.

By the 1980s, distinct and sometimes well-to-do middle classes were forming separately among blacks and Hispanics, who disliked being grouped with less fortunate minority group members.

As far back as the Roosevelt New Deal, these two ethnic groups had voted solidly Democratic. But political divisions were appearing in their ranks by the 1980s, especially among Hispanics who often hold conservative views. Further, many Hispanics disliked being grouped with blacks as "racial minority" citizens, and felt the interests of the two racial groups were often different.

Thus two racial minorities, rather than one, competed for attention in education, politics, and the job market.

PARTY LOYALTY BECOMES A POLITICAL ISSUE

The national Republican surge of 1952 dwindled by 1954, and Governor Shivers had a difficult race for reelection, winning the Democratic nomination over Ralph W. Yarborough 775,533 to 638,132 votes after an even closer first-primary contest that included two minor candidates. Shivers had no difficulty defeating Tod R. Adams in the general election.

A leader of Texas' political liberals, Yarborough proved to

be an indefatigable campaigner and three years later became United States Senator in a special election. The Shivers-Yarborough campaigns were bitter, and the stake included control over the Democratic party in Texas.

Shivers' reelection campaign was burdened by two negatives. Many Texans, particularly liberal Democrats, faulted him for supporting Republican Eisenhower in 1952 while Shivers ran as a Democrat for reelection — a persuasive party loyalty issue.

At the other end of the political spectrum, Shivers was criticized by some conservatives for attempting to break the state's two-term tradition for governors. They had strongly opposed Franklin D. Roosevelt in 1940 and 1944 for the same reason. Most of these voters, however, faced a choice between Shivers and abstaining from voting. They held Yarborough and his supporters in low regard philosophically.

The 1954 election also brought election of Bruce Alger of Dallas to the Congress, the first Republican elected from Texas in decades. Alger, a conservative, defeated Wallace Savage of Dallas, former state Democratic chairman and also a conservative, with the help of liberal Democrats punishing Savage for defecting to Eisenhower two years earlier.

That year, without a presidential contest on the ballot, Democrats regained control of the U.S. Congress and won nine governorships previously held by Republicans.

One reason Shivers had difficulty retaining the governor's office in 1954 was a tradition that chief executives should serve no longer than two terms. Shivers already had served more than five years, and the 1954 victory lengthened his tenure from July 11, 1949, when Governor Jester died, to January 15, 1957, an all-time record.

The adoption of a constitutional amendment effective in 1974 providing four-year terms for all statewide officials previously serving two-year terms makes it unlikely Shivers' record will stand, for any two-term governor will serve eight years.

The new state limit is two elective terms, as provided in the federal Constitution for presidents of the United States. President Roosevelt was elected four times and died early in his fourth term, leading to action to limit the chief executive to two terms.

With tidelands and the civil rights' controversy on voters' minds, Shivers made defense of states rights the theme of his campaign. The candidate's support of Eisenhower made his reelection more difficult, and Yarborough raised the party loyalty issue.

In his 1954 race for reelection, Shivers made clear that he would vote again for Republican President Eisenhower if the Democrats nominated Adlai E. Stevenson, Jr., which they did in 1956.

Independence of Texas voters from the Democratic voting tradition really started with the Shivers administration, and was helped along by the dissatisfaction over the award of the United States Senate seat to Lyndon B. Johnson in 1948, creating a large permanent block of anti-Johnson conservatives in Texas who formerly had been classed as Democratic or independents.

Despite his continued adherence to his decision to become a political maverick, Shivers in 1955 signed a bill passed by the legislature which abolished the authority for cross-filing of candidate names on more than one party's ballot.

Shivers never ran for public office after 1954 but remained a powerful political figure all his life, sometimes supporting Republican candidates but calling himself an independent Democrat.

His final term was marked with two scandals.

One was discovery of fraud in the veterans' land program, resulting in resignation of Bascom Giles, commissioner of the General Land Office, in January 1955 after having been reelected easily the previous November.

Elected eight times, Giles never took the oath for the final term to which he was elected and Governor Shivers appointed J. Earl Rudder, a World War II hero from Brady, to the office.

Giles later was convicted in the land scandals and served a term in prison. Giles originated the veterans land loan program which has been highly successful despite the scandal.

The second Shivers administration scandal involved activities at the insurance department, where the governor's appointees to the governing board proved to be untrustworthy. Two appointees were indicted but never went to prison.

The period was marked with numerous shenanigans by promoters of Texas insurance and investment firms, followed by bankruptcies. The department was reorganized in 1956 under a new State Board of Insurance, with such stringent administrative rules that an employee for the agency could not even accept a free cup of coffee from an insurance company representative. Previously, some commissioners and state legislators were found to be accepting financial favors from the operators of shaky companies.

Shivers encountered political difficulties during his final year of public office in 1956 as he attempted unsuccessfully to retain control of the Texas Democratic party against the challenge of Lyndon Johnson, the up-and-coming majority leader of the United States Senate, and the veteran, politically-shrewd Sam Rayburn, Speaker of the U.S. House of Representatives.

The State Democratic Convention held in September was supposed to be a "governor's convention" supporting Governor-elect Price Daniel. But the delegates endorsed the Democratic presidential ticket of Adlai Stevenson and Senator Estes Kefauver of Tennessee (for vice president) while Daniel didn't. Daniel did work out an accommodation with Senator Johnson and Speaker Rayburn, who ran the convention, with the result that hardly anybody in the Democratic party was satisfied.

During precinct conventions, which chose delegates to the state convention, Shivers' efforts generally were thwarted as the opposition elected liberal-moderate leaders and turned down Shivers' attempt to get Texas Democrats to endorse the principle of "interposition," an historic doctrine by which states were supposedly able to "interpose" their own policies such as racial desegregation and tidelands regulation, regardless of the federal government's desire to impose different policies.

The interposition doctrine was widely acclaimed as constitutional by Southern conservatives after the 1954 and 1955 U.S. Supreme Court rulings outlawed compulsory segregation in public schools. But the doctrine never won any recognition by the federal courts.

The liberal-conservative battle in Southern politics was fought on many fronts, usually on the issue of civil rights. Liberal Ralph Yarborough, an Austin attorney, lacked only 3,171 votes of winning the Democratic governor's nomination in 1956 against Price Daniel, then in his fourth year as U.S. senator and

GOVERNOR AND MRS. PRICE DANIEL, Sr. enter the Governor's
Mansion, 1957.

— Dallas Morning News Staff Photo

respected for his role in gaining congressional approval of Texas'
claim to its tidelands.

Despite the popularity of Daniel and Shivers, however,
Texas' long tradition of conservative Democratic control was
shaken in 1956.

The 1956 Democratic primary for governor also produced
one of the state's most colorful and conservative candidates —
rancher-historian J. Evetts Haley of West Texas.

Haley bluntly espoused the doctrine of states rights and individual liberty, and publicly criticized the inclusion of material

in public school textbooks of material which he considered to be un-American, subversive, or pro-Communist.

An example of Haley's directness came during the 1956 campaign when candidate Haley's automobile stopped for a traffic light alongside a car containing two women on an Austin street.

"I'm J. Evetts Haley," the pamphlet-pusher proclaimed to the two strangers. "I'm running for governor. Hope you will read this. If you disagree with me, by gosh, just vote against me." With that, both cars took off through a green light.

Haley finished a distant fourth in the governor's race, behind Daniel, Yarborough, and former Governor W. Lee O'Daniel.

Outgoing Governor Shivers and incoming Governor Daniel disputed how Daniel's successor in the United States Senate should be selected.

Daniel "resigned" from the Senate effective January 15, 1957, the day he was to be inaugurated as governor. Shivers called it an invalid "post-dated" resignation and wished to appoint a temporary replacement for Daniel pending the election of a successor. [14]

The argument did not end until inauguration day, when Shivers appointed Dallas oilman William A. Blakley to the Senate, shortly before Daniel took his oath as governor.

Blakley did not run for the office in the special election which Daniel called for the following April. The seat was won by Ralph Yarborough in a large field where Congressman Martin Dies, Sr. was runner-up and Republican Thad Hutcheson, a Houston attorney finished third. [15]

Yarborough received a plurality of 364,605 votes among 957,298 cast. The senator served until January 1971, twice winning reelection. He was defeated in 1970 by former Congressman Lloyd M. Bentsen Jr., a lawyer-businessman from Houston.

While Democrats fought among themselves for offices and party control in Texas, President Eisenhower and Vice President Nixon were reelected over Democrats Stevenson and Kefauver by greater majorities than in 1952.

The Democrats did better in Congress. They retained a thirty-three-seat majority in the House of Representatives and gained a two-seat majority in the Senate, where the two major parties previously were only one vote apart. Democrats also added an additional governorship in the 1956 election, making control of statehouses twenty-eight for Democratic governors and twenty for the Republicans. Hawaii and Alaska had not become states yet.

Civil rights remained as the boiling issue on the domestic scene, with Southern states resisting efforts to speed the racial integration process.

"The Supreme Court's decision in the school desegregation cases has been called a do-it-yourself plan," I wrote in the *Dallas Morning News.* [16]

"For the nation's highest court has given Southern school officials, including Texas, the biggest job they ever had without guidance on how to handle it.

"The court has said that compulsory segregation of races is unconstitutional. Beyond that, all questions must await future answers. 'A generation of litigation' is the predicted outcome."

A quarter century later, school officials, courts, Congress, and the taxpayers still wonder exactly what the Constitution requires to accomplish desegregation. And the "generation of litigation" forecast proved to be too modest. After two generations, litigation is more widespread than ever, throughout the United States and not just in the South.

By 1955-1956, school desegregation was well under way in the once-segregated South, both in public schools and colleges, while resistance remained strong and occasionally violent.

University of Texas regents voted to accept qualified Negro students in 1956, and sixteen other state colleges and universities did likewise, some starting earlier than the state university.

Public parks in the South were segregated until the Supreme Court declared this to be unconstitutional, and Texas Negroes brought a successful lawsuit in 1956 to open parks to all races. [17]

In October 1956, State District Judge Otis T. Dunagan of Tyler declared the National Association for Advancement of Colored People, a New York corporation, illegal on the ground that it was a profit-making organization that violated the laws of Texas.

Also at issue was whether the NAACP and its affiliates had

CIVIL RIGHTS Activist, Heman Marion Sweatt.
— *Courtesy Barker Texas History Center*

broken the state's barratry law (against paying litigants) in enlisting plaintiffs for Texas lawsuits.

Attorney General John Ben Shepperd, who filed the case against the NAACP, received wide national publicity and once had been considered a likely candidate for higher office. But he retired from politics after 1956 to become an Odessa business man. Will Wilson, elected attorney general after serving on the Texas Supreme Court, handled the state's case thereafter.

The state's case against the NAACP was settled when Judge Dunagan ordered the group to stop engaging in barratry (soliciting litigation) and allowing the corporation to continue operating in Texas.

The NAACP's chief counsel in the Texas cases, Thurgood Marshall, later was appointed to the United States Supreme Court. Marshall and his colleagues opposed the "gradualism" approach to racial integration. They insisted there is no way to have separate equality, contending only racial mixing satisfies the Constitution. The conflict of views on this question is still being litigated.

Governor-elect Daniel saw integration as a "local problem" which should be left to school boards.

"In the field of segregation, there is a question," said Daniel. "I feel that it should be left for the determination of the local district. Maybe the legislature could do something helpful." [18]

Legislators, particularly from East Texas where most Texas blacks resided, were eager to try to "do something helpful" mainly by impeding the desegregation process.

State Representative Jerry Sadler of East Texas had nine bills ready for the legislature which met in January 1957. Most of the proposals never were approved. Sadler's bills included one which would seek to prohibit any school employee from being a member of the NAACP, prohibiting closing any segregated school, and authorizing school administrators to assign pupils within the school system. [19]

Not all Texans shared the segregation view.

Tom Reavley, another East Texan who became a State Supreme Court justice and later a judge of the United States Circuit Court of Appeals, urged the state to take a positive approach to solving problems of racial discrimination.

Speaking as secretary of state, Reavley said:

"Equal education for all of our children is important. It is guaranteed by the constitution of this country and of that we should be proud. I believe any new legislation should be designed with the honest intention of affording equal education to every child in the state of Texas."

Reavley contended that Texas could defend — in federal court — equality of education, whether integrated or not, a prediction which fell short as federal judges began exercising increased influence over public education through their decrees. [20]

In September 1956, outgoing Governor Shivers took action in a Mansfield, Texas, school segregation dispute which attracted national attention.

The school near Fort Worth remained segregated under watch of a Texas Ranger ordered to the scene by Shivers, who

STATE'S RIGHTS never ceased to be an issue.

— *Reprinted from The Dallas Morning News*

acted in the belief that most citizens wanted continued segregation to prevent racial violence. Federal attorneys investigated the incident to see if Shivers had acted in an unconstitutional manner, but did nothing. [21]

Two continuing problems also attracted Shivers' attention during his final year in office. A drought, called the worst in Texas history, went through its sixth year, lowering reservoirs, drying up rivers, and causing serious shortages in crop and livestock-growing areas. [22]

The other familiar problem came from illegal aliens, mostly "wetbacks" crossing the Rio Grande from Mexico, who hampered efforts to control tuberculosis in South Texas. The disease was being brought under control in Texas, but additional cases came from the illegal in-migration. [23]

LITTLE ROCK, SPUTNIK,
AND TROUBLE IN THE SCHOOLS

The year 1957 brought momentous developments which are still shaking the nation's public schools.

President Eisenhower sent army paratroopers to Central High School in Little Rock to protect nine black children seeking to enter the all-white school by federal court order.

Soviet Russia launched Sputnik I, the first man-made satellite, into orbit around the world, leading to a critical examination of the educational systems and technology within the United States, as a rival world power. Americans later exceeded Russia's achievements in space, put men on the moon, and in 1981 presaged the beginning of commercial space transport by successfully launching the first reuseable shuttle aircraft.

Texans were shocked and concerned about events in Little Rock as they tried to cope with problems growing out of the Supreme Court decree for abolishing racial segregation.

And the Texas legislature's regular session was highlighted by investigations and legal actions concerning an East Texas representative caught soliciting a bribe from lobbyists for a group of naturopaths interested in preserving their authority to practice in Texas. The result was an exposure of legislative dishonesty and immorality which involved a small group of legislators but proved embarrassing to lawmakers in general.

The *Dallas News* assigned me to cover the events at Little Rock, where the world press gathered to report on the use of the military to enforce a civil rights order. Most Southerners were horrified at the situation, which some regarded as the *Second* Reconstruction, the first being that terrible period of military government in the South following the Confederacy's fall in 1865.

My own view, then and later, was that Little Rock was a much-maligned city, whose efforts to solve a very emotional and difficult problem was made much more difficult by efforts of outsiders, including President Eisenhower and his attorney general, Herbert Brownell, Jr.

The situation proved to be a blow to Eisenhower's popularity, especially in the South where voters had helped elect him to

129

two terms. The Republicans suffered huge losses in the 1958 congressional and statehouse elections. Democrats controlled the new Congress, almost two to one, and captured thirty-five of the forty-nine governorships, including the new state of Alaska. It was the most thorough Democratic victory since the Roosevelt landslide of 1936. [24]

On September 23, 1957, President Eisenhower announced the federal government would use "whatever force is necessary" to carry out court-ordered integration of the Little Rock public schools. [25]

Tempers became ugly before the president acted. Nine black children had already been to Central High School for one day, but were withdrawn for fear of physical harm and race riots, although they were protected by the Little Rock police and Arkansas National Guard on orders of local and state officials.

While the police and guardsmen did their duty, some found distasteful the task of helping promote racial integration against the wishes of their white friends and relatives.

While I stood with about two hundred other reporters and several hundred irate white citizens behind a barrier across the street from the school, a burly white policeman finally announced he was quitting his job and threw down his badge. The action brought cheers from the crowd, and someone started passing a hat to take up a collection to reward the officer. Such action today perhaps seems unthinkable, but this occurred at a time when the idea of compulsory racial mixing in the South still was almost unthinkable, to blacks as well as white.

While epithets filled the air against the black children and an occasional black adult who entered the school area from curiosity, there was some shoving, plus occasional rock-throwing. But the violence never got out of hand as many readers and television viewers away from the scene were led to believe.

In three years of watching the controversial and successful effort to enroll blacks at Central High, I confirmed three incidents of injury.

Here is what I saw:

A black reporter once was pushed off a sidewalk by a white man. The black was unhurt, but the action was certainly rude and uncalled for. On another occasion, a black girl's leg was hit by a rock, which caused a minor injury.

The worst-looking injury I witnessed was suffered by a white protestor, who was regularly one of the loudest, most unruly in the angry crowd of onlookers.

There were two hundred fifty paratroopers of the 101st Airborne Division deployed around the high school area to keep crowds at a distance while students were arriving, departing, or in class.

Several neighborhood residents invited protestors to stand in their yards where they could watch the proceedings. The soldiers, with bayonetted rifles, had orders to keep everybody out of the yards.

The heckler who got hurt was standing in a yard — with the owner's permission — and refused to move back when a trooper pushed him with a rifle butt. The man stumbled and received a bayonet cut across the chest, apparently accidental. The wound wasn't serious but blood stained his white shirt. A photograph of the episode made international news.

A few reporters were openly hostile to the protestors, although most went about their tasks simply trying to stay out of trouble. One writer for the *New York Times* was a particular problem. He required police protection for constantly upbraiding local residents about the immorality of their cause. The reporter finally became so obnoxious, the police kept him away from the schoolhouse area.

Whether white or black, Southerner or not, the whole situation was sad. I shall never forget the sight of the military camped on a high school football field, literally in charge of the school.

For three Septembers, *The Dallas News* sent me to Little Rock to report on school-opening, so great a symbol had this become.

General Edwin A. Walker, who later moved to Dallas and ran for governor, commanded the federal troops as head of the Arkansas Military District. His command was fair and evenhanded with regard for the prejudices involved.

The 101st Airborne, for example, brought black as well as white soldiers to Little Rock. General Walker assigned only whites to school guard duty, to avoid making the situation worse by giving local opponents cause to complain that "nigger soldiers" were enforcing integration in their community, a throwback to the deep resentment of military occupation of the South after the Civil War.

Despite General Walker's precaution, I overheard two observers in the neighborhood complaining that black soldiers were being used to force racial mixing. The "blacks" actually were a few dark-skinned Indians among the paratroopers.

Little Rock and Arkansas became almost dirty words around the world because of the sensational, adverse publicity.

An audience in another state booed when "Nellie from Little Rock" was sung in the musical "South Pacific."

My own view was expressed in a *Dallas News* article headlined "Arkansans Not All Hoodlums," [26] which was almost lost in the avalanche of anti-Arkansas publicity around the country.

The article follows:

> The smartly clad woman clerk in a Little Rock department store started crying when she learned I was a reporter.
>
> "Please, can't you tell that the people in this town are not all hoodlums," she said. "We're law-abiding people, trying to educate our children."
>
> Many citizens of Little Rock received calls from relatives elsewhere urging them to leave — or at least send their children away.
>
> It's hard to say anything good about the tragedy at Little Rock.
>
> First came mob violence by whites against Negroes because of a school integration plan, poorly timed. Next came the United States Army paratroopers, using rifle butts and bayonets against civilian objectors to integration.
>
> Little Rock's gradual integration plan became one long series of mistakes.
>
> Local sentiment was misjudged all along. Gov. Orval E. Faubus said there would be violence at Central High. There was. But observers believe the violence was much worse because Governor Faubus called out the Arkansas Na-

tional Guard to defy the United States District Court's integration order.

President Eisenhower blamed "outside agitators." Doubtless many from outside Little Rock were on hand for the opposition. Most came from nearby Arkansas counties where segregation sentiment runs deeper.

The violence was perpetrated by people you won't meet at the Rotary Club. Most of the preparation for integration was at the luncheon club level — speeches mainly by school officials asking everybody to cooperate in supporting the United States court order.

Integrationists were better organized than the other side.

The show of putting the nine Negroes into Central High was managed largely by Mrs. Daisy Bates, president of the Arkansas branch, National Association for Advancement of Colored People. Her husband publishes a Negro newspaper in Little Rock.

The Federal Bureau of Investigation reportedly advised the President there was no real threat of violence from carrying out the court order. If so, the FBI was wrong.

United States Dist. Judge Ronald N. Davies, who found officially that no threat of violence existed, must have wondered later at his judgment.

Little Rock is a tragic lesson in error. People in Dallas and other segregated cities should pray that it never happens to them. [27]

The racial integration controversy overshadowed all else in Texas during the late 1950s. Many bills were introduced and some passed by the legislature seeking to slow down the pace of changing the South's traditional system of segregation. Hispanics already had been declared by courts to be entitled to the same legal treatment as whites, and not separated as another minority group. By the 1980s Hispanics, some native Texans, and other immigrants from Mexico and Latin America, formed the state's fastest-growing racial group.

While the legislature was rather helplessly occupied with efforts to blunt the impact of the Supreme Court's racial equality ruling, events of great interest were occurring in Washington.

The Congress moved to get a better program under way for exploring space, following Soviet Russia's successful launch of Sputnik.

"The major domestic bill passed in the 20th century" was a federal Civil Rights Act, directing the U.S. attorney general to help enforce the right of Negroes to vote. [28]

This was followed in 1964 with a Civil Rights Act which penalized Texas and a few other Southern states (based on a formula) and gave the federal government supervision over election laws and elections where the racial mixture fit a prescribed formula. The avowed purpose was to safeguard against local pressures to deprive minorities of voting. But the formula did not apply to all states and subdivisions, only those which fit a certain criteria.

Two Texans with leadership roles in Congress were credited with steering the 1957 Civil Rights Act to passage:

Lyndon B. Johnson, who had become Senate majority leader four years earlier, and Speaker Sam Rayburn.

Dr. Joe B. Frantz, University of Texas historian and LBJ biographer, wrote in *L.B.J. — 37 Years of Public Service:*

". . . Three-quarters of a century of inaction (on civil rights) ended with the successful steering by Johnson and Sam Rayburn through Congress of an idea whose time was overdue. As Hubert H. Humphrey, then one of the Senate's firebrands, wrote to Johnson: 'I was never more proud of you.' . . . No one, whatever his views on civil rights, can deny that it was an historic occasion nor that Lyndon Johnson had been the chief architect and engineer.''

RALPH YARBOROUGH KEEPS HIS SENATE SEAT

When Ralph W. Yarborough, an Austin lawyer, won a United States Senate seat in 1957 at a special election, he received less than forty percent of the votes in a field of twenty-two candidates.

Conservative Democrats, long the dominant group in Texas politics, felt Yarborough could not get a majority in a head-to-head match against a well-financed, well-known conservative candidate.

Yarborough proved them wrong.

RALPH W. YARBOROUGH, United States senator from Texas, 1957-
1971, illustrates a point.

He defeated William A. Blakley, a Dallas rancher-financier,
who served in the Senate briefly in early 1957 by Governor
Shivers' appointment until a special election could be held.

The 1958 victory was Yarborough's first majority in six
statewide races for various offices. [29] Much of Yarborough's well-
organized support came from union workers and their wives,
and the candidate's main target was opponent Blakley's wealth.
Yarborough won by 760,856 to 536,073 and remained the idol
of the liberal faction throughout his dozen years in Washington.

Other liberal candidates fared less well with the state's voters, although a trend toward moderate victories was noted, particularly where the inflammatory issue of segregation was involved. [30]

Price Daniel won a new term as governor against State Senator

Henry B. Gonzalez of San Antonio (later elected to Congress) and W. Lee O'Daniel, former senator, then a Dallas resident.

Gonzalez actively supported integration of races. O'Daniel wanted to roll back the steps to integrate already taken in Texas under court orders.

Daniel, who established a moderate-conservative course on racial issues without open defiance, was elected in the first Democratic primary over both Gonzalez and O'Daniel, who split about forty percent of the votes.

In Dallas, pro-segregation Joe Pool lost to the more moderate Barefoot Sanders in the Democratic contest for a seat in Congress. But Sanders was upset in the general election by Bruce Alger, a conservative Republican, and the first member of his party to represent Texas in Congress in many years.

Both Pool and Sanders were state representatives. Pool later served as congressman-at-large, winning statewide election when the legislature failed to redistrict. Sanders became a Dallas attorney and later federal judge, ironically placed in the difficult position of having to decide the Dallas school busing case in 1981. As a legislator, Sanders had voted for some pro-segregation measures proposed by East Texans and opposed others.[31]

One race for the Texas Supreme Court attracted unusual interest.

Sarah T. Hughes, a former state legislator appointed to be a state district judge in 1935 by Governor Allred, challenged incumbent Associate Justice Joe Greenhill of Austin.

Greenhill, forty-four, had been appointed to an unexpired term and was running for an elective term. Mrs. Hughes, sixty-one, was the only woman serving as state district judge in Texas, and was an avowed exponent of women's rights and liberal causes.

She lost the race to Greenhill, who was backed by most of the state's lawyers and conservative voters. Later, President John F. Kennedy appointed Mrs. Hughes to a federal judgeship in Dallas, where she was still serving in 1982.

While politics were only moderately exciting during 1958, concerns turned to economic problems as well as the continued controversy over desegregation.

EAST TEXAS oil sold for as little as 10 cents a barrel in the early 1930s before conservation was ordered by the legislature and Railroad Commission. New oil brought more than $30 a barrel fifty years later.

— *Reprinted from The Dallas Morning News*

A seven-year drought which bankrupted many farmers and ranchers during the early 1950s ended with torrential rains and floods in the last half of 1957.

The other half of Texas' economic base — oil and natural gas — was undermined by the development of huge oil fields in the Middle East and the resulting drop in prices and demand for domestic fuel. Some producers were unable to find a market even at low prices for oil and gas.

While this seems strange to purchasers of high-priced oil and gas in the 1980s, the industry in Texas was seriously damaged by the immense competition of cheap foreign oil in 1958.

Well drilling and refining declined and many operators

"stacked their rigs" because of the lack of financial incentive to develop more domestic production. Paychecks dropped by $500,000 a week for oil production workers, either laid off or put on curtailed work schedules by the state's 8,000 drilling concerns. [32]

Texas had been producing about forty percent of all the oil consumed in the United States, and Railroad Commission proration kept production in line with the perceived "market demand," thus reducing the chance of disastrous price declines caused by wasteful over production.

But a dollar-per-barrel flood of foreign oil came to the eastern United States and even Texas. Eager customers replaced coal-burning furnaces with heating oil. Industry far beyond the state's boundaries already had contracted for cheap Texas natural gas to replace more expensive coal-fired boilers, which also brought pollution.

The result was to build an enormous appetite for gasoline, heating oil, and other products made from dollar-a-barrel oil, and for clean-burning natural gas purchased on long-term contracts for a few cents per thousand cubic feet.

After the Organization of Petroleum Exporting Countries raised prices in concert to thirty dollars to forty dollars per barrel starting in the 1970s, and restricted exports to maintain these prices, crash programs were launched in the United States to stimulate domestic energy sources. But the politicians waited almost too long to remove price restraints so American producers would again explore widely for domestic supplies. [33] Many old-time drillers, especially the fabled "wildcatters" who took large financial risks searching for new fields, already had gone out of business.

Texas oil production boomed in early 1957, after Egypt seized the Suez Canal from British control. The new country of Israel had attacked the Egyptians in October 1956, supported by the British and French. The vital canal was blocked by sunken and scuttled ships which halted much of the oil delivery from the Middle East to western Europe. The war lasted only a few days, when a United Nations peacekeeping force was stationed in the area.

But so much damage had been done to the canal that oil deliveries were impeded for many months, while western European nations called on the United States to supply its growing need for fuel.

A temporary result was record high oil production from Texas fields, reaching 3,250,000 barrels per day in April 1957.

The shortage caused by the Suez crisis proved to be relatively brief and by 1959 Texas oil fields were being allowed to produce only nine days per month in an effort to balance the supply against the demand.

The rising Middle East oil flow, much of it carried around South Africa on large tanker ships, had a severe impact on the treasury of the state of Texas.

"One field in Kuwait has more (oil) reserves than the entire state of Texas," explained Dr. Paul D. Torrey, an Austin petroleum engineer heading a committee which studied the plight of the domestic petroleum industry.

When the Texas legislature met in January 1959, it faced a ninety million dollar deficit in the state General Revenue Fund because of plummeting proceeds from the oil production tax. The deficit meant that the lawmakers had to raise taxes before they could make final appropriations for the 1959-61 budget.

Legislators agreed on a record $2.4 billion budget, but they wrangled long and hard over paying the bill. Much of the argument concerned whether Texas should levy a general sales tax, which Governor Daniel opposed.

Daniel was forced to call three special sessions before a tax program was approved to keep within the legislature's constitutional requirement for pay-as-we-go.

A gas pipeline "beneficiary tax" was the main part of the new finance bill, along with selective sales taxes, and higher levies on utilities and corporate franchises.

The gas pipeline tax later was declared unconstitutional, as were two others which Texas legislators enacted in an effort to tax gas going to customers outside Texas without placing the same amount on Texans.

Besides financial matters, the legislature in 1959 dealt moderately with questions involving segregation. And controversy erupted over a proposal to change the election laws to benefit Lyndon B. Johnson's bid for the presidency.

For a third September, I went to Little Rock to report on opening of its public schools. My reports indicate two impressions at the time: A reorganized Little Rock police force was dealing adequately and fairly with the problems of protesting segregationists, and with the large and sometimes troublesome visiting press corps.

It had become evident that some of the display, both of whites and blacks, was made in Little Rock for the benefit of the evening television news, an exhibitionism repeated in other Southern areas where racial confrontations occurred.

Little Rock's new police chief ordered the press to stay off the school grounds, avoid "setting up" pictures, and avoid interviewing students unless they were at least two blocks from the school building.

East Texans worried that redistricting the State Board of Education might cause the election of a Negro member, but moderates and liberals formed a majority to authorize election of a second board member from Harris County.

The legislature passed the "Lyndon Johnson Bill" to advance the date of political party primaries to May with runoffs in June, from the traditional July-August schedule. The idea was to give LBJ, the Senate Democratic majority leader, an opportunity to attend the 1960 presidential convention with a new six-year term nomination for the Senate in his pocket.

The legislation also changed the law and allowed a candidate's name to appear twice on the general election ballot, if one of the nominations was for president or vice president and the other for United States senator.

Although LBJ remained somewhat coy about his presidential aspirations, his Texas political followers and the Democratic leadership of the statehouse made an all-out effort to rearrange the election laws to accommodate Johnson's ambitions.

The passage brought criticism from the liberal minority of the Texas legislature, and from Representative Bob Mullen of Alice. They recalled how LBJ acquired his Senate seat originally on the dubious late votes from Box 13 in Jim Wells County.

"Two hundred and thirteen voters couldn't come to the polls that day," Mullen told fellow representatives discussing the 1948 runoff. "But they did get to vote, in a way." [34]

Johnson continued to ignore the criticism about his political past. He also tried to cast aside philosophical political labels, a necessity for his upcoming presidential race.

"I am a free man, an American, a United States Senator, and a Democrat," Johnson wrote for a University of Texas literary magazine. [35]

"I am also a liberal, a conservative, a Texan, a taxpayer, a rancher, a businessman, a consumer, a parent, a voter, and not as young as I used to be nor as old as I expect to be — and I am all those things in no fixed order."

While the election law didn't work out exactly as Senator Johnson desired, it did enable him to win two offices in 1960 and later to become president of the United States through the assassination of President John F. Kennedy in Dallas in 1963.

[1] *Politics in America,* 1945-1964, C.Q. page 13
[2] *Allan Shivers, the Pied Piper of Texas Politics,* Kinch and Long, page 180
[3] *Dallas News,* October 3, 1952
[4] *Op.cit.* October 19, 1952
[5] *Op.cit.*, October 17, 1952
[6] *Politics in America, 1945-1964, Op.cit.*, page 94
[7] Governor's Office transcription of December 1, 1953, broadcast over Mutual Broadcasting System (radio).
[8] *Ibid.*
[9] Comptroller's reports for 1980.
[10] *Ibid.*
[11] *Dallas Morning News,* May 1981, article by Terrence Stutz.
[12] *Houston Chronicle,* Susan Levine, June 16, 1981
[13] *The Dallas News,* Ed Sargent special, October 11, 1981
[14] Kinch and Long, *Op.cit.*, page 89
[15] *Texas Almanac 1958-1959,* page 455
[16] *Dallas News,* June 12, 1955
[17] *Op.cit.*, February 4, 1956
[18] *Op.cit.*, December 5, 1956
[19] *Op.cit.*, December 20, 1956
[20] *Op.cit.*, December 21, 1956
[21] Kinch and Long, *Op.cit.*, pages 188-189

[22] *Dallas News,* October 13, 1956
[23] *Op.cit.,* May 15, 1956
[24] *Politics in America 1945-1964, Op.cit.* page 28.
[25] *Dallas News,* September 24, 1957.
[26] *Dallas News,* September 29, 1957.
[27] *Ibid.*
[28] *Politics in America 1945-1964, Op.cit.* page 28.
[29] *Dallas News,* July 27, 1958.
[30] *Op.cit.,* July 30, 1958.
[31] *Ibid.*
[32] *Op.cit.,* March 2, 1958.
[33] *Politics in America, 1945-1964, Op.cit.,* page 22
[34] *Dallas News,* May 6, 1959
[35] *Texas Quarterly,* quoted in the *Dallas News,* December 31, 1958

4

JOHNSON AND KENNEDY

Politically-shrewd Lyndon Johnson carried his campaign for the Democratic nomination as president in 1960 largely to states without presidential primaries.

True to his schedule, he sought and won the Democratic nomination for United States senator from Texas in the advanced primary held in May 1960.

A new president was to be elected because Dwight D. Eisenhower was completing his second four-year term as chief executive, the maximum allowed under a new (22nd) amendment to the U.S. Constitution.

This left Vice President Richard M. Nixon, a former senator from California, in a commanding position to take the Republican presidential nomination. His only threat came from Governor Nelson Rockefeller of New York, who virtually gave up after a national survey indicated he was perceived as too liberal for the Grand Old Party kingmakers. [1]

Lyndon Johnson was regarded as the most conservative of four U.S. senators seeking the Democratic nomination for president, although many Southerners considered Johnson too liberal on civil rights and welfare issues to suit them.

Senators John F. Kennedy of Massachusetts and Hubert Humphrey of Minnesota fought each other in the primaries. Senator Stuart Symington of Missouri, like Johnson, remained aloof from the presidential preference voting and relied on contacts in non-primary states.

Lyndon Johnson easily won the Texas delegation's convention votes after crushing efforts of a liberal minority at the state

VICE PRESIDENT AND MRS. Lyndon B. Johnson in 1962.
— Dallas Morning News Staff Photo

Democratic convention. Some liberals predicted Texas conservatives at the Democratic state convention in June probably would vote Republican at the November general election. Some probably did.

Kennedy won the presidential nomination at the July 1960 Democratic convention in Los Angeles, with Johnson as the runner-up. To the surprise and chagrin of many followers of both Kennedy and Johnson, the new presidential nominee invited and Johnson accepted the vice presidential spot.

Since Kennedy and Johnson had been highly critical of each other and differed philosophically, the pairing seemed strange until it was realized that without keeping Southern Democrats in line, the Democrats' chance at victory was slender. The selection of Johnson made the ticket more palatable to Southern voters.

The story of what caused the sudden change of hearts in Los Angeles that convention night when Johnson received the invitation has been told various ways.

One version is that Speaker Sam Rayburn, a Texan friendly to both men, convinced Kennedy that Johnson was vital to the ticket and convinced Johnson that serving as vice president was more important than continuing as Democratic majority leader in the Senate.

Another version is that Rayburn originally advised Johnson against accepting the vice presidential nomination, and that the Speaker later changed his mind and declared the match a good one. [2]

Johnson gave the campaign his full attention, crisscrossing the South by air, often traveling with local Democratic officials. In the part of the campaign which I covered, Senator Richard Russell of Georgia traveled with L.B.J. and about forty newspeople.

The chartered plane, a late model prop-jet, was a model involved recently in several tragic accidents. When the plane landed in Austin ending the tour, cheers of relief arose from the passengers.

Campaigning by air sometimes is dangerous, and many candidates and reporters have hair-raising experiences to report. The hazard is increased because candidates feel they "have a schedule to keep" regardless of weather conditions and sometimes regardless of the quality of the aircraft and pilots.

Candidate Kennedy ran his own show, and very well, especially the handling of the controversial issue of his Roman Catholic religion.

While Johnson made a 3,800-mile campaign in Southern states, Kennedy emphasized the vote-heavy industrial, labor, and Roman Catholic areas of other states.

145

PRESIDENT JOHN F. KENNEDY.
— *Dallas News Library*

Religion was an issue that Kennedy handled very skillfully. He met the question head-on. Appearing before the American Society of Newspaper Editors April 21, 1960, Kennedy claimed the press was exaggerating religion as a political issue. He told the editors that the only legitimate question was whether he, as president, would be responsive to "ecclesiastical pressures or obligations"?

"My answer is . . . No," Kennedy asserted. [3]

More important to the campaign in Texas, on September 12 Kennedy told the Greater Ministerial Association in Houston:

"I believe in an America where the separation of church

and state is absolute — where no Catholic prelate would tell the president (should he be a Catholic) how to act and no Protestant minister would tell his parishioners for whom to vote."

Kennedy also reassured Protestant churchmen, that he opposed government aid to parochial schools. [4]

Although some Protestant leaders, particularly Baptists, continued to oppose electing a Catholic as president, Kennedy had succeeded in defusing the explosive issue and turned it to his advantage. Many Protestants felt sympathy for his position and did not want to be considered bigots by voting on religious grounds, while the polls and subsequent election results showed Kennedy rallied Roman Catholics en masse to his call for giving a member of that faith a chance to be president.

The Republican state convention had nominated John G. Tower, a thirty-four-year-old teacher of government at Midwestern University in Wichita Falls, to oppose Johnson in the November Senate race, and they nominated William M. Steger of Dallas to run against Governor Price Daniel's bid for reelection.

In my opinion, the real turning point in the election in Texas, whose twenty-four electoral votes were considered crucial to the national outcome, was an action surrounding an appearance by vice presidential candidate Johnson in Dallas late in the campaign.

A noisy, jostling crowd of women jammed the lobby of the Adolphus Hotel where Johnson and his wife were upstairs for a campaign appearance. Johnson chose to make the most of the incident, walking with his wife through the jeering lobby group and claiming he and his wife had been insulted, spat upon, and jostled. The pro-Johnson *Austin American* newspaper editorially termed it "a riot" and many lukewarm voters decided to support Johnson rather than be identified with such rude and unfair conduct. Democrats claimed the affair was inspired by Dallas Congressman Bruce Alger and senatorial candidate Tower. [5]

The Kennedy-Johnson Democratic ticket carried Texas by 1,167,932 votes to 1,121,699 for Republicans Richard M. Nixon and Henry Cabot Lodge. [6] Republicans attempted an election contest based on confusion over the marking of paper ballots on

147

which the Constitution Party had a presidential ticket but no other candidates.

More than 100,000 ballots were discarded as "mutilated" because voters reportedly failed to mark out the Constitution Party candidates while attempting to vote for candidates of one of the major parties. Attorneys for the Republicans pointed out that more such ballots seem to have been thrown away in counties where their candidates ran strongest than in the predominantly Democratic areas.

When Texas courts threw out the Republican lawsuit, Republicans nationally decided against contesting the results in Illinois where they claimed massive vote-packing by the Democratic-led Chicago city machine. Changing the results in these two closely-divided states would have given Nixon-Lodge the election.

Instead, the Democrats won nationally with 34,221,349 votes to 34,108,546 for the Republican ticket. Kennedy-Johnson won 303 electoral votes to 219 for Nixon-Lodge. Because minority parties polled 188,566 votes for president, the winners received less than a majority — 49.71 percent of the popular vote to 49.55 percent for Republicans. [7]

On election night, I was stationed at the Driskill Hotel in Austin to cover Lyndon Johnson's headquarters.

The results were so close that the totals were not known until Wednesday morning. About dawn, when the Kennedy-Johnson victory seemed certain, I called Johnson's headquarters at the hotel, hoping to find George Reedy, the senator's press secretary, to find out if they had a statement ready.

Johnson himself answered the phone.

I congratulated him on the victory.

"Senator, I believe you made the difference in winning this election," I commented, noting how the South voted Democratic.

"Why don't you write that?" he retorted, evidently smarting from slights from Kennedy backers.

"I intend to," I replied.

We chatted a moment and Johnson asked, "Why don't you come to Washington with me?" I told him I didn't want to go to Washington with anybody.

The next morning's *Dallas News* noted how strongly the

Democrats had run in areas where Johnson campaigned and Kennedy was hardly popular. Arthur Krock, a distinguished Washington correspondent for *The New York Times,* was the only other correspondent I noticed giving Johnson credit for making the difference in the election.

Years later, Johnson acknowledged the incident in a note to me. It seemed to please him more because he knew I never had been one of his real admirers.

TOWER AND THE REPUBLICANS EMERGE

While winning the vice presidency and reelection to the U.S. Senate in the same election, Johnson opened the way inadvertently for Republicans to gain an important political foothold in Texas.

Little-known John G. Tower of Wichita Falls, a college government professor, made an unexpectedly strong showing as the Republican nominee for senator against Johnson in November 1960.

Tower lost with 926,653 votes to 1,306,623 for Johnson.

But the Republican never stopped running. In May 1961, he won a special race for the Senate seat which Johnson vacated to become vice president.

Twenty years later, Tower was still a United States senator and powerful in the new conservative movement in Washington under President Ronald Reagan. The average tenure for a senator from Texas was eight years, and if Tower is reelected in 1984 he would set a longevity record for Texas. Also, he was the first Republican elected from the state since Reconstruction.

Although short of stature (five feet five inches tall), Tower seemed "seven feet tall" when it came to successful use of the new and powerful medium of television for political campaigning.

In the special Senate race in 1961, Tower won over sixty-nine opponents. His winning total was 448,217 votes to 437,874 for William A. Blakley, a wealthy Dallas conservative Democrat who had been appointed temporarily by Governor Daniel to the seat after Johnson's resignation.

Blakley also had served temporarily by appointment of Gov-

SENATOR JOHN TOWER of Texas.

— Photo courtesy Tower's office

ernor Shivers in 1957, losing to Ralph Yarborough in the special
election that followed. Thus Blakley had the distinction of being
the only Texan in history to be appointed twice to the United
States Senate, and twice to lose the office in the next elections.

In succeeding elections, Tower defeated three well-known
Democrats who considered a Republican vulnerable in a state
where Democrats won nearly all the offices. Unsuccessful challengers were former Attorney General Waggoner Carr in 1966,
former State Representative (later U.S. district judge) H. Barefoot Sanders of Dallas in 1972, and former Congressman Robert
Krueger of New Braunfels in 1978.

Tower's success came from several causes. The main one
probably is that he basically represents the conservative beliefs
of the majority of Texans, Democrats as well as Republicans and
Independents. Also, Tower campaigned tirelessly even between

150

elections, and he mustered young conservatives from college and university campuses for his campaign organization.

Further, the "solid" Democratic South became steadily more disenchanted with the national party's policies after the New Deal administration of Franklin D. Roosevelt. The region's voters supported Democrats more out of prejudice against Reconstruction practices and Northerners' pressure for civil rights and punishment of the South, without acknowledging the racial prejudices of other sections.

In a survey of the 1960 election, Dr. O. Douglas Weeks, professor of government at The University of Texas-Austin, noted that 500,000 more Southerners supported the Nixon-Lodge Republican ticket than had voted for Eisenhower-Nixon in 1956 when the Republicans won. Further, Dr. Weeks noted Republicans had their biggest vote in history in Texas, and that all over the South Democratic strength had been eroding in presidential elections since 1936.

"The day may not be far distant when many (former brass-collar Democrats) will become permanent converts to the Republican party," said Dr. Weeks. [8]

The analysis proved correct, although the transition was interrupted by the tragic slaying of President Kennedy in Dallas in 1963, followed by the five-year presidency of Lyndon B. Johnson of Texas. These events gave the Democratic party an unexpected benefit during those years, just when it appeared the South was slipping from the Democrats' grasp.

As vice president and later as president, Lyndon Johnson brought the national press and many distinguished visitors to Texas and to his ranch on the Pedernales River at Stonewall, west of Johnson City.

One of the first celebrities to visit Johnson in Texas was Chancellor Konrad Adenauer of the West German Republic, who expressed pleasure and surprise in April 1961 at a program in his honor performed by citizens of Fredericksburg, with songs and speeches in German. The Hill-Country town had preserved its German-ancestry culture since 1846 when immigrants there made a lasting peace treaty with the Indians. [9]

Democrats retained heavy majorities in both branches of Congress, and controlled more than two-thirds of the governorships when President Kennedy launched his "New Frontier" program in 1961. The eloquent new president promised to "get this country moving again" as he called on all citizens to "bear the burden of a long twilight struggle . . . against the common enemies of man: tyranny, poverty, disease, and war itself."

"Ask not what your country can do for you—ask what you can do for your country!" urged Kennedy in his inaugural address. [10]

While Kennedy did successfully sponsor some social legislation, such as establishing a $1.25 minimum wage and broadening Social Security benefits, his first year was marked by the Bay of Pigs fiasco, where a force of 1,200 Cuban refugees was landed in their home island, intent on overthrowing the government of Fidel Castro. They had been promised air support from the U.S. military, but it never appeared, leaving the beleaguered Cuban invaders at the mercy of Castro's forces. It was a blow to American prestige. [11]

The surviving Cubans were ransomed back to the United States in 1962.

In Texas, legislators faced the necessity of a large tax increase to pay higher salaries for teachers and other rising government costs in the face of a sluggish economy.

The legislature ended its 140-day regular session without a tax bill or a budget bill. The issue was settled later in a special session with passage of the state's first general retail sales tax at a rate of two percent, excluding food, prescription drugs, and some other items. By 1981, the total state rate had been increased to four percent and an additional one percent levied by most cities and towns, for a five percent total. A few large cities also added sales taxes to build transit systems.

In 1961 desegregation increased in public schools in Texas and other Southern states, although the courts still were sending mixed signals on what the districts must do to comply with the Constitution. One plan advanced was for "free choice" — letting parents choose schools their children would attend within an integrated system. This later was declared inadequate to meet the requirement of a unitary school system because most whites and blacks alike appeared to prefer neighborhood schools which left the systems mostly segregated, by choice.

Negroes gained in other ways, including more admitted to formerly all-white universities and into higher-paying jobs, especially in government, as politicians hastened to court the Negro vote.

A study of the 1960 election in Texas showed Negroes in big cities — Dallas, Houston, San Antonio, and Austin — had voted proportionately just as heavily as the white population. Nearly half of the state's black population lived in the four cities at the time. In San Antonio and Austin, Negroes were found to be voting in even greater numbers than upper-income whites, according to the study by Dr. Harry A. Holloway of The University of Texas-Austin government faculty. [12]

JOHN BOWDEN CONNALLY ELECTED GOVERNOR

Price Daniel announced he would seek a fourth term as governor in 1961, an unprecedented effort but one which would have made him the longest-serving chief executive in Texas history had it succeeded.

Governor Daniel had a strong sense of public service and history, and was related by marriage to the famous General Sam Houston.

He had been a state representative, Speaker of the Texas House, attorney general, and United States senator before winning the governorship in 1956. Later he was to become an associate justice of the Texas Supreme Court, the individual most honored by Texas voters in the state's history.

A formidable line-up opposed Daniel in the 1962 spring Democratic primary for governor — John B. Connally, a friend and sometimes political ally of Lyndon Johnson, and President Kennedy's secretary of navy; General Edwin A. Walker of Dallas, an ultra-conservative who became active in politics after retiring from the military; Attorney General Will Wilson; former Highway Commissioner Marshall Formby of Plainview; and Don

AT CAPITOL PRESS CONFERENCE with Governor John Connally in 1963 (left to right) Connally, Dawson Duncan of Dallas News, Kyle Thompson from UP International, R. M. Morehead of Dallas News, and Harley Pershing of Fort Worth Star-Telegram. In background, Ronnie Dugger. — *Author's files*

Yarborough, a young Houston attorney backed by liberal Democrats but no kin to United States Senator Ralph Yarborough.

Connally led the first primary with less than one-third of the total votes, while Yarborough united the liberal voters to finish second. Governor Daniel placed a disappointed third in the race.

Many conservative voters were skeptical or downright antagonistic to Connally, because of his Kennedy-Johnson connections, and he barely managed to eke out a 565,174 vote to 538,924 for Yarborough in the runoff.

Perhaps more surprising than Yarborough's strong showing against the well-financed, dynamic Connally was the close race

154

in the November general election against Jack Cox, a former
state representative from Breckenridge who was elected as a
Democrat but turned Republican. Connally won the election
with 847,038 votes to 715,025 for Cox.

When William P. Clements, Jr. became the first Republican governor of Texas in more than a century by winning the
1978 election, he credited Cox's strong showing against Connally — and subsequent Republicans against better-known Democrats — as one indicator which led him to believe that a Republican, with adequate financing and a strong organization could
win the state's highest office despite its generations-old tradition of Democratic domination.

Clements believed strongly in trends and figures, and he
calculated correctly on what it would take to make history by
winning his first bid for public office.

In addition to the strong showing by Cox against Connally,
the Republicans in 1962 elected Ed Foreman, an Odessa Republican, to the U.S. House of Representatives and sent eight members of the party to the state House of Representatives, most of
them from Dallas.

President Kennedy's popularity helped Democrats retain
strong control in Congress after the 1962 election, and Democrats won governorships in more than two-thirds of the states.

Reapportionment based on the 1960 census shifted more
congressional seats to the growing western states, while New
England was the big loser.

"Across the nation, voters showed a continuing tendency
to disregard traditional party lines in choosing men for high office. The success of Democrats in rock-ribbed Republican states
of northern New England and breakthroughs for Republicans in
the South — including a near-miss in the Alabama Senate race
— attested to the possible development of significant new voting patterns." [13]

While the South and West became increasingly conservative and Republican, the trend was offset by Democratic gains in
northeastern and midwestern states where Republicans formerly
were strong. The trend was to continue.

John Connally was far different from his predecessor, Price

Daniel. Where Connally was eloquent, dramatic, and sometimes bombastic, Daniel had been a low-pressure official who disliked controversy and tried to avoid it.

When holding a press conference at a time he had reason to believe reporters planned to ask difficult or embarrassing questions, Daniel often started the conference by talking about some other subject at such length there was little time left to quiz him about more controversial matters.

Reporters described Daniel's tactics as "filibustering" in his meeting with the press.

Daniel was an effective negotiator and earned decent box scores with his legislative program, even if he did lose on the largest one, opposing the general sales tax.

Connally came into office without previous experience as a candidate or elected official, although he had served as secretary of the navy.

It is my opinion, mentioned publicly several times, that Connally never really cared much for being an elective official, although his governorship rates among the state's best.

What John Connally enjoyed was the planning, execution, and intrigue of political campaigns, and he was good at it. To him, politics was like a giant human game, to be played for the love of the game as well as the hope of winning a big prize.

Connally did enjoy the exercise of power, and packed into his lifetime more excitement than most humans could generate in ten lifetimes.

In the last four years of his governorship, 1964-1968, Connally often represented his old friend and political ally, now President Lyndon Johnson, in promoting Mr. Johnson's program, particularly support of the war in Vietnam, to skeptical governors of other states.

In this, his main adversary was the governor of California, Ronald Reagan, who became president in 1981. Earlier, Connally, as a Democrat, represented the nation's majority political party. Republican Reagan was equally forceful in presenting the Republican, conservative viewpoint.

The confrontations between these two strong, eloquent men at National Governors' Conferences were classics. They were also great theatre, for Connally held his own against the veteran movie star, Reagan, on the platform.

Later, Connally became disenchanted with the Democratic national party and its liberal constituents in Texas. He turned Republican and ran for president against Reagan, Texan George Bush, and others in 1980. His style didn't sell in the Republican primaries and he withdrew, leaving Bush as Reagan's only opponent for the presidential nomination.

Observers speculated that Reagan would appoint Connally to a cabinet post, because the two held views that in many ways were parallel. I never believed it. It would be awkward to have two such strong personalities on the same team.

As governor, Connally paid less attention to details of the office than some of its occupants. He delegated authority well. While some capitol reporters were less than Connally fans, he generally satisfied them by allowing his press secretary, George Christian, to give replies to most questions regarding Connally's positions, even when the governor was away from his office. Connally always stood behind Christian's answers.

Christian, later a popular and effective press secretary to President Johnson, joined Connally's capitol staff in an unusual way.

A former capitol newsman, Christian served as press secretary to Governor Daniel and worked in Daniel's unsuccessful fourth-term campaign. When Connally's press secretary resigned, the governor appointed Christian despite his association with an erstwhile opponent. Christian was strongly recommended by the capitol press, which helped to overcome doubts Connally may have had about his loyalty and ability.

The results of Connally's first legislative session in 1963 were unspectacular. The high point in his program was to merge the state department, which administered parks, with the one regulating hunting and fishing. A new State Parks and Wildlife Commission was created, originally with three members in 1963 but increased to six members in 1971.

Appointments to the commission are the most sought-after within the governor's power, largely because of the impact on the state's vast recreational areas, particularly hunting and fishing.

Connally sometimes had difficulty getting Senate confirmation of his appointees. The most notable was W. St. John Garwood, a distinguished former Texas Supreme Court justice nominated by Connally to serve on The University of Texas Board of Regents, another much-sought appointment.

Garwood lacked one vote of receiving the twenty-one needed for Senate approval. An eleven-senator minority objected to Garwood's "liberalism" on admitting blacks to The University of Texas, which the federal courts already had ordered. Garwood was eminently qualified for the university appointment and the Senate's action disappointed many Texans.

The greatest accomplishment of Connally's six years in office was his support for improving higher education, and better salaries for teachers at all levels.

During his second term, Connally persuaded the legislature to reorganize the Coordinating Board, Texas College and University System. Though he reappointed some of its previous members, the agency did achieve more importance but still fell short of the goal of truly coordinating the higher education system to eliminate duplication, waste, and parochialism. The problem was, and to an extent continues to be, local pride in individual institutions whose backers have the political clout to expand the system unnecessarily, and then to prevent the legislature and Coordinating Board from effectively managing the programs. Considerable improvement was made in this direction during the 1970s, although the richly-endowed University of Texas and Texas A&M systems still resist efforts to coordinate them with other state supported universities, especially in sharing endowments.

During the early 1960s, President Kennedy, and later President Johnson, strongly supported huge expansion of the nation's space program, partly in response to the Russians' accomplishments in this field.

A major research and development center was established near Houston, and later named for LBJ. The multibillion-dollar expenditures also boosted research at universities and private firms. The race for federal funds nourished a practice known as "grantsmanship": the art of selling ideas for research to the federal government for financing.

By the early 1960s the Washington government, through huge infusions of money followed by regulations, had become so dominant that fears were openly expressed that local self-government was doomed. The worst example was the increasing number of school districts which were being operated under federal court jurisdiction in an effort to increase racial integration. The penalty for failure in such cases usually was the loss of federal "aid" to the school district, the end of financial rewards for following federal officials and racial minorities desired.

The lure of billions of federal dollars proved too much for most local units of government to resist. Some cities, counties, states, and universities employed lobbyists and established offices in Washington to cooperate with the new centralization.

Most members of Congress were eager participants in the system. It helped them politically. Also satisfied was the growing federal bureaucracy, including the military, as financial support and staffs increased.

The real losers were taxpayers and future taxpayers saddled with enormous debt. But federal subsidy was so widespread that few citizens or firms were excluded, although all was paid by increasing taxes or expanding government debt.

The situation was exacerbated by a United States Supreme Court "one-man, one-vote" decision requiring that all governing bodies—except the constitutionally-exempted United States Senate—be apportioned according to body count. Each state retained two senators, regardless of size or population.

The result was an enormous increase in the political power of urban areas with ethnic voting blocs. Rural representation was greatly diminished, where districts previously usually gave some consideration to area and natural boundaries.

The decision caused the thirty-one-member Texas Senate to lose its historic conservatism, largely because the cities gained so many seats at the expense of less-sparsely populated areas. Harris, Dallas, Bexar, and other populous counties assumed more political importance. Under the first "one-man, one-vote reapportionment in 1971, sixteen new senators were elected, the most in history.

The change was accompanied by great growth in state and

local governments, partly to deal with the new federal relationship and partly from natural growth and urbanization.

Texas, at least, enjoyed state government prosperity, because of large revenues from the new sales tax, and rising prices for oil and natural gas, whose tax payments are based on value of the fuel at the well.

An example is fiscal year 1963, when the state government spent about $1.6 billion, up more than $400 million over the 1960 figure. Even with greater spending, the legislature found a $200 million treasury surplus at the end of 1963. This appeared through increased appropriations for the next two years.

Few states proved to be as fortunate as Texas in pay-as-we-go government, required under the 1945 constitutional amendment. Recessions in the 1970s, for example, caused some states and cities like New York, to require federal help in extricating them from too-lavish budgets followed by debts which threatened them with bankruptcy.

Three major scandals rocked Texas during 1962.

Billie Sol Estes of Pecos and Abilene was discovered to be promoting an elaborate scheme to mishandle federal payments for grain storage, cotton acreage allotments, and the farm fertilizer business. He also contributed to Democratic political candidates, while currying favor with U.S. Department of Agriculture officials, one of whom was found murdered and others resigned or were fired.

Another highly publicized scandal was discovery that oil drillers in the congested, large East Texas field were stealing oil from beneath neighbors' leases by drilling slanted holes. The third scandal concerned illegal rice acreage allotments on the Gulf Coast.

A combination of public and private funds was used to build a $100 million laboratory in South Texas to produce sterile screwworm flies, an insect pest which was costing Texas livestock owners millions of dollars a year and greatly reducing the populations of deer and other wild animals. The damage came from infected sores on the animals' bodies. Scientists discovered that sterile male screwworm flies could be produced by radiation, and millions were released by airplanes over rangelands of South Texas and northern Mexico.

Since the flies mate once in a lifetime, the mating of a fertile female to a sterile male ended the insects' life cycle. The beneficial results were dramatic, and the fly almost eliminated, although it regularly recurs by moving northward from untreated areas in Central America.

1963: KENNEDY ASSASSINATED; JOHNSON BECOMES PRESIDENT

The year 1963 was one of the most tumultuous and tragic in the history of Texas and the nation. John F. Kennedy, a popular president, was assassinated in Dallas November 22, 1963, while on a trip to Texas to help pacify the warring liberal and conservative factions in the Democratic party of the state, led respectively by U.S. Senator Ralph W. Yarborough and Governor John B. Connally. It was a prelude to a 1964 reelection campaign.

The assassination catapulted Texan Lyndon Baines Johnson to the presidency, and enabled him to win an elective term in 1964.

Before the events in Dallas, speculation was widespread that Johnson might be displaced as vice president on the ticket with Kennedy in 1964. Johnson was an active vice president with strong friendships in the Congress from his days as Senate majority leader. Some of Kennedy's staff disliked Johnson's style, and there were rumors of a ''ditch Johnson'' sentiment for the next election.

One of the loneliest figures I ever saw was Lyndon Johnson one afternoon in late October 1963 when he came to Marlin for the funeral of an old friend, former Senator Tom Connally, who had retired from office in 1953 but continued to live in Washington where he died October 28, 1963.

I drove to Marlin to cover the funeral, which was delayed by the late arrival of Vice President Johnson.

He sat in a reserved pew of the Methodist church with Secret Service agents. After the church service, I drove to the cemetery for the burial. The vice president and I arrived about the same time, a quarter-hour before the funeral procession reached the cemetery.

161

Johnson sat alone on a bench in the shade of oak trees awaiting the arrival of Connally's cortege. I walked over to extend greeting. LBJ seemed surprised that I had spoken to him, and we chatted briefly. He invited me to fly back to Austin with him, but I declined since I had driven my car to Marlin. When I got home, I remarked how sad and lonely the vice president — the country's second highest official — seemed that afternoon.

Less than a month later, Lyndon Johnson was president of the United States, and an energetic one, surrounded by people seeking his company and favor.

All this resulted from the mail-order rifle of Lee Harvey Oswald, firing the fatal bullets at President Kennedy and near-fatal shots at Governor Connally as the two men with their wives were driven past Dealey Plaza in Dallas on November 22 en route to the Dallas Trade Mart for a luncheon.

The president came to Texas the day before, landing at San Antonio where he joined Vice President Johnson in dedicating a new U.S. Air Force School of Aerospace Medicine.

President Kennedy went to Houston later for a testimonial dinner honoring Congressman Albert Thomas, then to Fort Worth for the night.

He addressed a breakfast in Fort Worth on November 22, and flew to Dallas for the luncheon which he never reached. The president was pronounced dead at Parkland Hospital in Dallas.

Secret Service, Federal Bureau of Investigation, and other officers quickly surrounded Vice President Johnson, who officially became president of the United States at 1:39 p.m. aboard Air Force One parked at Dallas' Love Field. U.S. District Judge Sarah T. Hughes, an old friend and fellow Democrat, administered the oath to President Johnson as the dazed and blood-spattered Jacqueline Kennedy, wife of the fallen president, witnessed.

Kennedy's body was placed aboard the plane, which immediately departed with President Johnson and his party.

Wild rumors circulated that the shooting was a plot of right-wing reactionaries, but this proved completely false. The rumors persisted, however, and many people around the world continued to blame Dallas and conservative Texans for the crime, which they had nothing to do with.

162

Investigation proved Lee Harvey Oswald, who was charged with the shootings, was a Marxist who had recently come to Dallas after living in Russia, Cuba, Mexico, and other places. his political connections, if any, were never exposed but certainly there was no relationship with the conservative element of Dallas.

The case took a most bizarre turn two days later when Oswald was killed by Jack Ruby, a Dallas lounge operator who had befriended the Dallas police and was present with reporters when Oswald was being transferred between jails. The shooting of Oswald by Ruby at a Dallas police station was pictured live on television, and witnessed around the world.

Ruby's background was about as mysterious as Oswald's despite Ruby's close acquaintance among the local police. He was charged with murder, tried, and convicted. The case was overturned on appeal, and Ruby died before he could be tried again.

As in most other presidential assassinations and attempts, the motivation for Oswald's deed never became clear despite lengthy investigations. The consensus was that Oswald was a "loner" without any rational grievance against President Kennedy.

Unintentionally, the Kennedy assassination united Democrats of the state and nation, and the 1964 election of Johnson as president became a memorial to the fallen Kennedy.

It also erased previous opposition to Governor Connally, who recovered his health after Oswald's bullets ripped through Connally's chest and arm.

Afterward, Connally was asked frequently whether he accepted the theory that the Kennedy assassination was a plot involving more than one person and that shots had been fired simultaneously from another direction.

Connally maintained that he believed the assassination was solely the doing of one twisted mentality.

I was eating lunch at home in Austin when the radio started blaring excited reports that November day of "shots being fired at the president in Dallas." We joined the nation, listening in disbelief.

My assignment that day was to cover a party dinner at the City Auditorium in Austin that evening, where Kennedy was scheduled to speak after his Dallas appearance. Thirty-five hun-

163

LYNDON B. JOHNSON is sworn in as president in 1963 aboard
Air Force One at Dallas by U.S. District Judge Sarah T. Hughes,
Mrs. John Kennedy

— *Courtesy LBJ Library, Austin, Texas*

dred salads wilted at the places set for guests and 3,500 steaks
were never served by caterer Walter Jetton of Fort Worth. [14]

State legislators who had come to Austin for the Kennedy
Democratic ''Victory Dinner'' met instead for a twenty-minute
memorial service in the Texas House of Representatives.

The floor and the gallery were packed, with many univer-
sity-age students in the audience. Forty-five members of the
staff of Governor Connally, clinging to his life in Dallas' Parkland Hospital, also attended. Some of the visiting ladies wore
mink coats, which they had brought to Austin for the evening
dinner.

''For this to have happened anywhere would be tragic and
shocking to all Texans,'' said House Speaker Byron Tunnell of
Tyler. [15]

"For it to have happened in Texas is almost unbelievable."

After saluting the fallen president, Speaker Tunnell praised President Johnson:

"Lyndon B. Johnson has the qualities and the confidence to move into the presidency without delay and with calm confidence. In this respect we, and all the people of the free nations, are fortunate. He will dedicate his life to these vast new responsibilities—in the discharge of which John Kennedy gave his life today."

Senate Chaplain I. W. Oliver added: ". . . the Lord has prepared for times such as these" and he prayed that "we may feel forgiveness for those who perpetrated the foul deed of this day."

While the death of President Kennedy and the inauguration of President Johnson dominated the year 1963, some other events earlier in the year are worth noting.

Republicans and Southern Democrats meeting at the National Governors' Conference in July declined to endorse the civil rights program espoused by President Kennedy as part of his "New Frontier" administration. The president sent Vice President Johnson to the conference, disappointing members who had hoped Kennedy himself would meet with the governors. [16]

Four months later, the assassination melted much of the opposition to President Kennedy's program and it was enacted—and more — in President Johnson's "Great Society" administration.

Governor Connally complained that the other governors were too preoccupied with the civil rights issue, and should be paying more attention to the nation's need for better education and research. [17]

Connally's Committee on Education Beyond the High School recommended a ten-year program in Texas which would lead to limiting admission to the state's top universities to the top fifteen percent academically in high school graduating classes, and the next twenty percent become eligible for other state senior colleges. Junior colleges would be made available to those failing to qualify in the top thirty-five percent. The recommendation never got off the ground, and instead of restricting university enrollment to the better-qualified students, higher education as well as public schools were accused in the 1960s and 1970s of diluting their offerings to attract more students, particularly blacks. By the 1980s, the campaign was resumed at all education levels to end "social promotion" and "grade inflation," and to increase the discipline of education generally.

PRESIDENT JOHNSON

President Johnson moved quickly to establish his position as chief executive, both in Washington and Texas.

"Let us continue," he proclaimed five days after the assassination in an address to Congress, referring to his predecessor's plea to "let us begin" correcting the country's ills.

"This is our challenge — not to hesitate, not to pause, not to turn about and linger over this evil moment, but to continue on our course so that we may fulfill the destiny that history has set for us." [18]

The new president next asserted that the most fitting memorial Congress could provide in John F. Kennedy's honor would be "the earliest possible passage of the civil rights bill for which he fought so long . . . to eliminate from this nation every trace of discrimination and oppression that is based upon race or color."

The next priority, President Johnson said, would be to pass President Kennedy's proposed $10.3 billion annual reduction in business and individual income taxes to stimulate the economy. So much has been said about President Kennedy's social views that less attention has been paid to his conservative fiscal policies, which Ronald Reagan mentioned with approval during his campaign for president and at the outset of his administration, seeking credibility with the nation's host of Kennedy admirers.

Despite demonstrations for racial equality by blacks, and many whites including students and clergymen, the Kennedy civil rights program languished in Congress for many months.

With President Johnson lending his now-massive influence in Washington, the legislation was approved by a congressional conference and by February 1964, the U.S. House of Represen-

PRESIDENT LYNDON B. JOHNSON
— *Courtesy LBJ Library, Austin, Texas*

tatives had passed a substantially broader civil rights law than even President Kennedy had proposed. [19]

In July, a two-thirds majority of senators shut off a filibuster by Southern senators and the measure passed finally by Congress and was quickly signed by President Johnson.

It expanded federal authority over elections, provided federal power to insure nondiscriminatory access to public accommodations; authorized federal intervention to compel school desegregation; required equal employment opportunity regardless of race or sex by firms with more than twenty-five employees; extended the United States Civil Rights Commission and created a Community Relations Service to promote local civil rights program.

The principal clout of the new legislation called for federal prosecutors and courts to assist persons claiming themselves victims of discrimination.

While the debate went on in Congress, the United States Supreme Court was broadening its legal guarantees for rights to equal educational and job opportunities. [20]

While most Southern schools retained some segregation ten years after the historic Brown decision by the Supreme Court, the nation flamed with racial troubles. Three civil rights workers disappeared in Mississippi. Race riots erupted in New York, Chicago, Philadelphia, and other northern cities which had no laws requiring segregation.

"Though disowned by most civil rights leaders, these riots demonstrated the depths of frustration and often hatred demonstrated by young Negroes against the dominant white society." [21]

While the Congress was passing a law aimed at correcting injustices, it also heeded President Johnson's call to enact the tax cut which President Kennedy had recommended. Final passage came three months after LBJ took office, reflecting the speed with which the new president acted.

The politically-talented president, relying on skills and contacts acquired during his sixteen years in Congress, pushed through many other Kennedy proposals, some of which detractors said JFK really wasn't too keen about but endorsed to accommodate his liberal followers.

Included were Medicare, health care for Social Security recipients, which became a very expensive program; anti-poverty legislation, including food stamps for the poor; and legal aid for indigents. He even defused conservative opposition by reducing President Kennedy's budget request by nearly one billion dollars for 1964.

"The president, although he also benefitted from a 'honeymoon' period with Congress and fresh cooperation resulting from President Kennedy's assassination, did indeed seem to know how to work effectively with the Legislative Branch. [22]

"Above all, President Johnson seemed to have an unusual sensitivity in dealing with Congress which his predecessor sometimes lacked. It was largely a matter of knowing when the president's role should be muted, so as not to offend, and of sensing when a specially strong presidential voice and strategy was called for."

Lyndon Johnson was living in the best of political worlds — a Southerner who sometimes seemed conservative yet attractive to liberals because of his support of FDR's New Deal and his successful promotion of the legislative package left on his White House desk by the death of President Kennedy.

While he quickly made his presidential mark in Washington, President Johnson's impact on his beloved Hill Country of Central Texas — Stonewall, Johnson City, Fredericksburg, and Austin — seemed no less dramatic to those of us who watched him at home.

Johnson quickly transformed the LBJ Ranch at Stonewall into a retreat and summer White House beside the Pedernales River. A few days after he took office, many extra telephone lines were being strung to the ranch, roads improved, an airstrip started, and Secret Service quarters installed.

Reporters could predict where the president was going by the way emergency telephones were installed along his expected route, whether to Austin's Headliner Club in the Driskill Hotel or the home of a friend. The activity generated by President Johnson on the home front was enormous, reflecting the man's own great energy as well as the importance of his office.

Chancellor Ludwig Erhard of West Germany was one of his first big-name visitors to President Johnson, although the previous chancellor had come to Stonewall while Johnson was vice president.

Chancellor Erhard flew to Bergstrom Air Force Base outside Austin aboard a Lufthansa plane directly from Bonn, accompanied by other high government officials and West German newspeople.

A story which I wrote for *The Dallas Morning News,* appearing December 30, 1963, reflects the reception the Germans received:

> STONEWALL, Texas—President Lyndon B. Johnson put a western style hat on German Chancellor Ludwig Erhard here Sunday afternoon to climax a folksy international festivity.

The ruddy, rotund West German leader appeared to enjoy the whole affair — from the hat act to a concert by famed Texas pianist Van Cliburn.

It was a day of great contrasts, the leaders of two great nation's carrying their own plates of barbecue and beans across the drafty wooden gymnasium of Stonewall High School.

Inside were jammed some 400 persons—including dignitaries of the United States government, the state, and the Stonewall, Fredericksburg, and Johnson City areas.

The day's greatest applause came for tall, curly-haired Van Cliburn's program of Beethoven, Brahms, other German composers, and American Samuel Barber. These were played on a grand piano against a backdrop of baled hay and a saddle on a makeshift cedar corral.

There were songs by the St. Mary's parochial school choir and dances by Billyettes, Fredericksburg school groups. But the high point came as the president of the United States called up his old friend, German-born rocket scientist Wernher Von Braun, now heading an American rocketry research in Alabama.

"If America reaches the moon in this decade and is the first to be there, it will be more due to Wernher Von Braun's effort than any other living man," said Johnson.

Then President Johnson explained that a difference in mathematics (Germany follows the example of the world generally in using the metric system) caused difficulty in matching American hat sizes to the heads of German visitors.

"Forty liters or a 10-gallon hat," said Johnson, offering the first to Chancellor Erhard and the second to Von Braun. The chancellor wore his for the rest of the program.

Hats, some badly-fitted, also were given to the whole delegation of German visitors including about thirty-five reporters. For variety, the President gave one also to Pierre Salinger, the presidential press secretary. With this went a tribute to Salinger as "one of the most trusted, able people working for the government. I don't know what I would do without him."

Like most of President Johnson's staff, Salinger was brought to Washington originally by the late President Kennedy.

While Johnson was distributing hats, he called on Sal-

170

inger to play the piano. He played a brief original selection, after remarking how difficult it is to follow Van Cliburn on the program.

Master of Ceremonies Cactus Pryor, member of the staff of KTBC-TV Austin, owned by the LBJ Company, recalled that in 1922-1923 Lyndon Johnson rode a donkey four miles from his home to the same school where Sunday's ceremony was held.

"Where else is there greater opportunity?" asked Pryor.

The president noted that his community had entertained "heads of state . . . and camel drivers. We do not measure men by their wealth here. We measure them by their love of freedom," he said.

The president engaged in much hand-shaking after the ceremony and earlier, and left the main rostrum to greet friends at a nearby table. He also said the blessing before the meal, expressing thanks for friends "from across the waters . . . and neighbors here at home."

George McGhee of Dallas, U.S. ambassador to West Germany, was among thirteen seated at the head table. Also on the guest list were German Consul and Mrs. Gershon Canaan of Dallas.

Johnson and Erhard, in more formal remarks, both attested to the warmth and success of their two-day meeting in Texas. Mrs. Johnson drew special praise from the chancellor.

"The homelike atmosphere she created brought about a spirit for our talks which already was a guarantee of our success," he said. "I feel at home with you."

Erhard also praised "this wonderful state of Texas" and German-ancestry citizens of this Hill Country. They left the old country and became "loyal citizens" of this new land, the visitor observed.

Chancellor Erhard was the first of many distinguished visitors to the Johnson White House at Stonewall.

Most of the president's staff and press remained in Austin, seventy miles away, and commuted to the ranch when invited, usually traveling by chartered bus.

While the president held a few press conferences on the ranch-house lawn, most were conducted by his press secretary or other administration officials at the Driskill Hotel in Austin, where the big Crystal Ballroom had been converted into a press center.

This also gave the Washington press corps access to the Headliners' Club downstairs, which became one of the nation's more famous drinking places despite its small size.

When the president needed quarters in Austin, this was arranged by the Driskill, Johnson's favorite campaign headquarters dating from his days in Congress and the United States Senate.

My introduction to White House press conferences and briefings brought some surprises, although I was somewhat acquainted with the procedures through the visits of other presidents to Texas.

Senior correspondents for the Associated Press and United Press International got to ask the first questions; then there was a scramble for attention from the other reporters. Cameras were arranged along a raised platform in the rear of the room and not allowed to block the sight of reporters sitting out front, contrary to the practice of photographers at the state governor's office. Camera lights were arranged before the White House briefings or conferences started, and mostly placed where they didn't blind the reporters with glare. Also, recorders could be plugged into circuits in the back of the room, rather than putting dozens of individual microphones on the speaker's rostrum.

Besides the daily announcements by the press secretary, or an assistant, on what the president was doing that day, or planned to do, various cabinet members and high federal officials calling on LBJ at the ranch met with reporters at the Driskill.

It came as a surprise to me that so many of the explanations and remarks were made on a "nonattribution" basis, meaning the reporters could use the information without identifying any source.

This placed us in the position of being blamed if the remarks or "expert" backgrounding didn't pan out later. The press was being used to send up trial balloons to test public opinion on various proposals. If the information given the press in such manner drew an unpopular reaction, the president or someone around him could deny any such intention, and the press would be criticized for wrongful speculation or being ill-informed.

A few of the more famous television and newspaper people also got special treatment, occasionally an official "leak" to stir public interest.

I did not think then or now that such "nonattribution" news reporting is good journalism. While such "news" from sources unwilling to be identified may have a place in communications, such as protecting the source from bodily harm, the casual control of news to test public sentiment does nothing for good government but serves only to benefit politicians and the bureaucracy at the expense of press credibility.

Many Washington newspeople were close friends and admirers of President Kennedy and were shocked by his assassination. The same group disliked Lyndon Johnson's style and almost resented his presence in the White House. The same went for some of the White House staff which President Johnson inherited from the slain Kennedy. These drifted away in a few months, and were replaced by Johnson loyalists, often old friends from Texas.

Scholarly, pudgy George Reedy served as President Johnson's press secretary, as he had been for Vice President Johnson. Pierre Salinger of President Kennedy's staff stayed a short while. President Johnson also employed Bill Moyers, a young Baptist preacher and writer from Texas, but broke with Moyers when the latter went to New York to become a newspaper and television commentator.

The president sometimes frustrated Reedy to near despondency judging from the latter's reactions, although a mutual link remained until Reedy gave up to become a university professor.

George Christian was hired away from Governor Connally to become White House press secretary, and there appeared to be misgivings among the White House press as to Christian's ability.

The amiable, straightforward Christian quickly dispelled the doubts, however, and became one of the most popular and respected persons ever to hold the position.

President Johnson started early to court the Washington press and a few of them became almost maudlin over the attention and small gifts he gave them — such as an ashtray and a beautiful White House snow scene Christmas card.

The visitors were invited to the ranch, where the president donned cowboy attire and rode horseback to show some Texas color. He also drove around the ranch in an open car, trailed by the Secret Service.

Once I took a reporters' bus tour of LBJ Ranch with Mrs. Johnson as the guide.

"There have been so many changes recently, I don't recognize my own ranch," she said plaintively. "We hope the neighbors don't mind." [23]

While touring the ranch with Mrs. Johnson, more than two hundred reporters and photographers observed Hereford cattle and sheep along with two large presidential helicopters. We finished the tour with an outdoor luncheon of barbecued pork spareribs, furnished by a Fort Worth catering service.

Back at the hotel, a few of the Eastern correspondents wrote lurid accounts of their visit to the Wild West sighting "antelope" and "pine trees." The "antelope" were Texas goats in the distance, and the "pine trees" were Texas cedar, really a juniper, a pest in the Hill Country.

Although president, Lyndon Johnson remained unpopular with some of his neighbors, including Hill Country conservatives. Most Texans paid their respects to the new president and the high office, however.

"I've never been for Lyndon Johnson before," an older Austin woman remarked when I made an interviewing trip down Congress Avenue. "But I've made a resolution since he is president to stop cussing him and start praying for him."

Said an Austin businessman:

"I'm having a hard time adjusting. We've had Lyndon Johnson around here for years — but this is the first time he's been president. I hardly know how to act." [24]

Both the president and Mrs. Johnson received honorary doctoral degrees from The University of Texas at Austin at commencement in 1964. Mrs. Johnson graduated from the University, but there was grumbling among anti-LBJ alumni for granting the honor to her husband, whose degree is from Southwest Texas State University in San Marcos.

Residents along Lake Granite Shoals northwest of Marble

174

Falls expressed irritation by the president's visit to lakeshore property which he owned there. The surge of security helicopters overhead, and the waves from Secret Service boats and the president's big cruiser, some residents claimed, disturbed the tranquility of the area.

The criticism became even louder when the Lower Colorado River Authority changed the name from Granite Shoals to Lake LBJ.

After being nominated for an elective term, President Johnson and his vice presidential running mate, Senator Hubert Humphrey of Minnesota, drew a big display of neighborhood affection with a birthday party at Stonewall, which served as a Democratic party political rally.

The sponsor was the Gillespie County Democratic Committee, hoping to reverse the results of the 1960 election where Republican Richard Nixon had received more than seventy-five percent of the votes against Democrats Kennedy and Johnson, even though Gillespie, where LBJ ranch is located, is Johnson's home county.

A great effort was made by Gillespie County civic leaders to stir support for President Johnson; and in the 1964 election, the local resident won his victory at last — a tribute to the office as much as the man. [25]

THE 1964 ELECTIONS

While President Johnson was highly visible and active on the national and international scene in 1964, Governor Connally recuperated slowly from the severe wounds inflicted by Lee Harvey Oswald in Dallas.

By February 1964, the governor was well enough to discuss the assassination with the Associated Press managing editors meeting in Austin. [26]

"Like a sharp jab . . . numbness . . . frankly, I thought I was killed," Connally described the bullet that struck him.

He also revealed, what this reporter noticed without Connally saying so, that the near-fatal shooting had changed him in ways other than physical. Connally became a more compassionate person.

He called a statewide conference on morals and ethics. Connally said the convalescent period gave him time to "think, ponder, and reflect . . ."

"The thought crossed my mind that Lee Harvey Oswald was the end product, in an extreme way, of many of our own failures in dealing with young people," he told the editors. "Even if we cannot have prayers in school, it would still seem we could devise simple courses in kindergarten or the first grade to teach children not to lie, not to cheat, not to steal, not to covet . . .

"The answer lies not in a decree from Austin. It lies in each school district, with the actions of each school board, and the determination of each teacher and parent that more must be done to make good morals an accepted custom rather than a far distant target."

Unfortunately, the governor's philosophical advice went largely unheeded, as showed later by increasing central control over education, a growing permissiveness regarding young people, a breakdown of discipline and frequently of criminal law enforcement.

In September, Connally told state capitol reporters he agreed basically with the findings of a federal commission headed by Chief Justice Earl Warren of the Supreme Court blaming Oswald alone for the assassination tragedy.

"This Marxist — this mentally deranged man — was not a product of Dallas . . . not a product of its schools, its environment, or its culture," Connally commented. "To condemn a great city is unwarranted and does the state and city a great disservice."[27]

Many persons outside Texas, including members of the eastern media, continued to blame Dallas and Texas long after the event for providing the environment which brought President Kennedy's demise.

By August 1964, Connally had recovered sufficiently to make a good will tour of Mexican states bordering Texas, accompanied by reporters.

From Victoria, Tamaulipas, the third stop, I wrote that

"Connally—whose name Mexicans associate with the late President Kennedy—is scoring a personal triumph on his tour . . ."

His only references to the assassination, in response to questions, were brief comments that the deed was "the work of one demented man rather than a conspiracy."

The hospitality was warm and security heavy as Connally and his wife visited the Mexican state capitals, a reception described as "befitting a president." "President Kennedy was very popular with the Mexican people and the tragedy of last November apparently gives Connally an extra-warm place in their hearts."[28]

Texans also displayed greater affection for Connally after his shooting. While his election victory in 1962 had been a hard fight both in the Democratic primaries and general election, re-election in 1964 was relatively easy.

In the Democratic primary against his previous runoff opponent, Don Yarborough of Houston, and two other candidates, Connally received about sixty percent of the votes. In the November election against Republican Jack Crichton, a Dallas petroleum engineer, Connally captured about two-thirds of the total vote, a somewhat better showing in the state than President Johnson's 63.3 percent against Republican Barry Goldwater.

Nationally, the Johnson-Humphrey ticket received 61.1 percent of the popular vote, the highest percentage in history. Even the second-term triumph of Franklin D. Roosevelt in 1936 netted a smaller majority, 60.8 percent.

President Johnson's "broad coattails helped the Democrats score major gains in the House of Representatives and increase their already heavy majority in the Senate."[29]

The Democratic ticket carried forty-four states and the District of Columbia. The Republican ticket of Goldwater and William E. Miller of New York, Republican National Chairman, for president and vice president, lost all of the traditional GOP strongholds of the North and East. The Republicans carried only Goldwater's home state of Arizona and the Southern states of Alabama, Georgia, Louisiana, Mississippi, and South Carolina.

Another effect of the 1964 election was to replace some conservative Southern members of the Congress with liberals, with the effect shown in 1965 when the Johnson administration quickly pushed to enactment a huge package of social programs.

Goldwater and his candidacy did remove control of the Republican Party power structure from the northeastern states, where even Republicans are inclined to more liberal philosophy than most Republicans in the West and South. The center of Republican power shifted westward. Two of the party's next presidential nominees, Richard M. Nixon and Ronald Reagan (both of whom were elected), came from California.

Another, President Gerald Ford came from Michigan. But Ford reached the office through the resignation of Nixon.

Criticism of President Johnson's political past hurt his campaigns in Texas. Former Governor Stevenson, Johnson's opponent in the still-controversial 1948 Senate election, endorsed Goldwater but did little else in the 1964 campaign.

One factor, which the Johnson-Humphrey campaign directors attempted to offset, was the effect of a book called *A Texan Looks at Lyndon,* a highly critical review by J. Evetts Haley, a well-known conservative historian-rancher. Eight million copies of the book were distributed.

Johnson-Humphrey campaign headquarters distributed favorable editorials about President Johnson. Writer A. C. Greene of the *Dallas Times Herald* called the Haley book "evil." [30]

The 1964 political year brought a new young Republican to statewide attention, George Bush of Midland and Houston, who ran more strongly against incumbent Democrat Ralph Yarborough than fellow GOP candidates did in Texas races for president and governor.

Nevertheless, Yarborough received 56.2 percent of the total Senate race vote, and Bush went down in defeat along with most of the other Republican candidates across the nation. It was a real landslide for the Democrats in the wake of the event in Dallas of November 22, 1963.

Republicans also lost all ten seats they held in the Texas House of Representatives (none in the Senate). Nine of the Republicans elected in 1962 came from Dallas.

The Democratic ticket of Johnson and Humphrey won a 1,663,185 to 958,566 majority over Goldwater and Miller in

Texas. Nationally, Democrats dominated the presidential vote by 43,128,956 votes to 27,177,873.

It was the Democrats' greatest victory since 1936, when the Republican candidate (Landon) carried only two states against FDR. In Southern states carried by the Democrats, a heavy turnout of black votes were credited with the victory margin.

Goldwater doubtless would have done better except for the huge sympathy vote for Democrats in the wake of the Kennedy assassination. He also took a more conservative stance than his voting and personal record represents in other ways, particularly on civil rights. The senator came away with a worse image than he deserved.

The tragedy of President Kennedy's death closed, at least temporarily, a widening gap among Texas Democrats.

The top-level rift among Democrats in Texas had brought Kennedy to the state in an effort to promote harmony.

There was speculation that Kennedy planned to ditch Johnson as his running mate in 1964. Johnson and Senator Yarborough were so much at odds they refused to ride together in parades led by the president in Houston and San Antonio, before his ill-fated trip to Dallas where they did ride in the same car. [32]

While President Johnson and Governor Connally remained friendly on most matters, they disagreed sharply about the 1964 Democratic choice for U.S. senator. Connally favored Joe Kilgore, a former congressman from McAllen who moved to Austin to practice law. Former Governor Shivers also wanted a conservative candidate. But President Johnson, looking at the national as well as state political scene, supported Yarborough.

At a victory party in Austin, Yarborough took note of his opposition in Texas, as well as his supporters in and out of the state.

The senator thanked the *New York Times* for "having endorsed me editorially." [33]

"I was recognized by the best paper in the country even if the big dailies of Texas were against me," Yarborough told his followers.

Much of the Texas press' criticism of Yarborough came from allegations that he once took $50,000 from West Texas promoter Billy Sol Estes. The senator called this an "infamous lie." [34]

179

While the 1964 election turned on personalities and historic happenings, rather than issues, the civil rights issue remained strong in the South, and to an extent in Texas.

Governor Connally and Attorney General Waggoner Carr both criticized the Civil Rights Act of 1964, passed by Congress at President Johnson's urging. Connally did declare that "our own (state) failures are the cause of much of the troubles" from federal intervention in civil rights disputes.

Republican presidential candidate Goldwater and gubernatorial candidate Crichton termed the new federal law "unjust and unconstitutional." [35]

Ten years after the Supreme Court handed down its 1954 school desegregation opinion, Texas public schools were progressing gradually toward integration. It still was being argued whether actual integration (racial mixing) or desegregation (an end of compulsory segregation) was required to meet the constitutional requirement.

A *Dallas News,* survey in 1964 indicated 325,000 blacks attended public schools in Texas. While 200,000 of these were in districts which had abandoned official segregation, only 20,000 were enrolled in classes with whites. [36]

Segregation in higher education in Texas had virtually disappeared, although most Negroes by choice still enrolled in predominantly black institutions.

The University of Texas at Austin, which admitted its first Negro student in 1949 by Supreme Court order, made another "first" in 1964 when the engineering department appointed Ervin S. Perry, a black graduate student, to its faculty, the first member of the race ever to teach in a formerly all-white Southern university.

Dr. John J. McKetta, dean of engineering, noted that Perry was a top scholar, considered the best doctoral candidate in engineering "anywhere in the world." [37] Perry was one of six children reared on a forty-acre cotton farm near Coldspring, San Jacinto County. All graduated from Texas universities.

1965: A BANNER LEGISLATIVE YEAR

"This year, John B. Connally must be rated as the most effective governor in modern Texas history," I wrote for *The Dallas Morning News,* following the biennial session of the Texas legislature. [38]

Assistance in passing the Connally program came from Ben Barnes, a personable young representative from DeLeon, who was elected Speaker of the House after Connally appointed Speaker Byron Tunnell of Tyler to a vacancy on the Texas Railroad Commission, as legislators went into session in January.

"None within memory has proved to be such a strong leader in proposing programs for state government, and seeing them adopted," said my summary of Connally's legislative success.

"The success of Connally's programs will depend on future operations. But his ability to get ideas approved is unmatched.

"The Connally program in the 59th Legislature has been enacted in most cases without change. Other governors can claim numerical success for the bills they wanted, but often the content differs vastly from the proposal. This is not so in the 1965 Connally year."

The governor's chief compromise during the session dealt with salaries and other funds for public schools. The appropriation contained an effort, sponsored by Connally, to obtain a merit pay system for teachers, which was never implemented by local districts to any noticeable extent. A three-year study of public school finances and programs was ordered by the legislature.

The legislature appropriated substantially more money for higher education in 1965, established a new coordinating board for higher education, and proposed an eighty-five million dollar loan fund, backed by the state, for students in public and private education.

To finance a pay increase for public school employees, the lawmakers raised the tax on cigarettes and required earlier payments on inheritances.

Public school teachers and administrators, whose associations opposed Connally's recommendations in their area, proved to be his most formidable legislative opposition. They obtained more money than Connally wanted allocated for them, but the governor effected a compromise of sorts by having the legislature include provision to establish a merit pay system for teachers, whose pay scale was based on college degrees and longevity rather than any consideration of teaching ability.

While merit pay became part of the education appropriation, experience later showed that little was done on the local level to implement the provision. Connally and representatives of school districts—board members, administrators, and teacher representatives — disliked his insistence that greater effort be made to finance public schools locally.

". . . Drop your bucket where you are," he once quoted a poem in responding to demands for the state to take over a greater share of financial responsibility for public schools. [39]

The governor insisted that all taxes are "local" which must be paid ultimately by individual taxpayers — whether levied at the national, state, or local levels.

In 1965, the federal government got much farther into the effort to equalize the financing of public education by making affluent people and districts pay relatively more than the poor.

President Johnson's new Great Society legislative program allocated extra federal funds for public schools based on how many school-age children in each district came from families with less than $2,000 annual income. The act brought eighty-six million dollars to impoverished Texas districts the first year, increasing total federal contributions to $125 million, an amount substantially increased in following years. [40]

Governor Connally complained that some districts failed to pass along to teachers the full amount the legislature appropriated for salary increases. Instead, administrators and boards sometimes spent part of the money for other items in the school budget.

While the state set minimum salaries to be paid from state funds by local districts, some districts, particularly cities and oil-producing areas, set salaries higher than the state minimum scale.

In Connally's second term, the legislature also adopted his proposal for $200 million more in bonds for water development, which voters later approved, and four-year terms for governor and other statewide elected officials. This became a reality in terms starting in January 1975, replacing two-year terms. The 1965 proposal was defeated but voters adopted a later plan in 1972.

Another accomplishment sponsored by the governor was reorganization and improved financing of the state program to aid the mentally-handicapped.

As Connally enjoyed good response to his recommendations from Texas legislators, President Johnson was doing much more in influencing Congress.

With an overwhelming endorsement by the voters in winning his own four-year term in 1964, President Johnson "led the 89th Congress in an amazingly productive session."[41]

"Measures which taken alone would have crowned the achievements of any Congress were enacted in a seemingly endless stream. . . . Congress approved programs which long had been on the agenda of the Democratic party — in the case of medical care for the aged under Social Security (Medicare) for as long as twenty years. . .

"The pace of the 1965 session was so breathless as to cause a major revision of the image, widely prevalent in preceding years, of Congress as structurally incapable of swift decision, prone to frustrate the demands for progress . . ."

The Voting Rights Act of 1965 greatly expanded the authority of the federal government to intervene in local electioins in the name of protecting civil rights.

It applied only to Texas and a few other Southern states on a formula designed to help minorities politically. In 1982, Congress revised the law slightly and continued its operation.

The law declared that federal supervision over elections was needed in districts where fewer than fifty percent of voting age citizens had registered in 1964. Ostensibly, this was designed to protect the voting rights of blacks in Southern states. Six Southern states including part of Texas were placed under its jurisdiction, over the complaint that a civil rights law should apply to the whole nation, not just areas selected by formula.

One result was to increase registration in eleven Southern states by 500,000 for the 1966 election.[42]

Meanwhile Congress also liberalized greatly the immigration law allowing natives of other lands to come to the United States.

It created a cabinet-level department of Housing and Urban Development and enacted a wide range of benefits for higher education, including federally-backed loans for students.

The outpouring of legislation from the Congress was viewed apprehensively by conservatives.

"Of the many domestic programs which will pump billions into our domestic economy, there can be no other result than inflation, which in turn means an increase in the cost of living, which in turn saps all other benefits of a prosperous economy," commented U.S. Representative Omar Burleson, a Democrat from Anson. [43]

"There can be no perpetual prosperity through perpetual deficits.

"It seems all too common to ignore the fact that the nation's resources are limited and must be allocated. No magic in the new economics can change this basic fact."

"The Congress and the administration must eventually find out they are burdening people with an oppressive new saturation, and should see that trying to do everything at once is a course filled with incalculable risk. It is one thing to meet a threat against our national security at whatever cost, but no idle joke that a prudent Congress can be the best kind.

"A hurry-up-and-do-everything Congress is doing a disservice to its immediate constituency and to our nation's future. (Congress) has constructed the greatest colossus of government in its history . . .

"Programs created by the fancy of lawmaking are bound to grow in size, bureaucratic control, and confusion and cost."

By the 1980s, Congressman Burleson's appraisal of President Johnson's milestone in lawmaking had proved to be prophetic.

And the voters in Burleson's old West Texas district had elected as his successor Representative Charles Stenholm of Stamford, a conservative Democrat-cotton farmer, who joined Republicans in supporting painful budget-balancing measures necessitated by the huge cost of these federal programs. In this, Stenholm and other conservative Southern Democrats formed a majority coalition supporting President Reagan's economic program.

President Johnson also persuaded Congress to support a much greater participation by the United States military in the long-running war between North and South Vietnam.

As billions of dollars in federal taxes were poured out to assist state and local governments in a wide variety of social and environmental programs, as well as education, these lower-echelon governments established offices in Washington to deal more directly with Congress and federal agencies making the payments.

In 1965, the number of states with liaison offices in Washington increased from two to twenty and within a few years nearly all the states including Texas had set up such offices in the national capital. So had most large cities and universities.

THE VIETNAM WAR AND GREAT SOCIETY

President Johnson's smashing victory in the 1964 election and his success in persuading Congress to enact his Great Society domestic program into law climaxed his long career.

By 1966, the country began to feel seriously the double strain of financing a greatly expanded war effort in Vietnam and the expense of the programs for welfare and other programs that had been adopted under LBJ.

In the tragic month of November 1963 when President Kennedy was assassinated, an event taking place in faraway South Vietnam led to ultimate heavy involvement of the United States in a war that caused deep division among the American people and doubtless influenced President Johnson's decision not to run for reelection in 1968, a move that surprised most supporters and political observers.

The event was the overthrow of the South Vietnam government of President Ngo Dinh Diem, a Roman Catholic, by a group of military leaders. The Diem government had been beset by corruption, failures in fighting the insurgent Viet Cong, and opposition from the country's large Buddhist population. [44]

Soon after President Johnson took office, the military coup government was displaced by another military group, and the country's leadership remained unstable for years.

The United States was drawn increasingly into the war. Its participation was small before the Johnson presidency, although State Department officials admitted the department "might have encouraged the proper climate" for the revolt against Diem. [45]

While President Johnson was leading his government in establishing the Great Society at home, shuttling back to Texas often for long weekends at his "Summer White House" at Stonewall, the Viet Cong with help from Communist North Vietnam were stepping up the pace of war.

On August 2, 1964, a U.S. destroyer was attacked by hostile vessels in international waters of Vietnam's Tonkin Gulf. Two days later, the Vietnamese attacked two more ships of the U.S. Seventh Fleet in the same area, and President Johnson announced that "appropriate armed action" had been taken after the "deliberate . . . unprovoked" attack. [46]

Eight days after the initial attack, President Johnson signed the so-called "Tonkin Gulf Resolution" which launched the United States into nearly full-scale war against the North Vietnamese and Viet Cong.

Congress adopted the resolution by 502 to two vote. It was not a formal declaration of war, but a proclamation which produced a sort of U.S. military action that disappointed both citizens favoring a full-scale war and those who wanted the U.S. to stay out of the Vietnam controversy.

Signing the resolution, President Johnson explained:

"The position of the United States is . . . to any armed attack upon our forces we shall reply.

"To any in Southeast Asia who ask our help in defending their freedom, we shall give it." [47]

It was presented to the American public as a war against the encroachment of Communism. After the Tonkin Gulf Resolution, U.S. "hawks" among the population wanted all-out bombing of Hanoi, capital of North Vietnam, using nuclear weapons if necessary to stop the flow of arms and manpower to the Viet Cong.

It proved to be a very long and bloody war, lasting until 1973 when the United States withdrew the last of its troops from

South Vietnam and stopped bombing in nearby Cambodia during the administration of President Richard M. Nixon. About 50,000 Americans lost their lives in the war. Victory went to the Communists of North Vietnam, and a spirit of isolationism rose in the United States.

The military build-up which eventually led to more than 600,000 U.S. personnel being put into Vietnam began during the first full year of President Johnson's administration when he ordered troops increased from 20,000 to 140,000 and more bombing of the North Vietnamese. [48]

The president meanwhile authorized sending 30,000 U.S. military men into the Dominican Republic to stop a civil war which he said threatened Communist control. [49]

The huge outlays for military and domestic programs accelerated the rate of inflation at home.

The Johnson administration became an increasingly unhappy period and the quiet of the Texas Hill Country saw more and more of LBJ as the nation's problems mounted.

For *The Dallas Morning News* of July 14, 1965, I wrote:

> With the help of jet aircraft and the long-distance phone Lyndon Johnson is making Texas into the second capital of the United States.
>
> Others have talked about putting the brain-center of the national government somewhere besides the exposed and often-troubled District of Columbia.
>
> President Johnson is doing it by the simple expedient of coming home to Texas almost every weekend. His three-day visits to the LBJ Ranch are becoming a habit. Opening of his new offices at the Federal Center in Austin will make operations of the presidency in Central Texas even more convenient.
>
> This year, Mr. Johnson has probably spent more time "at home" in this area than during any similar period since he went to Washington as congressman from the Tenth District of Texas in 1937.
>
> Ever since the then-lanky protege of President Franklin D. Roosevelt won his first election, he has spent most of his weekends running for higher office or at least tending to his political fences.
>
> There is no higher political office than president of the

187

United States. Now that Lyndon Johnson has achieved this pinnacle, he can usually choose where—if not always how—he will spend his time.

Jet aircraft carry Mr. Johnson from Washington to his ranch (usually with a change to a helicopter) faster than he could travel from Johnson City to Austin (sixty miles) during his boyhood.

The telephone—that symbol of fast, personal communication which LBJ loves—keeps him in close contact with everybody he wants to talk to.

The ranch gives Mr. Johnson both freedom and isolation that is impossible in Washington. He attacks recreation with the same boundless energy which has marked his long public career. When he flies in from Washington, the next step usually is to ride a helicopter to Lake Lyndon B. Johnson (formerly Granite Shoals) at Kingsland, where the president refreshes himself with a fast spin in a motorboat.

There are official guests along sometimes, but mostly President Johnson surrounds himself at the ranch with old friends and longtime staff members. He feels comfortable with them, as he does in the familiar surroundings of the Hill Country where he grew up.

Mr. Johnson's activity Monday before returning to Washington illustrates how he spends a day "at home." Much of the day was spent talking from the ranch on the long-distance phone about affairs in Vietnam, the Dominican Republic, and other distant places, considering appointments and other decisions which he must make.

He interspersed these with (1) a swim in the ranch pool, (2) a trip to the family graveyard on the ranch to arrange for some shrub plantings, (3) a trip to the bank at Johnson City, and (4) a one-hour nap.

The president can swim at the White House, but his visitors often use even this period to talk business. At home on the Pedernales, Lyndon Johnson is much more the master of his own life than he is in the White House at Washington.

LBJ turned to his old political counselor and ally, John Connally, for help. He obtained Connally's support and influence at the National Governors Conference held in Minneapolis the summer of 1965 and received the state executives' endorsement of LBJ's prosecution of the war in Vietnam. The war was becoming increasingly unpopular and President Johnson sought all the support he could muster following the Tonkin Gulf Resolution and escalation of the war.

While Congress had given the resolution bipartisan backing, Republican governors and some Democrats were beginning to criticize the president for his actions. In 1965, Governor Connally was still a Democrat and a leader among governors nominated by that party.

Visiting newspeople, including the White House press, usually described Connally as "protege" or "political student" of President Johnson.

Such a relationship never existed. Connally was never Johnson's protege, but rather a manager and director of LBJ's rise to the top.

As the 1966 elections approached, I wrote that Connally occupied a "position of unusual independence" in relation to the president "and he is playing the part." On the contrary, longstanding opposition to Johnson by many of the state's Democratic conservatives had made Connally's task of getting elected governor much more difficult in 1962.

After the 1963 wounding in Dallas, such opposition toward Connally virtually disappeared and he was more and more "his own man" in politics.

[1] *Politics in America, 1945-1964,* Congressional Quarterly Service, page 36
[2] *L.B.J. — 37 Years,* Frantz
[3] *Politics in America, 1945-1964, Op.cit.,* page 34
[4] *Ibid.*
[5] *Texas in the 1960 Presidential Election,* O. Douglas Weeks, page 61
[6] *Politics in America, 1945-1964, Op.cit.,* page 95
[7] *Ibid.*
[8] *Dallas News,* February 15, 1961, quoting from a brochure published by The University of Texas Institute of Public Affairs.
[9] *Op.cit.,* April 16, 1961.
[10] *Politics in America 1945-1964, Op.cit.,* page 41
[11] *Ibid.*
[12] *Dallas News,* November 8, 1961
[13] *Politics in America 1945-1964, Op.cit.,* page 47
[14] *Dallas News,* November 23, 1963

[15] *Ibid.*
[16] *Dallas News,* July 25, 1963
[17] *Op.cit.,* July 23, 1963
[18] Frantz *Op.cit.,* (year 1963)
[19] *Politics in America 1945-1964, Op.cit.,* page 48
[20] *Ibid.*
[21] *Ibid.*
[22] *Ibid.*
[23] *Dallas News,* December 28, 1963
[24] *Op.cit.,* January 5, 1964
[25] *Op.cit.,* August 30, 1964
[26] *Dallas News,* February 4, 1964
[27] *Op.cit.,* September 26, 1964
[28] *Op.cit.,* August 18, 1964
[29] *Politics in America (May 1979),* Congressional Quarterly Inc., page 19
[30] *Dallas News,* October 2, 1964
[31] *Politics in America 1945-1964, Op.cit.*
[32] O. Douglas Weeks: *Texas in 1964: A One-Party State Again.*
[33] *Op.cit.,* November 4, 1964
[34] *Op.cit.,* June 28, 1964
[35] *Dallas News,* September 15, 1964
[36] *Op.cit.,* May 10, 1964
[37] *Op.cit.,* May 12, 1964
[38] *Dallas News,* May 28, 1965
[39] *Op.cit.,* March 21, 1965
[40] *Op.cit.,* May 19, 1965
[41] *Politics in America, Op.cit.,* page 21
[42] *Op.cit.,* page 22
[43] *Dallas News,* September 13, 1965 (Morehead column)
[44] *Politics in America, Op.cit.,* page 15
[45] *Ibid.*
[46] *Public Papers of Presidents,* Volume II, U.S. Government Printing Office.
[47] *Ibid.*
[48] *Politics in America, Op.cit.,* page 22
[49] *Op.cit.,* page 15

5

REPUBLICANS BEGIN A COMEBACK

The enormity of the Democrats' election victories in 1964, from courthouses and statehouses to the White House, caused some observers to predict the two-party political system in the United States was dead.

But the strength of the system was demonstrated anew in 1966 when the Republican party proved itself alive, if not completely healthy.

On the national level, Republicans recaptured forty-seven seats in the United States House of Representatives and three in the Senate, although Democrats retained a majority in both. The parties drew even in number of governorships held, with twenty-five each after a Republican gain of six. [1]

The minority party also fared batter in Texas than had been expected when political campaigning started that year.

U.S. Senator Tower, for example, was an underdog in his race for reelection, as published polls showed him far behind.

Democrats nominated Waggoner Carr, a popular and well-known state attorney general from Lubbock, whose victory over Tower appeared likely during most of the campaign.

State and national Republican leaders concentrated on helping Tower, and they paid little attention to other statewide races. John Connally easily won reelection for a third term as governor and Preston Smith for lieutenant governor. Crawford Martin, Connally's former secretary of state, was elected to succeed Carr as attorney general.

The Tower victory and general election was analyzed as follows:

John Tower, the ex-professor of political science, showed them how to write the textbook on campaigning in his successful race for the United States Senate this year.

His victory over Waggoner Carr and the combined forces of Governor John Connally and the Democratic Establishment will long be studied by those wanting to know "How to Win As a Minority Party Candidate."

The first-term senator, who came into politics from the faculty of Midwestern University at Wichita Falls, had liberally been setting his sights for November 8, 1966, since the day he took office at the national capitol in 1961, succeeding Lyndon B. Johnson as a lawmaker from Texas.

The Republican debacle of 1964, leaving President Johnson almost unchallenged on the national political scene and John Connally even more firmly entrenched in state politics, offered John Tower a less than an optimistic outlook for 1966.

But the five-foot six-inch Texan campaigned with an astuteness and energy that provoked the admiration of the experts in the practical science of political campaigning. His shock troops were an enthusiastic band of Texas Republicans led by State Chairman Peter O'Donnell, Jr. of Dallas. They attacked the problem of getting back on the victory road by using computers, personal calls, rallies, and advertising.

John Tower's campaign was low-keyed. As in the Senate, he sided with President Johnson on conduct of the war in Vietnam and he refused to criticize Mr. Johnson even on points where they disagreed.

He declined to rehash the 1964 race, in which he actively supported Barry Goldwater against Mr. Johnson.

Along the way, Tower picked up support—as he did in 1961—from many liberal Democrats who disliked the Connally-Carr "team" that for years has controlled the Democratic party in Texas. U.S. Senator Ralph Yarborough said early he would vote for Carr as a matter of party loyalty, but he did nothing else to help his fellow Democrat and indeed seemed pleased at the discomfiture of his conservative rivals within the party.

Unlike Carr, whose campaign wandered and who had difficulty finding any issue against Tower, the Republican candidate spread a gospel of the desirability of conservative two-party representation. He shuttled back and forth by airplane between Washington and Texas almost like the bird in a badminton game, spending part of each week on congressional duties and the other days speaking wherever he could find an audience.

No racial backlash vote was evident here, but many Negro voters apparently stayed away from the polls in Harris County and places other than Dallas. Here, they turned out strongly for Democratic candidates.

Tower had voted against the 1964 Civil Rights Act and a law which gives federal agents permission to intervene in registering voters in certain areas.

Likewise, he voiced strong opposition to the politically popular Medicare program and helped hold a thin line in the Senate for retaining Section 14B of the Taft-Hartley Act which permits Texas and other states to enforce "right to work" labor laws.

Tower stated his views on these and other problems around the state, but managed to do so without raising the ire of those who disagreed with him.

Even in his hour of victory Tuesday, Tower refused to take an I-told-you-so attitude about President Johnson and Governor Connally trying to defeat him. Instead, he said he didn't think the election had cost the president or governor any prestige, and he viewed the returns mainly as evidence that Texas is continuing the development of a two-party political system which was interrupted temporarily in 1964.

Governor Connally remains as the strong man of Texas politics, even more than President Johnson. While Connally lost his attempt to rescue Waggoner Carr's faltering candidacy, an all-Democrat slate was swept into the top positions of state government.

The only newcomer on this level will be Crawford Martin, who will succeed Waggoner Carr as attorney general in January. Martin is a former state senator from Hillsboro and served as secretary of state by Connally's appointment until he resigned to make the attorney general's race this year.

Returned for new two-year terms were Lieutenant Governor Preston Smith, Comptroller Robert Calvert, Land Commissioner Jerry Sadler, Agriculture Commissioner John White, Treasurer Jesse James, and Railroad Commissioner Byron Tunnell.

Republicans did not make a serious effort to beat any of these men.

But they did score modest success in the races where they put forth major effort. Republicans George Bush, 42, of Houston and Bob Price, 39, of Pampa were elected to Congress, along with twenty-one Democrats. Senator Tower is 41, giving Republicans three youngish lawmakers from Texas.

The Texas legislature's single Republican, Representative Frank Cahoon of Midland, will be joined at the January session by Senator Henry C. (Hank) Grover of Houston; Representatives Chuck Scoggins of Corpus Christi; and Abraham Malouf of Canadian. Eleven Republicans served in the state House of Representatives before most were exterminated at the polls in 1964. [2]

One result of Governor Connally's effort to elect an all-Democrat ''team'' probably was to give a winning margin to several lawmakers beset by serious Republican opposition. Included were Congressmen Joe Pool of Dallas and Graham Purcell of Wichita Falls, and legislative slates in Dallas and Harris counties.

Governor Connally thus retains his position as top hand in the Texas political corral. But looking ahead to 1968, state legislators may exercise increasing independence in the next two years—at least more than they would have if Democrats had swept the U.S. Senate, congressional and all legislative races. At least, the reelection of Senator Tower, election of two Republican congressmen, and four GOP men in the legislature leaves the party with a better foothold than it had two years ago.

The transition in Texas politics will continue as more power shifts to growing metropolitan areas. The new legislature will show the effect of major reapportionment, and further reshaping of the districts — reducing the brass-collar rural Democratic influence—is in prospect for 1967, because of court orders.

One reason for Tower's success was his choice of Kenneth Towery, a former Pulitzer-prize winning reporter from Cuero, as public relations director.

''He hasn't made a mistake since Ken Towery took over,'' a Democratic political professional praised Tower's adviser. [3]

Towery succeeded in destroying the image Tower's opponents were trying to create that the senator was reactionary.

Towery depicted his candidate as really "a pretty good guy. . . . He's not just negative. He considers a vote against waste is a vote for the people. Some fellows up in Washington believe if you vote against giveaways you are 'against the people.' " [4]

Meanwhile another Texas political public relations man, George Christian, newly employed by President Johnson, proved to be an excellent choice. Like Towery, Christian is a low-key, good-natured person who is loyal to his employer but never distorts truth even for political gain.

Christian was Governor Connally's public relations man after having served in a similar capacity for Governor Daniel.

"It is typical that nobody around Christian seemed to know how he feels about Lyndon Johnson, the man, about whom nearly everybody here expresses opinions. But his friends look upon Christian as a fellow who would accept such a position as a patriotic duty without much question about the personalities involved. This sets Christian apart in a political world, where cynicism is too often justified." [5]

Christian's first assignment in Washington was to help Dr. Walter W. Rostow (who later joined The University of Texas staff in Austin) digest reports from federal agencies.

When fellow-Texan Bill D. Moyers left as presidential press secretary, Christian was appointed to that position where he served during the stormy last half of President Johnson's elective term.

The "White House shuttle" between Washington and Texas brought a sort of Chamber of Commerce war between Austin and San Antonio.

During the first months of Johnson's presidential administration, Austin had been headquarters for the White House press and others who accompanied the president. The Johnsons usually went to the LBJ Ranch with occasional trips into Austin.

A new federal building was built in Austin, with elegant offices for Johnson. He continued to use these the remainder of his life.

Occasionally, the White House staff and press stayed in San

Antonio when the president came to Texas. The visitors numbered from about fifty to one hundred fifty and rooms often were required for them on short notice. Sometimes, the Driskill Hotel in Austin was unable to furnish the Washington visitors immediately the quarters they wanted and irritation resulted. President Johnson's administration brought business to Austin and Central Texas in many ways. Local restaurants, hotels, and car rental agencies were the immediate beneficiaries.

Republicans increasingly criticized the administration of some new Great Society programs, but their support of the Vietnam war effort was greater than from the president's own party, the Democrats.

Speaking of the rising Republican hopes for the election, one nonpartisan publication reported:

". . . the odds had shifted significantly to the benefit of the Republicans. Behind this change was the escalation of the Vietnam war, with its heavy toll, both in American lives and dollars. The Republicans did not pretend to have an easy solution to the Vietnam war; indeed most Republicans tended to support the Johnson administration's Vietnam policies, and the Republicans were sharply critical of Democratic critics of the war for failing to give solid support to the American war effort. But like the Korean war, the conflict in Vietnam, because of its limited nature, increased frustrations across the country and began to undermine public support of the administration in power.

"The war effort, in turn, generated inflationary pressures that were being felt throughout the country by mid-1966. The Republicans were able to argue with some effectiveness that the Johnson administration should be cutting down, rather than increasing, national expenditures for a wide variety of Great Society programs. Moreover, these very social programs that had looked so politically attractive at the end of 1965 were beginning to encounter serious administrative difficulties, with wide gaps between the promises of the Johnson administration to improve educational standards, end conditions of poverty and assure racial peace, and the administrations' actual ability to deliver on these promises.

"President Johnson's own personal popularity plummeted

during the year; wide splits appeared in the Democratic party in many key states; and at the very same time a number of attractive Republican candidates appeared to head the GOP in critical states — in sharp contrast to the unpopularity of Goldwater, the party's 1964 standard bearer . . .

"Republicans concentrated their fire increasingly on Vietnam, crime, and the alleged 'credibility gap' between what President Johnson and his administration said they were doing and their actual performance." [6]

Many young men left the United States to avoid being drafted into military service in Vietnam, thousands of them fleeing to Canada. The war was becoming an embarrassment to the president and his party, partly because of restraints on the military against using its full strength against the North Vietnamese. Critics called Vietnam a "no-win war" and it proved a catastrophe for both South Vietnamese and Americans.

REAGAN MOVES TO CENTER STAGE

My first acquaintance with Ronald Reagan, except in motion pictures, took place in 1966 when I went to California to cover the wind-up of his campaign for governor against the incumbent, Democrat Edmund (Pat) Brown, father of Jerry Brown, a later governor of the state.

The handsome Reagan was a celebrity from his movies before he became involved in politics. At the 1964 Republican convention in San Francisco, where Barry Goldwater was nominated for president, Reagan's speech on the need for a return to more conservative government almost stole the show.

Reagan established national political recognition even before running for office by his eloquent remarks against big government around the country, delivered in person, on radio, and in written columns.

While I was around Reagan several times before he became president, the closest I ever had to a conversation with him occurred in Lampasas, Texas, long after he had left the governorship and two years before his 1980 election as chief executive.

The occasion was a 7:30 a.m. speech by Reagan arranged by

197

U.S. SENATOR John Tower, R-Texas, (right) and President Ronald Reagan (left) in discussion.

— *Photo from Tower files*

a Lampasas banker and local Republicans. The high school auditorium was filled with enthusiastic citizens from all over Central Texas, despite the early hour.

While some national pundits, particularly in Washington, were virtually writing off Reagan's chances to be elected president because of his outspoken conservatism, I sensed from the reaction of the crowd in Lampasas that here was a candidate who could win grassroots support. After all, most in the cheering audience considered themselves Democrats, while the man on the podium among the signs made by Lampasas High School art students was an unabashed Republican.

After the speech, I was invited to a private reception for Reagan at the home of a local business man. In my few seconds with the man, we talked of the California governor's race which I had covered.

Reagan the candidate and officeholder was never much for

small talk. Because of his celebrity status, even before entering politics, he seemed always surrounded by staff and security people, with wife Nancy frequently at his side.

Everywhere he went, Reagan became a center of attention. His only rival at the National Governors' Conference was John Connally of Texas, who became famous when he was nearly killed by Lee Harvey Oswald. Connally also was a man of imposing presence and eloquence.

The most dramatic confrontation between Reagan and Connally took place aboard the USS Independence, a passenger ship which became a floating convention center for the governors on a cruise from New York to the Virgin Islands.

When the shipboard-Virgin Islands conference was held in 1967, Connally served as the chief defender of President Johnson's increasingly-criticized Vietnam war policy.

The president assigned former Texas Governor Price Daniel aboard the ship as a White House liaison with the governors.

The trip south from New York's harbor, after rough seas around Cape Hatteras, became more play than work and real news was scarce for the horde of reporters and photographers aboard.

One morsel they seized upon to make headlines across the country was "The Case of the Purloined Message."

By interviews and press conferences, the governors made known their like or dislike for President Johnson's programs, usually divided along party lines.

Reagan and the Republicans accused the president of trying to influence the governors unduly into supporting his actions, a charge which the Democrats and White House denied.

Once a radiogram from the White House addressed to liaison man Daniel was accidentally delivered to Reagan's cabin. The governor of California claimed it was evidence of President Johnson's attempted interference in the conference.

The Democrats asserted the wrongful delivery resulted from shipboard chicanery engineered by the Republicans. What really caused the mix-up was never made clear. The whole affair was a tempest in a teapot.

The main conference session, to discuss resolutions, was held in the ship's lounge as the vessel sailed from St. Thomas to

St. Croix, a nearby island. Both Reagan and Connally waxed oratorical in the smoky room. It resulted in a nominal victory vote on resolutions by the Democratic majority.

After Connally later became a Republican, and dropped out of the 1980 presidential primaries because of his poor showing, it was speculated in Washington that President Reagan would appoint Connally to the Cabinet or some other high position in the administration.

I never believed it. First, the two charismatic characters were too much alike. There would hardly be room for them both in the same administration. Second, Vice President George Bush and Connally, both from Houston, were hardly political friends and Bush might feel threatened from upstaging Connally.

During the 1968 campaign, a few backers of Republican Nixon, including some conservative Democrats, urged Governor Connally to support Nixon for president or at least to "go fishing" rather than help Democrat Humphrey in Texas.

Those making the pleas included William P. Clements of Dallas, an oil and gas drilling company executive little known in politics at the time. Ten years later, Clements was elected governor.

Connally spurned the Republicans' advice in 1968, and late in the campaign joined President Johnson in campaigning for the Democratic ticket. The effect was to carry Texas for Humphrey, who received 1,266,804 votes to Nixon's 1,227,844. Governor George Wallace of Alabama, candidate of the American Party, drew 584,269 votes in Texas. Without Wallace in the race, Nixon could have carried Texas easily.

Despite Connally's assistance to Humphrey, liberal Democrats accused the governor of helping Nixon raise money in Texas. The charge was renewed in 1971 after President Nixon appointed Connally to be secretary of the treasury. Later Connally formally joined the Republican party, saying he had lost faith in the Democrats' national leadership and goals. As a presidential candidate in the 1980 Republican primaries, Connally failed to get enough delegates pledged to finish the race before the nominating convention.

Reagan is a man of great personal charm and wit, and he differs from other politicians I have met.

He is aloof from the press, and seems to regard reporters as a necessary nuisance. Early in his administration as governor of California, Reagan discovered the press is much less powerful than some members like to believe. In controversies with California lawmakers, Reagan effectively used television broadcasts to bring his views to the public, without filtering his message through regular news channels.

Reagan continued the practice effectively as president, going "over the heads of Congress and media" to speak directly to the public. He also held press conferences less frequently than any of his predecessors since Herbert Hoover. Reagan added a new dimension in political communication, for which his personality and training were ideally suited.

1967 — A POOR YEAR FOR JOHNSON AND CONNALLY

The year 1967 was hardly a memorable one for President Johnson in the White House, or Governor Connally in the statehouse.

Even as Connally took the oath January 17, 1967, for his final term the governor and his family suffered from a viral infection. A cold norther added to the gloomy atmosphere.

Before the year ended, the popular Connally found himself increasingly in disagreement with his friend, the president, and he surprised his many friends and supporters by announcing he would not seek a fourth term in 1968.

Two days after his last inauguration, Connally asked the legislature to authorize $125 million in new taxes, mostly for a teacher pay raise. He also recommended authorizing cities to impose a one percent sales tax by local option. Most observers predicted voters would never approve such a tax, but most of the state's municipalities voted for the tax just as soon as it became legal.

Other Connally proposals included four-year terms for statewide elective officials (later adopted) and annual sessions of the legislature (later defeated).

In March, Connally told a New York audience of his growing disenchantment with President Johnson's Great Society operation.

201

"John Connally of Texas lashed out (March 2, 1967) at restrictions accompanying federal aid to the states, calling them the work of 'average men without any divine wisdom'." [7]

Connally commended the "worthy aims" of many of the social programs "enacted in good faith by the Congress."

"The damaging mischief comes all too often when the design is worked out in endless, tedious detail by middle management and clerical personnel in dozens of bureaus, to be handed down to state and local governments for exact compliance to uniform regulations, or else."

After the 1967 legislative session, Connally claimed he got most of what he had recommended including increased appropriations. Increasing taxes was delayed until 1968. Public school teachers were given a pay raise.

Meanwhile in Washington, President Johnson's troubles worsened. The Vietnam war was costing the United States more than two billion dollars per month, while 486,000 Americans fought beside 750,000 South Vietnamese. National leaders in 1967 remained optimistic about victory over the Communists. [8]

After Johnson's earlier honeymoon with Congress, which adopted about everything he had recommended in 1964-66, a stalemate developed between the president and the Congress. Southern Democrats joined Republicans in trying to put brakes on the Great Society's huge spending, especially in ghetto areas where blacks were rioting and destroying property. [9]

U.S. Representative Adam Clayton Powell, Democrat from New York, was excluded from the Congress for misappropriating federal funds. Senator Thomas J. Dodd, Democrat from Connecticut, was censured by the Senate for spending campaign money to pay personal bills. Further, the senator had tried to get a federal tax exemption on $100,000 of "campaign" funds collected in a year when he wasn't running for office.

The practice of accepting donations, usually from those with an interest in legislation, in noncampaign years had begun to flourish and remained widespread, sometimes to the embarrassment of recipients.

Often politicians pay too little attention to the source of the contributions, and had rather not know too much about sources.

For as long as government exists, the giving of gifts to public officials will continue, despite repeated efforts to regulate the practice.

During the controversy over the Dodd case, I related an anecdote about a colorful South Texas legislator who was always looking for "campaign funds."

Once a lobbyist approached the lawmaker just before Christmas, and asked whether the member would prefer to have a new suit or venison for Christmas, the story goes.

To the lobbyist's surprise, the legislator said he would take the meat.

"Why?" asked the lobbyist.

"Well, I can take that venison and have it cooked, and charge twenty-five dollars a plate for folks to attend a testimonial dinner for me," replied the official. [10]

Except that the dinner ticket today might cost $100, the testimonial fund-raising or "appreciation" dinner remained commonplace.

As the unhappy year 1967 drew toward its close, President Johnson called Governor Connally to the White House.

Reporter David S. Broder of the *Washington Post* wrote perceptively of that occasion: [11]

WASHINGTON — It was hardly coincidental that in the midst of last week's critical events in Washington — with Robert S. McNamara leaving the cabinet and Eugene J. McCarthy challenging the president's renomination — Governor John B. Connally of Texas turned up as an overnight guest at the White House.

In almost every political crisis in Lyndon Johnson's life, Connally has been the man to whom he has turned. The association goes back thirty years to the time when the president was a young Texas congressman and Connally was his administrative assistant.

It was Connally who supervised the bitter recount battle that preserved Johnson's 87-vote victory over Coke Stevenson in the 1948 senate primary; Connally who looked after his interests in the cutthroat world of Texas politics; Connally who came to Washington to manage his unsuccessful campaign for the 1960 presidential nomination and then to aid his vice-presidential candidacy; Connally, who from his seat as Texas' governor, has served as the president's liaison man, lightning rod, and, occasionally, layer-down-of-the-law, with, for and to the other Democratic governors.

They have had their differences, which is hardly surprising when one recalls another Texan's remark that "you could take either one of their egos, slice it up, and have healthy portions for any six ordinary men." But the governor and the president, like the professionals they are, have simply agreed to disagree on certain matters within the framework of an enduring political alliance.

Part of the element in that alliance in recent years has been their mutual determination that Robert Kennedy shall not take the Democratic Party away from Lyndon Johnson. Year-in and year-out, summer and winter, Connally has been the most anti-Robert Kennedy man in Lyndon Johnson's circle.

Connally has never wavered for a moment in his belief that the junior senator from New York is out to ruin Lyndon Johnson and take over the wreckage of the Democratic Party, and his suspicion extends to everyone who has ever been associated with the Kennedys. Two years ago, when Bill D. Moyers was still riding high at the White House, Connally was vocally insisting that Moyers was a Kennedy man (apparently because of his work at the Peace Corps with Sargent Shriver and his personal friendship with the Kennedy brothers) whose advice was leading the president into serious political trouble.

With virtually everyone at the White House now convinced that McCarthy's candidacy is being encouraged by Robert Kennedy, Connally's long-held conspiracy theory seems to be in the ascendancy.

Connally's visit to the White House last week produced rumors that he might succeed McNamara at the Pentagon, probably because he is familiar with the department from his tour of duty as secretary of navy in 1961-62, and he has announced he will not seek reelection to a fourth term as governor next year.

But McNamara is expected to leave early in 1968, and most Texas politicians doubt that Connally would quit his job before the primary next May. His resignation would give the advantage of incumbency to Lieutenant Governor Preston Smith, a declared candidate for governor but not a Connally favorite. It would also weaken Connally's control of the convention that picks the Texas delegation to the national convention.

A more interesting speculation, among those who believe the president may not run next year, is the thought that Connally could be groomed as his successor. It has been assumed by most that if Mr. Johnson stepped down, he would back Hubert Humphrey for the nomination.

THE EMERGENCE OF PRESTON SMITH

An editorial writer once compared Preston Smith to The University of Texas and professional football star Bobby Layne in the famous quarterback's declining years on the gridiron:
". . . He doesn't look very good . . . all he can do is beat you." [12]

When that was written in 1970, Smith had just become the first Democratic candidate in history to win an unopposed nomination for governor of Texas. Smith went on that November to defeat Paul W. Eggers, an energetic and popular Republican nominee, for the second time in as many elections.

The 1970 vote was Smith 1,232,506, Eggers 1,073,831.

This was closer than the result in 1968 when Smith won his first race for governor: Smith 1,662,019, Eggers 1,254,333.

Although political life was never easy for Smith, a self-made Lubbock business man, he was a successful practitioner of the art. He also was a better governor than his critics contended.

Smith learned statecraft and government from the bottom up. He served six years in the Texas House of Representatives, six years in the Senate, and six years as lieutenant governor, before winning two two-year terms as chief executive. Although he tried again in 1972 and 1978, the hard-working candidate failed to achieve his goal of serving six years in every office he sought.

Better than most governors, Smith understood the feelings of legislators, particularly those in the Senate where a few members wield great power.

One reason for Smith's image problem was that he fol-

GOVERNOR PRESTON SMITH and Author Morehead.

lowed Connally as governor. Connally came closer to being a movie fan's idea of a leader than anybody I knew in public office: handsome, wavy-haired, tall, and articulate with a high sense of drama.

"(Smith) suffered in physical and oratorical ability, compared to Connally," wrote one capitol correspondent. [13]

While Smith, a physical fitness buff, was above average in personal appearance, his conservative approach failed to bring any waves of enthusiasm from the press and many other observers of the political scene. We think they underrated his abilities.

Smith's trademark was a polka-dot necktie, which he adopted as a candidate when former Governor Daniel advised him to wear something distinctive.

When the state bought a prop-jet airplane for the governor's use, Smith had polka-dots painted on its nose, and named the craft after his two-year-old granddaughter, Kelly Michelle Smith. [14]

Smith related that he had announced his ambition to become governor when he was an eight-year-old farm lad, one of thirteen children in a family living near Lubbock. He worked hard for everything he got, including an education at Texas Tech University, where he graduated to become a prosperous motion picture theatre owner in a period when that entertainment was very popular.

Although many low-rated Smith's chances of becoming governor, hardly anybody was surprised when the lieutenant governor announced for the higher office:

"I'm running for governor . . . it doesn't make one iota of difference to me (whether John Connally seeks a fourth term) or not." [15]

This statement came while Connally was in Africa on a six weeks' safari. Most observers expected Connally to run again, and considered him a strong favorite if he did run.

But Smith demonstrated his instinct for making sound political judgments.

He told Connally of his intention to run when the governor returned to his office from Africa and asked for Connally's support which was not forthcoming. Connally waited to make his decision.

So Smith announced formally anyway, commenting that he sensed deep unrest among the people: "These riots, the Vietnam war, and taxes are something about which people are troubled." [16]

He correctly read the mood of the times and drew his main support from conservative Democrats who still dominated the state's elections.

Early in his Austin career, Smith tried as a state representative to get legislative approval of a constitutional amendment dividing the Permanent University Fund endowment income among all state universities, then numbering fourteen. This incurred bitter opposition from legislative supporters of The Uni-

GOVERNOR AND MRS. PRESTON SMITH at an inauguration. Lieutenant Governor Ben Barnes at left.

— Dallas Morning News Photo

versity of Texas and Texas A&M, the fund's sole beneficiaries.

Once talking to a West Texas senator, Smith asked:

"Hear that?"

"Hear what?" asked the senator.

"Hear that West Texas oil and gas that The University of Texas and Texas A&M are draining from beneath our West Texas land," said Smith.

The fountainhead of the multibillion dollar fund was from oil and gas found on the 2.1 million acres bestowed on the state university when it was founded more than a century ago. The grassland was virtually worthless until the discovery of oil, and Texas A&M waited years to claim a one-third share. Earlier, Texas A&M preferred to get its money from general legislative appropriations.

Governor Connally and Speaker Barnes were close friends, socially and politically. Smith developed an adversary role in dealing with them, and sometimes the coolness was very evident.

As with most achievements in his life, Smith won the governorship the hard way. Ben Barnes of DeLeon was elevated from Speaker of the House to lieutenant governor, where he continued his feud with Governor Smith.

Smith got into the 1968 Democratic primary runoff as a runner-up to Don Yarborough, a Houston man backed by party liberals. This is a different Yarborough from another man of similar name later elected to the Texas Supreme Court and later forced to resign.

Eight Democrats were eliminated in the first Democratic primary, among them Secretary of State John Hill, former Attorney General Waggoner Carr, rancher-banker Dolph Briscoe, and Dallas attorney Eugene Locke.

The party's conservative majority rallied behind Smith in the runoff and he won the nomination by a margin of 146,264 votes.

Senator Yarborough earlier had shown an inclination to run for governor, and Republicans hoped that he would, for they believed a well-financed conservative Republican could beat the senator — leader of the state's liberal voters.

As it turned out, the general election was between two conservatives, Democrat Smith and Republican Eggers.

Campaigning with Smith was rigorous. Up at dawn, he took calisthentics before scheduled breakfast meetings.

The candidate crisscrossed the state many times. At one breakfast ''rally'' at Marshall which I attended the guests seemed to be all Smith's local workers. His county manager told Smith there was no need to come back again before the election.

''You're wearing us out,'' said the manager.

As did other candidates, Smith faced dangerous travel on occasion. After taking off from Marshall in a chartered DC-3, our pilots received radio advice from the ground against trying to land at Daingerfield, the next scheduled stop. A strike was in progress against the Lone Star Steel Company, and occasional gunfire accompanied the strife.

So we landed at Mount Pleasant, which was not scheduled, where Smith borrowed an automobile from a friendly dealer and we sped over backroads to Gilmer, arriving right on time for a noon luncheon. The auto trip over rolling country roads at high speed didn't seem to bother Smith, who sat calmly in the front seat beside an aide who was driving.

I sat in the back seat, white-knuckles grasping an arm rest.

In his first legislative session as governor, Smith scored two major victories.

Because of a miscalculation by legislative opponents, the governor saw a ten-year pay raise program enacted for teachers and legislation for expanded public education including state-financed kindergarten. Whether the Constitution permits a legislature to authorize spending for longer than a two-year period is doubtful, but Smith did it with a schedule increasing teacher pay.

This came about because the legislature insisted on limiting the main state budget appropriation to a single year, while the governor held out for a two-year bill.

When the one-year budget bill reached his desk late in the session, Smith vetoed it. He then signed the teacher pay-raise legislation and other bills which the comptroller could certify as payable since they were not competing with the big budget.

Next, the governor called a special legislative session to approve a two-year budget and taxes to make up the amount needed over anticipated revenues.

The second big goal of the governor was submission of a State Water Plan, costing several billion dollars, which would authorize a system to transfer water from areas with surpluses, either from outside the state or East Texas, to water-short areas such as West Texas where the governor lived. The plan failed narrowly, largely because of negative votes from Harris County and East Texas.

Smith was the hardest-working governor I ever knew, and he sometimes was misunderstood as a result.

A caller might telephone the governor's office and Smith would answer personally, instead of letting a secretary screen the calls. Likewise, the governor frequently placed his own calls to others.

Once, according to a story which went around *The Dallas News,* office, the city editor was startled to pick up the phone one morning and hear:

"This is Preston Smith."

The startled editor hesitated.

The caller continued: "I'm Preston Smith, the governor. I sat with you at a luncheon in Dallas the other day."

The city editor remained unstrung by this beginning and laughed nervously.

This irritated the governor, who had called to complain about an item in the paper.

After the city editor laughed, Smith delivered his message, then promptly called the publisher to complain that the city editor had laughed at him.

A very sensitive man, Smith resented such descriptions as "colorless" and stories comparing him unfavorably with Connally. I hardly blamed Smith for his attitude. Younger reporters of the Smith era regarded themselves as a new breed of adversaries to the Establishment and enjoyed making cutting remarks about public officials with whom they disagreed philosophically.

Particularly in the first part of his four-year administration, Smith went out of his way to accommodate the press. He was accessible both by telephone and in person, and once got in trouble — with ensuing critical publicity — for taking a group of reporters and wives to a governors' assembly in Williamsburg, Virginia, aboard a Texas National Guard airplane.

A dissident Guard officer complained to national headquarters in Washington that the trip was an unauthorized use of the aircraft, although some governors of other states did the same thing.

After the embarrassing publicity, the National Guard was repaid several thousand dollars from private funds for the trip. I offered to repay my share, but Smith's staff assured me that the expense already had been covered.

Later, when a National Governors' Conference was held in Puerto Rico, new regulations from Washington permitted staff

GOVERNOR AND MRS. PRESTON SMITH.
— From LBJ Library

members and working press to accompany governors flying aboard National Guard aircraft.

So Smith traveled aboard an old-style National Guard transport plane with staff and media people. Mrs. Smith and several ladies flew to Puerto Rico on the governor's state furnished prop-jet.

The trip aboard the National Guard plane proved to be rather harrowing.

We joined several other governors and their parties on a National Guard plane leaving from Florida for the over-water flight. Not quite halfway to San Juan, our plane developed engine trouble and had to turn back to Homestead Air Force Base in southern Florida.

It was nearly midnight by the time another National Guard plane was obtained and passengers and baggage transferred. An Air Force officer at Homestead summoned off-duty enlisted men to transfer the baggage, and they seemed unhappy at the Saturday night assignment.

When our plane eventually reached San Juan about 2 a.m. on Sunday, we discovered that name and hotel labels on the baggage had been shuffled to the extent that some passengers were separated from their baggage for a day or two.

Governors follow different policies toward association with reporters on trips and at social events.

Relationships were cordial with Governors Allred, Stevenson, Jester, Shivers, Daniel, and Connally. O'Daniel kept reporters away except when he wanted them for political purposes and Molly's wedding.

Smith's relations with most reporters outside business hours cooled toward the end of his administration.

Dolph Briscoe had a few friends among the press, and he was unfailingly courteous to all, including the press, who often failed to respond in kind. Many reporters treated Governor Briscoe, as they had Smith, in an adversary manner, sometimes rudely.

Briscoe never learned how to cope with the media, except a few old friends like me. I had known him and his wife Janey since his days as a young state representative after World War II.

William P. Clements, the Republican following Briscoe, became a master at handling the media. He maintained accessibility, and practiced the salesman's (which he once was) art of remembering names and faces. Clements seemed to enjoy putting reporters down when he deemed they deserved it.

Governors Smith and Briscoe had difficulty getting across to the media. On the other hand, Governor Clements proved adept at one-upsmanship in his news conferences and other media relations.

1968 — A YEAR OF TURMOIL

Despite a lively governor's race state politics in Texas were tame in 1968 compared to the stormy national campaign for president.

As rioting and looting continued in black areas of several cities, protest demonstrations arose in many places including Texas over miseries of the Vietnam war.

President Johnson and his programs became increasingly unpopular. Joking references were made to military bases "being the only place it is safe for President Johnson to make a personal appearance."

Nevertheless, Johnson surprised most Americans by announcing in a nationwide broadcast on Sunday evening March 31 that he would not run for reelection. The verbal bombshell was dropped almost casually at the end of Johnson's discussion of domestic and foreign affairs.

At the time, I was attending an American Press Institute seminar on political correspondence held at Columbia University in New York City. A group from the Institute visited a student-faculty tavern across the street from the university campus to hear the president on television.

Our group was mostly silent, but others in the place were openly hostile to Johnson. When he announced his impending retirement, some listeners appeared stunned. It was as if the young hecklers had lost their main target.

While I was in New York the following week, the country was shaken by the assassination in Memphis, Tennessee, of Martin Luther King, a black leader of the civil rights movement.

Despite appeals for calm, unrest gripped the nation as police searched for the killer. A white man later was arrested and convicted.

Tension ran so high on Manhattan Island that the press seminar visitors stayed close together, heeding warnings of possible violence in the city, especially against whites in Harlem, New York's black center.

Columbia University is located between Harlem and downtown where crowds, mostly blacks, milled around Times Square.

I purchased a small radio to follow the news, and could see smoke rising from Harlem where some stores were looted and burned.

An all-news radio station kept broadcasting advice for citizens to stay at home, and especially for parents to keep their children at home. A "crisis center" at city hall provided information about conditions in New York, especially responding to rumors of race riots (which did not occur).

It was my first experience with racial tension in a non-Southern community and more eerie than other places where I had covered civil rights demonstrations.

Even before Dr. King's death, police patroled with dogs around the Columbia campus. This surprised me, because much criticism had been directed against Southern police for using dogs in crowd control in civil rights demonstrations.

Because Columbia is located in an area noted for violence, a fortress-like wall had been built around its campus long ago, with stout gates which could be locked to repel any attempted invasion. This surprised me almost as much as seeing U.S. paratroopers camped at Little Rock's Central High School during its earlier racial troubles.

During the seminar, those attending the Institute were luncheon guests of *The New York Times* management. Guests included Mayor John Lindsay.

Half-jokingly, I asked the mayor if he knew large dogs were being used for police patrols around Columbia University.

"We do not talk about that," he smilingly replied.

Within a month, more than five hundred students and outside radicals captured Columbia University's main building, held administrators hostage, and staged a sit-in on the campus which caused classes to be suspended for days. Police were unable or unwilling to handle the demonstration, and the event became a blight on higher education. The radicals eventually lost, after claiming they intended to "take control of your world, your corporation, your university, and attempt to mold a world in which we and other people can live as human beings." [17]

President Johnson's withdrawal was just one surprise in the presidential race.

On the Republican side, moderate Governor George W. Romney of Michigan was considered the frontrunner until his unfortunate comment that he had been "brainwashed" about the Vietnam war.

Except for a storm of criticism which followed, the remark seemed of little importance to me. Nevertheless, adversaries in both parties made the most of it and the Romney-for-President bandwagon stalled.

Former Vice President Nixon forged ahead in the Republican nomination primaries with California's Governor Reagan, and New York's Governor Nelson Rockefeller as his principal challengers.

Nixon finally emerged as victor at the Republican convention, after Reagan switched his vote to Nixon.

Former Attorney General Robert Kennedy, brother of the late President John F. Kennedy, ran well in Democratic presidential primaries, until he was slain following a victory celebration in Los Angeles June 4. The assassin apparently had no political motivation for his act.

With Kennedy and Johnson both out, the Democrats' nomination battle was between Vice President Hubert H. Humphrey, President Johnson's choice, and U.S. Senator Eugene McCarthy of Minnesota, the most liberal and anti-war candidate on either side.

Another factor was Governor George C. Wallace of Alabama, a favorite of segregation-minded conservatives. He ran as a candidate of the newly-formed American Independent Party.

McCarthy's campaign, which attracted thousands of college-age youths, drew the most attention. At the national convention in Chicago, its tactics turned to violence which not only wrecked his "Be Clean with Gene" image, but hurt the Democrats generally.

Governor Connally became the leader of the Texas delegation to Chicago and its "favorite son" candidate for president. Several party leaders around the country also had expressed hope that Connally would run for president, but the Texan never held serious expectations that would happen in 1968.

Connally's generosity to liberal Texas Democrats during the delegate-selection process proved a headache for him.

"Last June (1968) Connally went into the state Democratic convention with more than eighty percent of the delegates. His forces had been dominant in 253 of the state's 254 counties," wrote Robert E. Baskin, chief of the *Dallas Morning News* Washington Bureau.

"The liberal wing of the party had been utterly defeated all along the route — from the precinct to the state convention.

"If Connally had followed procedures normally used in Texas politics, he would have set up a delegation to the national convention absolutely committed to him in word and spirit.

". . . Connally chose to be magnanimous. He allowed the liberal pro-Ralph Yarborough element of the party to be represented on the delegation to Chicago." [18]

At the national convention, liberals in the Texas delegation ignored Connally's majority leadership and challenged the seating of his delegates. His opponents were backed both by Senator McCarthy and Vice President Humphrey, making the Texas governor a "most indignant man."

The only pleasant experience concerning the Democratic national convention was the trip aboard a special train, carrying the Texas delegation. Everybody had a fine time until we reached Chicago.

There, Texans quickly discovered that long-paid-for hotel room reservations already had been claimed by others, mostly McCarthy followers who reportedly just asked the keys to a certain room, parked unlabeled luggage inside the rooms, and disappeared. Perplexed hotel officials explained it was illegal for them to remove luggage without the owners' permission. After a hectic day, most Texans with reservations were assigned rooms in the large hotel.

Across the street in Grant Park, McCarthy enthusiasts held forth boisterously.

In the beginning, the noisy demonstrations were tolerable but the agitated youths — almost all whites — became aggressive as their political hero's fortunes waned at the convention hall several miles away.

Once they smeared a foul-smelling substance into the lob-

217

MOREHEAD boarding the Santa Fe at Fort Worth for the Chicago convention of Democrats, August 1968.

— *Dallas News Photo*

by carpets of the convention hotel, leaving an odor that literally sickened its guests.

Downtown Chicago was miserable, as police and Illinois National Guardsmen struggled to keep the McCarthyites under control.

In Chicago, I scribbled notes for a column which I never sent, because it sounded so unreal.

"On a grand scale," I wrote, "Chicago has experienced its same trials as Southern communities invaded by (civil rights) troublemakers — and reaping an avalanche of bad publicity.

"Compared to what happened in this city during the Democratic national convention, Little Rock's school integration difficulty was like a Sunday School picnic.

"Oxford, Mississippi, brought two deaths when James Meredith (a black) enrolled (at the University of Mississippi) with the help of U.S. marshals and the U.S. army.

"But the great Chicago disturbance did more than any of these to disgrace the nation. It was a planned insurrection with trouble-making organized by professionals.

"Except for actions of the police and National Guard, the city might have been in flames, for riots feed on themselves.

"Chicago citizens, many of whom probably criticized Southern officials during racial traumas, reacted as did much of the South.

"Television networks were accused of distorting coverage to emphasize 'police brutality' rather than conveying accurately the days of taunts and planned obscene heckling which the demonstrators employed . . .

"As one working man at the convention, my thanks to the police and the Illinois National Guard."

It was closer to domestic revolution than I ever witnessed before or afterward.

The convention was more orderly than downtown Chicago, but still hectic. President Johnson stayed away, probably on advice of security people but also fearful that he would be booed by the delegates of his own party.

Whenever a speaker at the convention mentioned the Kennedy name it brought a standing ovation.

219

A boomlet started just before the convention for Senator Edward M. Kennedy of Massachusetts, the sole surviving brother. McCarthy forces challenged seventeen delegations, including the one from Texas, without avail, as Humphrey supporters maintained control.

Humphrey, a popular liberal-moderate favored by union labor and most of the party's power blocs, easily won the nomination for president, with Senator Edmund S. Muskie of Maine as his vice presidential running mate.

The anti-war faction led by Senators McCarthy and George S. McGovern of South Dakota gained one victory which later weakened the Democratic party.

They succeeded in abolishing the "unit rule" which bound a whole delegation to vote with the majority at every level of the Democrats' presidential nominating process.

By approximately sixty to forty percent, the convention rejected a resolution to stop the war in Vietnam. The majority endorsed President Johnson's Vietnam war policy, despite the rising criticism.

The Democrats left Chicago bitterly divided. [19]

Besides Nixon versus Humphrey, a third important candidate in the presidential race was Alabama's feisty Governor Wallace, who showed strength in northern industrial states as well as the conservative South. Wallace's candidacy worried conservatives backing Nixon more than it did Humphrey and the Democrats, for Wallace could attract support which otherwise probably would go to Nixon and Spiro (Ted) Agnew, governor of Maryland and Republican choice for vice president.

My first impression of Agnew was favorable. He became governor of Maryland in 1966 in part of a political reversal from the Democrats' sweep in 1964. Several times I witnessed Agnew in action at governors' conferences.

I wrote that Agnew was a "natural" running mate for Nixon, and would help the Republicans offset the threat from Governor Wallace and his American Independent Party.

During the first Nixon-Agnew administration, my original judgment appeared to be sound. During the later trauma of Watergate, Agnew also was unseated from office. In fact, he went out ingloriously before President Nixon resigned in 1974. Agnew's folly was alleged conspiracy and bribery while serving as a public official in Maryland, and he resigned after pleading "no contest" to a federal charge of income tax evasion.

It wasn't the first time my judgment proved wrong. Before Land Commissioner Bascom Giles' conviction of misusing his office in the 1950s, I had voted for him without hesitation every time he ran.

The well-managed, well-financed Nixon-Agnew campaign started well in front of the disunited Democrats, according to the early polls.

But the likeable "candidate Humphrey" proved to be a tough campaigner with assistance from his running mate, Senator Muskie.

Humphrey quickly disassociated his campaign from the unpopular Johnson administration, and promised to stop American bombing of North Vietnam if elected. The move sought to appease the noisy anti-war faction led by Senators McCarthy and McGovern. [20]

Texas Governor Connally remained cool to the Humphrey appeal, after being slighted in the delegate fight in Chicago as well as being less than enthusiastic about the Democratic ticket and platform.

As the contest narrowed toward election day, Connally finally gave the Democrats the push they needed to carry Texas, although Nixon won the nation's electoral vote after an extremely close popular vote.

Both Humphrey and Nixon visited Texas in the final days of campaigning. The Democratic candidate for governor, Preston Smith, revised his own schedule to attend a Humphrey rally at Austin's Municipal Auditorium, and was rewarded with a chorus of boos when he appeared with the presidential candidate. [21]

The election proved Smith a better vote-getter in Texas than Humphrey, however.

"Although John Connally appeared with Humphrey in Fort Worth, Dallas, and Austin, the governor has many friends who are quite active in the Nixon campaign," I wrote.

"Some Republicans claim to have a list of Connally's principal political contributors, and are soliciting funds for Nixon with the governor's consent if not his assistance.''

When the Texas votes were counted, Humphrey had 1,266,804 (41.1 percent), Nixon 1,227,844 (39.9 percent), and Wallace 584,269 (19 percent). [22]

The national popular vote was very close. While Nixon ran ahead of Humphrey, he received only 43.42 percent of the total to Humphrey's 42.72. [23]

The Electoral College, representing pluralities if not majorities in each state, gave a majority to Nixon — 320 votes to 191 for Humphrey and forty-six for Wallace. The Alabama governor's electoral votes all came from the South.

The 1968 results again proved the wisdom of the United States Constitution provision for the Electoral College, giving the total vote in each state to the candidate receiving the most votes, regardless of how small the plurality or majority.

Three times in the 1931-1981 period, the Electoral College prevented the United States from being governed by a ''plurality president.''

Both Presidents Truman in 1948 and Kennedy in 1960 took office with a majority of the Electoral College votes, but less than half of the popular votes because of minor candidates in these races.

Efforts continue to change the winner-take-all-in-each-state Electoral College system. This would be a mistake, in my opinion, based on the record above.

Electoral College majorities have kept ''plurality presidents'' from taking office at crucial times in our history. By following the Constitution's requirements, each winner held a constitutional majority.

In event that no candidate receives a majority in the Electoral College, the choice goes to the U.S. House of Representatives, a responsibility it has never been required to exercise. Partisan politics in such a situation could be extremely divisive in the nation.

Even though the Electoral College system works, it may not be just what the Constitution's writers intended.

Probably the originators wanted the final choice for president to be made by designated electors, usually substantial citizens of each state, to avoid the possible election of some completely unqualified person as president. Electors seldom vote except as directed by the popular vote for the leading candidates in each state.

In 1968, for example, one Republican elector from South Carolina cast his ballot for Wallace rather than Nixon. It did not affect the outcome.

A negative effect of the Electoral College plan has been to magnify the importance of large blocs of ethnic, labor, religious, or other special-interest voters, in two-party states.

Candidates make special appeals to such "swing" voting blocs, while paying less attention to the views and needs of voters in so-called "safe" states, such as the South was for Democratic candidates until recent years.

The rise in two-party strength among all fifty states has diminished the impact of bloc-voting, but various groups still insist on special consideration.

The 1968 presidential race reemphasized the conservatism of most Texas voters. Together, Nixon and Wallace received fifty-nine percent of the votes.

The election also demonstrated the growing independence of American voters, particularly in the South.

Arkansas, for example, gave a majority to presidential candidate Wallace (American Party), to Winthrop Rockefeller (Republican) for governor, and J. William Fulbright (Democrat) for U.S. senator — men of quite divergent views.[24]

LBJ COMES HOME TO TEXAS

Thirty-two years after Lyndon Johnson went to Congress as a tall, thin young congressman, he returned to Texas in 1969 to spend the last five years of his active life.

With an eloquent tribute to old friends like Speaker Sam Rayburn and former President Harry Truman, Johnson paid his official farewell to Washington the night of January 14, 1969, with an appearance in the House of Representatives chamber before an audience of legislators, military men, newspeople, and others who had known LBJ best during his public career.

He spoke of the Great Society programs passed under his guidance, particularly social and civil rights programs.

"Now, it is time to leave," he said. "I hope it may be said a hundred years from now, that by working together we helped to make our country more just, more just for all people, as well as to insure and guarantee the blessings of liberty for all of our posterity." [25]

After turning the reins of power over to his successor, President Richard M. Nixon, Johnson flew to his Hill Country ranch at Stonewall. He remained busy with writing his memoirs, overseeing the transfer of his papers from Washington to Austin, and the financing and construction of the Lyndon Baines Johnson Library on The University of Texas campus at Austin.

While I found much to criticize about LBJ during his rise to the presidency, and wrote considerably in that vein, I always believed Johnson tried his best to make a good president.

Regardless of his methods in reaching the top, Johnson (many persons I met outside Texas thought I looked and talked like him) wanted history to record him as a compassionate and effective president, and he toiled in that direction, both in the White House and in arranging for the presentation of his life and times for future generations.

I agreed with President Johnson's role in the tragic war in Vietnam, except that he should have given the military more leeway to use the necessary force to win the war after we got into it.

The Great Society program, well-intended, went too far and cost too much. Included were programs to which former President Kennedy gave political service, but never tried very hard to write into law.

President Johnson (unfortunately for the country) got the whole package implemented, and by the 1970s the Great Society was being crushed under its own weight of rapidly-increasing inflation and a national debt that turned into a millstone for the nation's economy.

One result was the election of conservative Republican Ronald Reagan as president in 1980, on his promise to attempt to restore the nation's economic health and security.

Writing of the task President Reagan inherited, Toby Cohen, a New York researcher in the social field, commented:

"It was President Johnson, not President Reagan, who forsook the New Deal goals of social and economic democracy. The Great Society tied all its social-welfare programs to the dole, and thus consigned millions to that hidden population of almstakers Roosevelt so feared creating.

"Medicaid, legal aid, job training — all the Great Society programs — levied means tests. To be eligible, one had, in effect, to be on welfare . . .

"To be sure, much good was achieved: people who never had decent medical care now received it and capable legal aid as well. Thanks to job-training programs, many longtime welfare recipients were able to find their first jobs. But the awful irony is the fact that these noble experiments of the Great Society coincided with an unprecedented national effort in desegregation, and designed largely to benefit poor blacks and other minorities, enforced a new segregation.

"The Great Society, at least in the cities, established separate medical and legal systems, one public and mainly black, the other private and mainly white.

"Worse for economic and social democracy, the white taxpayer — any taxpayer — was made to pay for medical and legal services that were provided to welfare recipients but not to him — services he often could not afford to buy for himself in the private sector." [26]

The above is an accurate analysis, in my opinion.

Much of the criticism of LBJ came after his death. While he was alive, he and his family largely ignored all critics, which seemed to increase the longer Johnson was out of office.

The former president appeared genuinely to enjoy retirement. The eight-story LBJ Library opened in 1971 and included an almost lifesize replica of the White House Oval Room which Johnson used during his five years and two months as chief executive. It was for the president's use during his lifetime although his trips there were irregular.

Many receptions were held inside the marble building, with its reminders of history, and the Johnsons often attended such affairs. After he died, Johnson's body lay in state inside the Library before being sent to Washington for further tributes, and eventually buried in the family plot at the LBJ Ranch.

Johnson basked in the achievements of his wife, Lady Bird, who sponsored roadside and park improvement projects in Texas and the District of Columbia. She also wrote a best-selling book, *A White House Diary*.

Once at an autograph party honoring his wife, Johnson joked that the ''rare copies of her book will be the ones that are not autographed.''

PRESTON SMITH, THE GOVERNOR

Preston Smith's first term as governor was marked by success in passing laws designed to benefit the public school system, and by a well-meaning but unsuccessful attempt to gain public approval of a $3.5 billion water development plan, looking toward transfer of water from surplus areas in East Texas to other areas.

In the beginning, the new governor followed a genuine ''open door'' policy. He was, in his first term, the most approachable governor I ever knew, but less so after the Sharpstown scandal brought a barrage of unfavorable publicity.

Smith personally answered many phone calls to his office, without asking who was calling first.

''This is Preston Smith . . . I am your governor'' often was his opening remark.

Occasionally, Smith received calls from drunks as important figures do. It is said that hearing the governor personally answer the phone was a sobering experience for such callers.

Once a visiting minister asked Smith if being governor made him feel ''a little like God.'' His reply: ''Well, I can say that I enjoy being governor.''

His fascination with the telephone became legend.

Once he got the wrong person when he punched one of the buttons on his telephone console.

Exasperated at first, Smith then broke into a little half-smile that was his trademark. Turning to a visitor in his office, he remarked: "You know, as smart as I am, it looks like I ought to be able to use the telephone."

While Smith could laugh at himself, for a politician he was extremely sensitive to ridicule, and was said to have the longest memory for slights and derogatory remarks of any governor in history. Descriptions such as "colorless" and "humorless" by the media deeply offended Smith.

His differences with the media mounted steadily after Smith's first months in office. Evidently, he did not believe the old politicians adage that "I don't care what you say about me, but for gosh sakes don't ignore me."

During his first six months, Smith held more press conferences than Connally had done during his whole six years in office. While reporters grumbled over lack of access to Connally, Smith gave them almost more access than they wanted, for it is almost compulsory for capitol news reporters to attend a governor's press conference for fear of missing something important.

Over the years, Smith built a public image of being determined, hard-working, and sincere, and he genuinely liked people. This was his real character, although Smith never succeeded in projecting the personal magnetism of a John Connally, who was a hard act to follow as a personality.

A United States Supreme Court decision establishing the "one-man, one-vote" principle for electing public officials became fully effective during Smith's administration.

The court decision came in 1965 while Smith was lieutenant governor, and he found himself with a less compliant conservative majority of senators than had his predecessor, Ben Ramsey.

When Ben Barnes succeeded Smith as lieutenant governor, liberals were awarded the best committee chairmanships and assignments in the Senate that the group had ever had. Power in the Senate, in effect, shifted from conservative rural to more liberal urban members in a transition taking several years.

Small-town philosophy still influenced the legislature, however. Lieutenant Governor Barnes came to Austin from DeLeon, Speaker Gus F. Mutscher from Brenham, and the governor reared on a dryland cotton farm in West Texas cared deeply about preserving his roots.

U.S. SENATOR Lloyd Bentsen, Democrat from Texas.

Smith's legislative battles with Barnes became legendary, and the governor frequently won. Their biggest fight in 1969 resulted from Barnes' determination to restrict appropriations to one year, requiring annual sessions of the legislature.

The governor opposed annual sessions, and vetoed the one-year appropriation, then calling a special session to enact a two-year budget and taxes to pay the bill.

Smith's open door policy at the governor's office was matched by hospitality at the Governor's Mansion, supervised by his wife Ima.

During his first 100 days in office, Smith posed for photographs with an estimated 5,000 visitors to his reception room. [27]

The thirty-one senators were invited separately to bring as many constituents and other guests as they desired for refreshments at the Mansion, giving them a chance to meet the official family.

During this period, the famous "chicken salad" case opinion was revived, with the result that the Smiths had to pay personally for large quantities of food and drink not covered by state appropriations. The "chicken salad" case was a 1915 decision by the Texas Supreme Court that the governor's state expense allowance did not cover food and drinks even though the state furnished the house, utilities, and utensils.

Some, if not all, other states give their governors an entertainment allowance. In Texas, this frequently comes from private donations rather than public funds.

NATIONAL POLITICS: BACK TOWARD THE CENTER

As President Nixon steered the nation out of the Vietnam war and back toward a less liberal domestic policy, politics in Texas remained rather tranquil in 1970 except for the United States Senate race.

The early favorite was incumbent Ralph Yarborough, who was upset in the Democratic primary by Lloyd Bentsen, a former congressman from McAllen, who had become a Houston businessman-lawyer.

John Connally, an old political foe of Senator Yarborough,

helped manage the Bentsen campaign. After the Democratic primary was over, Connally accepted appointment from President Nixon to the cabinet post of secretary of the treasury.

Yarborough attributed his unexpected defeat to his votes against G. Harrold Carswell of Florida, and Clement F. Haynsworth, Jr. of South Carolina, two conservatives named to the United States Supreme Court by President Nixon but rejected by the Senate controlled by Democrats.

Since the Texas electorate was much more conservative than the Senate, Bentsen developed Yarborough's votes against the Nixon nominees into a winning issue, forcing Yarborough into the defensive of trying to explain the reasons for his votes.

"Ordinarily, most citizens probably would neither know nor care much about such appointments, but the Carswell-Haynsworth debates have given the public a broad exposure to the issues involved," I wrote. [28]

"Nobody can disprove President Nixon's conclusion that prejudiced Northern liberals in the present Senate will effectively bar any conservative Southerner from the U.S. Supreme Court, regardless of how well qualified."

The Senate confirmed Nixon's third choice, Harry Blackmun of Minnesota, for the court vacancy created in 1969 when Associate Justice Abe Fortas, a confidant of Democratic presidents, was forced to resign because of revelations that he accepted a $20,000 fee from the family foundation of a man later imprisoned for illegal stock manipulation. [29]

Yarborough said after his loss that "the vote on Carswell affected the outcome more than I realized." He gave less weight to the impact of rejecting Haynsworth. [30]

East Texans and labor union members who had formerly supported Yarborough voted for Bentsen, and many of the liberal senator's former friends stayed away from the polls in protest of what they considered his anti-Southern votes.

Yarborough's defeat also proved a blow to the aspirations of George Bush, congressman from Harris County, to be elected senator. Bush considered his chances would be good to win a general election victory over Yarborough, who defeated Bush in

1964. But Bentsen, much more conservative, proved a more formidable Democratic nominee.

In addition to conservatives rallied by Bentsen's record and his friend Connally, Bentsen drew support in the fall campaign from former President Johnson, making a rare foray back into politics during his retirement.

His appointment afterward to Nixon's cabinet marked a turning point in Connally's career, and he proclaimed himself to be a Republican while maintaining close contact with the conservative Democratic leadership in Texas. Former Texas Supreme Court Justice Will Wilson already had joined the Republican Party after being named to a high post in the U.S. Department of Justice.

The new situation resulted in three "conservative" Democratic factions in the state. A Connally-Bentsen-Shivers set, including former President Johnson, appeared to be deteriorating. LBJ never gave up his ties to Yarborough and the liberals who had helped promote his political ascendancy.

The second "conservative" Democratic faction belonged to Governor Smith, a "loner" who had just achieved the historical precedent of being renominated for governor without an opponent in the Democratic primary.

The third "conservative" band then operating was headed by Lieutenant Governor Barnes, an up-and-coming young political star and adversary of Smith. Businessmen interested in state legislation and regulations tried to follow both Smith and Barnes, despite their differences. [31]

With Nixon in the White House, Connally in his cabinet, and Smith in the governor's office, politicians in Texas sought to establish conservative positions, or at least the philosophical center. The liberal movement following Senator Yarborough's defeat was left in disarray within the state, a blow from which it never recovered.

In 1971, reports from Washington — later proved incorrect — were that President Nixon would seek Connally as his running mate in 1972. This was viewed as a further threat to Democratic dominance in Texas and the South, since Connally was much admired by Southern conservatives.

231

Among those whose political fortunes were hurt by this situation was Lieutenant Governor Barnes, Connally's close friend and protege.

Barnes enjoyed much of the same support in Texas that Connally did among conservative Democrats.

Sensing that Barnes would make an effort to unseat Smith in 1972, the governor early attacked Barnes for allegedly obstructing legislation which Smith deemed desirable.

As it turned out, neither Smith nor Barnes made the runoff in the 1972 Democratic primary for governor.

The winner was a quiet, gentlemanly rancher-banker from Uvalde named Dolph Briscoe who had served as a state representative in 1949-1957.

DOLPH BRISCOE ELECTED

A few days before Christmas in 1971, Briscoe invited about 150 friends to his big ranch at Catarina. As a guest on that occasion, my respect for Briscoe increased along with my wonderment over why a man in such fortunate private surroundings would be interested in becoming governor.

One evening during the gathering at the sprawling ranchhouse, expressions were sought from various guests on the prospect of Briscoe winning the race which he wanted to enter. I was asked for an offhand opinion as a member of the Austin press.

"Briscoe could win it," I commented, amid applause from Briscoe's friends who wanted a favorable report.

While I believed then what I said, my confidence was hardly absolute in that prediction, though it proved accurate.

Back in Austin, I wrote:

CATARINA, Texas—One of the most interesting political movements in Texas history is being shaped here in the big rambling ranch house of Dolph Briscoe.

Long before he started running for governor, Briscoe entertained friends and kinfolks by the hundreds. Some hunt the huge brush country whitetail deer. Some go for Mexican and bobwhite quail. Others fish Briscoe's kingsize tanks which offer lots of big black bass.

GOVERNOR AND MRS. BRISCOE campaigning in Dallas, 1978.
— *Dallas Morning News Staff Photo*

Many of the guests—more than 150 for overnight isn't uncommon—come here just for relaxed talk, fresh air, and ranch country cooking that features Texas beef with a Spanish touch—side dishes of peppers and chili, hot biscuits, and skillet bread.

Talk Is Of Politics

The talk these days is of politics and Briscoe's race for governor. Four years ago, the Uvalde rancher-banker, once a Texas legislator, ran fourth in an eleven-candidate race for the Democratic nomination for governor. Preston Smith won in a runoff against Don Yarborough, the liberal lawyer from Houston. Third place went to Waggoner Carr.

Briscoe vowed to try again after Smith had served two terms. Some persons tried to coax him into running against Smith in 1970, although Briscoe may have been uncertain whether this was much more than an overture by the incumbent governor's political enemies rather than a sincere elect-Briscoe effort.

The crowds of sport-shirted men passing these days through the rambling ranch house sixteen miles southwest of Catarina come from all over Texas. Most are helping in Briscoe's campaign, although this isn't the sole or even principal method of getting invited. Many are old friends from University of Texas and legislative days.

Congressman Jack Brooks of Beaumont has been Briscoe's close friend and frequent visitor since they were freshmen in the Texas House of Representatives a quarter-century ago. Brooks is more liberal than Briscoe, whose background marks him as a fiscal conservative. But this doesn't interfere with their friendship.

Many groups visit the ranch, especially during hunting season, when Briscoe's friends from the Uvalde area load up the hunters in pickups and jeeps and head for the thousands of acres of brush and cultivated grasslands where roam the big bucks along with herds of cherry-red Santa Gertrudis cattle.

This fall the ranch is the most luxuriant ever. Rain last June broke an eight-month drouth and rainfall has been "just right" ever since. Buffel grass which Briscoe had seeded from airplanes fifteen to twenty years ago has reached fencepost high, rippling across hills as far as one's eyes can see.

One wonders why the head man of such an empire would want any public office. Briscoe has always been involved — head of cattlemen's, sheep and goat raisers, South Texas Chamber of Commerce, and more organizations than we could list.

The political visitors appear mostly to be volunteers, amateurs, and successful business and professional men who don't ordinarily engage in politics.

Their enthusiasm for Briscoe is impressive. Money as well as workers is coming into his campaign. Some funds come from backers of other candidates for governor, who have decided to "hedge" on the chance that Briscoe just might get elected. This is encouraging to Briscoe supporters concerned over the possibility that Ben Barnes and Preston Smith would tie up all the campaign funds.

Here in his own setting, Briscoe is confident and relaxed, a warm host with a laugh that rings the rafters. In the cities, among strangers, Briscoe appears shy and less polished than his competitors. He isn't a glad-hander.

Briscoe's few paid campaign workers are hoping the sincerity that comes across from Briscoe in person can be translated into a television personality by next spring when the Democratic primary campaign reaches a climax. Since eighty percent of Texas' people live in the cities, Briscoe must win there.'' [32]

This view of Briscoe volunteering to leave a very comfortable life for the more rigorous and often frustrating political arena reinforced an opinion which I had expressed two years earlier in another *Dallas News* column concerning a U.S. Senate race:

"Sometimes we wonder why men who seem to 'have everything' for the good life choose the rigorous course of running for public office . . .

"Just one (of three candidates) can win. And the winner will be committed to six years or more of hard work, including frequent separation from family and the required attendance on a constant series of time- and energy-consuming, and often boring, public meetings to stay in touch with the voters.

"Perhaps the candidates themselves don't know why they do it. Ego — the desire to exercise authority and help make decisions affecting the lives of others — certainly is one reason candidates run for public office.

"But the same drive causes writers to work for by-lines and athletes to risk injury and defeat by taking the risk they can enjoy the sweet taste of victory and the roar of the crowds.

"Some candidates run for an office because it is a well-paying position, with fat fringe benefits, and often the opportunity to exercise influence as a public official that will enable one to make bigger money through government-franchised business operations of getting 'cut in' on deals with outsiders seeking favors from the government.'' [33]

None of the above answers fully the question of why they do it.

The desire to perform public service is doubtless a major factor in many cases, perhaps most. It provides an opportunity to participate in government and policy-making.

For all its faults, the political world is fascinating. Its characters are almost uniformly interesting, if not always admirable. Politics and government is where the action is. Once a participant, even as an observer, one seldom leaves without regret. The attraction is so great that many ex-officials and ex-news people continue to live and work around the government even though they would probably fare better financially some other place.

Certainly Dolph Briscoe did not need the job or money when he tossed his rancher's hat into the governor's race. He spent about a million dollars of his own which he never recovered.

The Sharpstown scandal presented the opportunity that Briscoe needed. He projected the image of "Mr. Clean" at a time when confidence in the integrity of some of the state's highest officials was being questioned.

The Sharpstown affair surfaced in 1971 with the revelation that several state officials had been involved in the bank-insurance-legislative case, one way or another.

The Sharpstown Bank of Houston had sponsored, through friendly legislators, two bills designed to establish a deposit insurance system on state banks that could provide a competitive edge over national banks.

The legislation passed the House and Senate in a 1969 special session, but was vetoed by Governor Smith at the request of supporters of national bank interests.

Meanwhile, the Sharpstown Bank got into financial difficulty and closed after a federal investigation into its operation. Later it reopened under another name.

The investigation disclosed that Governor Smith had profited $62,500 from a non-collateral loan from the Sharpstown Bank, which he used to buy stock in National Bankers Life Insurance Company of Dallas, which was owned by the same interests. Smith denied any illegal action and claimed the loan and stock purchase were arranged by his business partner without his direct knowledge.

House Speaker Gus F. Mutscher of Brenham fared worst of any state official involved. He had borrowed large sums from the Sharpstown Bank and expedited passage of the so-called

"Sharpstown bills." Later, Mutscher drew a probated sentence on charges of conspiracy to accept a bribe.

Although not involved financially in the Sharpstown case, Lieutenant Governor Barnes drew politically-damaging criticism for assistance in passing the bills through the Senate.

Even former Attorney General Waggoner Carr felt the blast, because of his involvement in security deals and for lobbying in behalf of the Sharpstown legislation.

The political fallout in 1972 was widespread. Neither Barnes nor Smith made the runoff for governor in the Democratic primary.

Attorney General Crawford Martin was unexpectedly defeated for reelection by John L. Hill, a Houston lawyer. While Martin had no connection with Sharpstown, Hill charged he should have investigated it more vigorously.

Many legislators likewise lost to opponents who charged them with being members of a corrupt governing body. While support for the Sharpstown legislation was almost unanimous among the representatives and senators, few apparently knew enough about the subject to expect the controversy it aroused.

A later legislature passed laws to require more exact reporting of campaign finances, and a lobbyist regulation act.

While such statutes serve some useful purpose, no system has been devised to stop unscrupulous interests from gaining favor with weak and willing lawmakers, particularly those with strong political ambitions.

Fortunately, most lobbyists are highly ethical and useful additions to the lawmaking scene. They furnish expert information on the subjects under legislative discussion.

Lobbyists who get in trouble and cause scandals in the lawmaking process are usually amateurs without any real understanding of how the system works. The professional lobbyists, many of them former legislators, do establish contacts and friendships with public officials and their staffs and support favorable candidates for election. Most are discreet in this relationship.

Few people realize how false is the public perception of lobbyists, because of the publicized image projected by the un-

GOVERNOR AND MRS. DOLPH BRISCOE, 1978.
— *Dallas Morning News Staff Photo*

scrupulous minority. Some of the finest persons of my acquaintance have served clients in dealing with the legislature.

Many lobbyists are unpaid except for expected benefits to their personal interests. My check with the secretary of state's lobbyist registration list in a recent legislative year disclosed that by far the largest number registered were school teachers, backing legislation for higher pay and other benefits to public schools. The regular full-time lobbyists are a much smaller group paid to represent business or labor corporations, or trade and professional associations.

Despite the advantage the Sharpstown scandal gave Briscoe's candidacy in 1972, his victory was far from easy.

Many conservative Democrats already had ties with Smith and/or Barnes. Liberals supported former State Representative Frances Farenthold of Corpus Christi.

Briscoe led the first primary with 963,397 votes to Farenthold's 612,051. Barnes ran third with less than 400,000 votes while Smith trailed with only 190,709.

Democratic nominee Briscoe encountered surprising difficulty in the November general election.

The Republican choice was Henry C. (Hank) Grover, a very conservative legislator from Houston. He won the nomination over Albert Fay, a wealthy Republican who was also from Houston. Fay had worked for the party's candidates and causes for years, while Grover was a relative newcomer.

The presence on the November ballot of Ramsey Muniz, nominee of La Raza Unida party, complicated Briscoe's election problem. Muniz drew from the liberal Democratic areas, mainly Mexican-Americans.

Briscoe eventually forged ahead with 1,633,493 votes to Grover's 1,533,986 and Muniz' 214,118.

That election night, I worked in Dallas on my newspaper's coverage of the gubernatorial race.

Early returns, from which some news organizations based quick projections that Grover might win, showed Briscoe trailing. This was reflected in pre-midnight editions of some newspapers and in broadcast reports.

After a conference of news executives in *The Dallas Morning News* about 10:30 p.m., we decided to follow a conservative report rather than speculate on Briscoe's possible defeat.

At that time, the Texas Election Bureau showed only scant reports from rural areas where Briscoe was expected to run strongest. Often these tallies come much slower than the mechanized, computerized metropolitan election boxes.

Our decision proved to be proper and the final count showed Briscoe a solid winner by a plurality, which caused some critics to continue calling him a "minority" governor.

One of Briscoe's handicaps in the 1972 election was the fact that he ran on the same ballot with Senator George S. McGovern, the Democratic presidential candidate, and R. Sargent Shriver, the vice presidential nominee. Texas conservatives disliked them both.

With the Republicans' Richard Nixon and Spiro Agnew seeking reelection on the same ballot, many independents and conservative Democrats failed to support Briscoe, as they would under other circumstances.

Offering a clear choice between conservative and liberal tickets at the top, the Republicans carried Texas in the presidential race by approximately a two to one majority.

[1] *Politics in America,* Congressional Quarterly, page 23 (1979)
[2] *Dallas News,* November 10, 1966
[3] *Op.cit.,* November 20, 1966
[5] *Op.cit.,* June 4, 1966
[5] *Ibid.,* June 4, 1966
[6] *Politics in America Op.cit.*
[7] Associated Press in *The Daily Texan,* March 3, 1967
[8] *Politics in America, Op.cit.*
[9] *Ibid.*
[10] *Dallas News,* May 5, 1966
[11] *Austin American,* December 12, 1967
[12] *Dallas News,* August 10, 1970
[13] *Houston Chronicle,* Bo Byers, October 16, 1969
[14] *Op.cit.,* November 23, 1969
[15] *Dallas News,* August 25, 1967
[16] *Op.cit.* September 5, 1967
[17] *The Daily Texan,* November 3, 1981
[18] *Dallas News,* August 27, 1968
[19] *Politics in America Op.cit.,* page 27
[20] *Op.cit.,* page 29
[21] *Dallas News,* Morehead column, October 28, 1968
[22] *Politics in America, Op.cit.,* page 25
[23] *Ibid.*
[24] *Dallas News,* November 24, 1968 (Morehead column)
[25] *LBJ — 37 Years of Public Service,* Joe B. Frantz
[26] *Dallas News,* August 21, 1981
[27] *Op.cit.* April 27, 1969, Morehead column
[28] *Dallas News,* April 12, 1970, Morehead column
[29] *Politics in America, Op.cit.,* page 33
[30] *Dallas News,* May 5, 1970, Morehead column
[31] *Op.cit.,* December 17, 1970
[32] *Op.cit.,* December 23, 1971
[33] *Op.cit.,* January 15, 1970

NIXON AND WATERGATE

President Nixon's tremendous victory in 1972 was to be followed by two years of humiliation, disgrace, and finally resignation from the nation's highest office.

The series of historical events was unsuspected as both Democrats and Republicans held their national presidential nominating conventions in Miami Beach, Florida.

The Democrats meeting in July nominated McGovern and Shriver. Conservatives went home dispirited and defeated, as liberals took complete control of the party. The split extended into the state level and sometimes locally.

Noisy anti-war, anti-Nixon demonstrators tried to disrupt the Republican convention, but lessons learned during the Democratic fiasco in Chicago four years earlier taught security officials how to cope much better with such antagonists.

Nixon's attempt to end U.S. involvement in the Vietnam war were ignored by his enemies, even though he finally succeeded in extricating American forces from that bloody, unpopular war. The president's problems with domestic affairs overshadowed his achievements abroad.

Two months before Nixon's renomination in Miami, an event occurred which was to bring down his administration by forced resignation on August 9, 1974, beset by a hostile Congress, press, and even judiciary, and a disenchanted, bewildered public. Impeachment was offered as the alternative to resignation.

The dramatic chain of events started in June 1972 with the arrest of five burglars inside the Democratic National Headquarters in Washington's Watergate Building. They were caught in

PRESIDENT RICHARD NIXON visiting the Connally Ranch at Floresville in 1972.

— *Author's files*

an amateurish effort to install electronic listening devices in the Democrats' offices, ostensibly to keep opponents informed of what the Democrats were doing. The burglars were connected with a Nixon reelection committee.

At first, Watergate made a relatively small ripple. Espionage in political campaigns is rather commonplace. Yet the Watergate Affair, coupled with Nixon's own personality and his deceptive attempt to conceal his own knowledge of the case proved to be the president's undoing shortly after he reached the zenith of his career and influence.

Nixon could have prevented the tragic result.

The man was neither an evil person nor a bad president. But under fire he bungled his response to the Watergate charges. Had he been more forthright and truthful to his friends, rather than try to cover up the controversy, Nixon could have completed his second term in the White House and perhaps be recorded in history as a good president, on balance.

The depth of opposition among his adversaries reflected clearly outside the Republican convention hall at Miami Beach in 1972.

Demonstrators were mostly confined to a park away from the convention except on specified occasions permitted by police; but they kept trying to disrupt the meeting. On the night of Nixon's acceptance speech, police dispersed a crowd across the street from the convention center with tear gas, some of which got into the auditorium where the convention was being held. Pepper was dumped into the air-conditioning system, causing further discomfort.

Military units were assigned to help protect the president in the neighborhood, which to me was a sad sight comparable to the paratrooper encampment on the grounds of Little Rock Central High School in the 1950s. The use of military forces inside this country to protect its institutions against its own citizens is hardly the American way.

The renomination of Vice President Agnew came to complicate Nixon's difficulties. In 1973, the vice president resigned under fire because of corruption charges arising from his political career in Maryland.

The 1972 Democratic presidential convention was unhappy for most Texas delegates and party supporters.

Governor Wallace of Alabama, paralyzed from the waist down from an attempted assassination two months earlier in Maryland, came to Miami Beach in a wheel chair. He announced he would not seek the presidency in 1972 as he had done previously as an American party candidate.

Conservatives put his name into nomination at the Democratic convention, and the Alabaman received 387 first-ballot votes despite his noncampaign.

Senator McGovern won on the first ballot. Wallace was the first choice of fifty-two of Texas' one hundred thirty delegates, including Governor-nominate Briscoe and his wife, Janey. When the final roll call showed McGovern the winner, the Briscoes and eleven others changed their support to McGovern in a spirit of "party unity."

As it turned out, Briscoe drew criticism both from the liberals, for supporting Wallace, and later from the conservatives, who disliked McGovern.

On the roll call, forty-one Texas delegates had voted for McGovern, thirty-two for moderate U.S. Senator Henry Jackson of Washington, and five for other candidates.

The complaint about Briscoe from both the right and the left made more difficult his November victory over Republican Grover and Raza Unida's Muniz. Texas' political middle ground was shrinking.

Most Democratic officeholders in Texas put as much distance as possible between themselves and the national ticket, but didn't defect openly as top state officials did in 1952-1956 during the tidelands controversy.

R. Sargent Shriver, brother-in-law to the Kennedy dynasty of Boston, ran for vice president on the ticket with McGovern.

The Democrats carried only Massachusetts and the District of Columbia. Texas went for Nixon-Agnew with 66.2 percent of the vote, slightly higher than the Republicans' national margin of 60.69 percent. [1]

John Connally campaigned hard for Nixon, and held a colorful reception for the president at the Connally Picosa Ranch near

JOHN CONNALLY aboard President Nixon's plane, 1971.

— *White House Photo*

Floresville. Several prominent Democrats attended the party.

George Wallace's decision to remain in the Democratic party helped give the Republicans larger margins in the South than elsewhere, because Wallace conservatives hardly had any place to go except Republican.

Three weeks before the general election, I wrote for the *Dallas News,* that the political situation recalled the story of a football coach whose team had just lost to the national champions, 60 to 0.

Locker-room reporters asked what the coach considered the turning point of the game.

"—It was the moment we walked onto the field," replied the coach. [2]

The turning point in the 1972 presidential race was the moment George McGovern won the nomination.

Two days after the general election, I wrote:

"The old order was shattered in 1972, a year which may be recorded in political history as Reconstruction II, ending a century of brass-collar domination of the Democrats as a result of the Civil War.

"President Nixon's sweep; Senator John Tower's reelection (against Democrat Barefoot Sanders of Dallas) in a presidential year when many experts said a Republican couldn't buck the Democratic tradition; Hank Grover's astonishing performance in the governor's race; and GOP gains in Congress and the legislature . . . these signal the end of the Democratic nomination being 'tantamount to election' in Texas as was the case for decades." [3]

In the Senate race, incumbent Tower had defeated the challenger Sanders, later appointed a U.S. district judge in Dallas, by almost two to one. Sanders had scored an upset victory over former Senator Ralph Yarborough to win the Democratic nomination.

While the Republicans won nationally, their efforts to gain political dominance across the country suffered a major blow with the Watergate scandal, which handicapped the party's candidates for several more years.

A decade later, Democrats still were trying to overcome the damage done to their party by the 1972 McGovern debacle.

The Watergate scandal helped another "Mr. Clean" candidate, Democrat Jimmy Carter of Georgia, with the presidency in 1976. The old Democratic coalition of Roosevelt, Kennedy, and Johnson years never reformed. They won by skillfully blending labor, ethnic groups, intellectual liberals, and brass-collar Southern Democrats into an unbeatable combination which had faded into history with the 1980s.

BRISCOE TAKES OVER

Even before Governor Briscoe and Lieutenant Governor William P. Hobby, Jr. of Houston were inaugurated on January 16, 1973, the governor-elect had taken steps to strengthen the Democratic party.

Briscoe controlled the machinery of the Texas party, and

successfully sponsored Robert Strauss, a Dallas lawyer, for the national Democratic chairmanship, removing a management linked to the McGovern-liberal candidacy. The move helped the divided Democrats, for Strauss was both respected and well-versed in political circles. One of his best friends was John Connally, who he had declined to follow into the Republican party.

In his inaugural address, Briscoe cited as his philosophy the credo of his fellow-townsman, John Nance Garner, the former vice president:

" 'There are just two things to government as I see it. The first is to safeguard the lives and property of our people. The second is to insure that each of us has a chance to work out his destiny according to his talents.' "

Briscoe drew applause by pledging "no new taxes," a pledge he was able to fulfill during six years as chief executive, partly because of the state's booming economy.

Leaving office six years later, Briscoe felt he had kept faith with Texans by avoiding new taxes during his administration.

"It hadn't been done in recent years," Briscoe said of his no-new-tax policy in an era when the federal government, along with many states and local governments, ran up large deficits despite tax increases. [4]

"I'm proud of the proof that it could be done, and that the policy still generates more income for the state, and more jobs for its people, through building a healthy business climate."

He called this the major accomplishment of his administration. It was made possible, in part, by the twenty-seven-year-old constitutional amendment barring deficit spending. The fact that Texas was booming as part of the industrial "Sunbelt" also was a major factor, as income from sales and other taxes rose with inflation and increased business volume.

One factor which the governor had not anticipated was the effect of the Organization of Petroleum Exporting Companies (OPEC), composing of oil-producing countries of the Middle East, South America, and Africa.

Texas crude oil sold for an average of four dollars per barrel and natural gas for less than fifty cents per thousand cubic feet in 1973. The state levies a percentage tax on the value of oil and gas at the well, hence higher prices bring higher tax returns. In Texas' case, this occurred despite the fact that the state's oil and gas production had begun a slow decline due to the aging of its wells without any comparable discovery of new reserves.

In October 1973, the OPEC countries caused a near-panic in the United States by placing an embargo on most exports of oil.

About forty percent of this nation's oil was imported at the time, mostly from OPEC producers.

Within weeks, gasoline and heating oil shortages developed in the United States and motorists fought for places in lines at filling stations which had gasoline. Stations operated shorter hours and many closed permanently.

Congress and the public blamed everybody for the difficulty, although spokesmen from the energy industry, particularly Texas, Louisiana, and Oklahoma, had been warning for a quarter-century that over-reliance on "cheap" imported oil rather than developing a more dependable domestic supply could disrupt our economy and threaten our military capability.

The discovery of huge oil reserves in the OPEC countries, mostly by American companies, changed the balance of power in the petroleum world, once centered around Texas.

OPEC oil originally sold in this country for as little as a dollar per barrel, so eager were the poor producing companies to obtain cash. One result was proliferation of inefficient uses for energy, especially in the United States, where large "gas guzzling" motor vehicles became the style when gasoline cost only thirty or forty cents a gallon and it made little difference to the owner if the car burned a gallon of gasoline in less than ten miles.

Likewise, many industries and homes that formerly burned coal for fuel switched to heating oil or natural gas, both cleaner and efficient.

When OPEC called the sudden embargo to raise prices, the industrial, consuming countries were in turmoil. Just as soon as OPEC members agreed to hold out for a higher minimum price, originally six dollars per forty-two-gallon barrel, buyers eagerly paid whatever the producers asked for the oil.

By 1982, the OPEC price was thirty-four dollars per barrel. But the effect of higher prices in promoting conservation and increasing drilling had created a surplus of oil which had begun to reduce prices. Industry economists predicted oil prices long-range would continue to rise, however.

When Governor Briscoe attended his first meeting of the National Governors' Conference (now Association) in Stateline, Nevada, the principal topic discussed by the governors was how to expedite the construction of a pipeline from Alaska's long-discovered Prudhoe Bay oil field on its Arctic North Slope to warmer southern waters where the oil could be shipped to the lower forty-eight states.

The construction had been delayed for ten years by lawsuits and objections of environmentalists, mostly from California, northeastern states, and opponents in Congress. With Briscoe and Governor William A. Egan of Alaska as the chief proponents, the governors by twenty-three to twelve vote recommended that construction be permitted. [5]

Since the OPEC embargo had not yet started, northeastern and midwestern governors voted against the recommendation, contending their energy needs should be filled from existing sources, mostly southwestern states and OPEC.

The mood of the country on another matter was reflected in an article I wrote from Stateline after the conference:

". . . The national press seemed interested almost entirely in Watergate while the governors wanted to talk about the energy problems more vital to them." [6]

Governor Milton A. Shapp, Democrat, of Pennsylvania was quoted: " 'The press is more interested in trying to get this conference involved in the Watergate situation than in the important issues facing state governments . . .' " [7]

Most of the governors declined to speculate on the rising controversy in Washington.

At the conference, Texas reporters were introduced by Governor Briscoe to Governor Carter of Georgia. The two men became friends, although Briscoe later suffered disappointment when Carter as president rejected a plea for the federal government to release the oil and gas industry from burdensome price controls to help restore the nation's energy independence.

Carter explained to the reporters the "zero-based budget-

249

ing'' concept which he had applied to state government in Georgia. The idea appealed to Briscoe. After the explanation, I remained unconvinced that Carter had done more than regroup his state's agencies without any significant change in expense or state employment.

In December 1973, after the OPEC embargo, Governor Briscoe called his first special session. Under threat of losing $240 million in federal highway funds unless it acted, the legislature quickly reduced the highway speed limit from seventy miles per hour to fifty-five. Many motorists in Texas and other places with long distances to travel objected to the reduction, which was designed to save gasoline. High-speed driving increases gasoline consumption, according to experts.

During the regular session of the legislature, held earlier in 1973, Briscoe had signed into law what he called ''the most far-reaching package of ethics and reform legislation in Texas history — legislation designed to restore public confidence in their officials and to open the doors of government more widely to public scrutiny.'' [8]

This came in the wake of the Sharpstown scandal, and with the help of legislators who made Sharpstown and official integrity a campaign theme.

While Briscoe fared well with the legislature and public during his first year as governor, some reporters kept questioning his style, his wealth, and his infrequent press conferences.

This group remained frustrated over inability to find out the Briscoes' finances and how much land they owned. The governor, unaccustomed to such situations, seemed uncertain as to how to respond.

One Uvalde friend told me that, besides Briscoe's reserved nature, the governor considered discussing finances and property both personal and improper.

''Where he comes from it's impolite to ask how many acres or how many head of livestock a man owns. And it's considered bragging if he told you'' was the explanation.

While Briscoe learned better how to deal with the media and other critics as his administration progressed, he was never at his best on television or before large, strange audiences.

GOVERNOR DOLPH BRISCOE talks in his office with Reps. John H. Poerner of Hondo (left) and Tom Massey of San Angelo (sitting on desk). Briscoe's Executive Assistant Kenneth Clapp in background.

— *Author's files*

"Briscoe is at his best in small gatherings and in a one-on-one basis with individuals," I wrote. [9]

A Dallas attorney, who worked on Briscoe's staff, once told me: "He's the best one-on-one man I ever saw."

During 1974, a Constitutional Revision Commission headed by former Supreme Court Chief Justice Robert W. Calvert, comprised of 181 legislators and other citizens, drafted a proposed new Constitution for the state.

But the legislature, serving as a constitutional convention, rejected the proposed new charter in 1974, and the next year similar revisions were defeated by the voters.

Governor Briscoe thought the state of Texas was getting along rather well as it was, and said so.

SHAKE-UP IN WASHINGTON

During Governor Briscoe's first term, the United States got a new president and vice president without holding an election.

The nation was shaken by the Watergate episode, and demands increased for removal of Nixon.

First came the resignation of Vice President Agnew on October 10, 1973, after he pleaded "no contest" to charges of income tax evasion. Other charges of corruption involving Agnew as a public official in Maryland were dropped. Two days after Agnew resigned, President Nixon appointed Gerald R. Ford of Michigan, leader of the Republican minority in the House of Representatives, to be vice president. [10]

The Watergate controversy put a severe strain on the government in Washington, as the president's critics demanded his impeachment. Newspapers and airwaves were filled with the story. Court action forced the president to release tape recordings of conversations in the White House with many persons. Nixon contended the tapes were private.

A House of Representatives investigating committee employed well-known Houston attorney, Leon Jaworski, former president of the State Bar of Texas, as special prosecutor in the inquiry.

As the pressure grew more intense, Nixon resigned on August 9, 1974, the first president to do so in U.S. history. The tapes which the Supreme Court unanimously decided should be made public disclosed that contrary to Nixon's protestations, he really did know about the attempted cover-up of the burglary at Democratic national headquarters in 1972.

This revelation shocked Nixon's friends in Congress and the nation, who had accepted his word. Had he chosen to be truthful about the matter, I believe he would have completed his presidential term although under a cloud. Deception finally did the president in, although his bad judgment followed a barrage of criticism and hostility that lasted for many months and preoccupied the nation.

Immediately upon the Nixons' departure from the White House, Gerald Ford was sworn in as president. Under constitutional authority, he selected his own vice president. Former Governor Nelson A. Rockefeller of New York, one of the nation's richest men, was chosen. Reports indicated that Ford deliberated until the last over whether to appoint Rockefeller or George Bush of Houston, who later became an elected vice president in 1980 as a running mate with Ronald Reagan.

Bush had been a member of Congress, ambassador to the United Nations, and Republican national chairman.

One month after taking office President Ford pardoned Nixon for "all offenses against the United States which he, Richard Nixon, has committed or may have committed." [11]

President Ford acted to cool the passions and divisions which had arisen during the Watergate hearings period. Some anti-Nixon partisans had demanded that Nixon be further humiliated by trial for alleged criminal actions. While Ford did largely succeed in putting the matter to rest for most Americans, the pardon probably was the principal cause of Ford's defeat in a bid for election two years later against Democrat Jimmy Carter.

While the tapes proved to be Nixon's downfall, and many critics lamented publicly that recording confidential conversations without the knowledge of other parties involved was reprehensible, later it was revealed that President Roosevelt, Kennedy, and Johnson, at least, had made secret recordings.

The revelations contradicted members of other administrations who claimed Nixon's tapings were unprecedented.

As Democrats in Congress began exercising more responsibility in dealing with the unelected President Ford, the nation began to resume normality.

U.S. military involvement in Vietnam ended under President Nixon in 1973, but fighting continued in nearby Cambodia. U.S. assistance ended in mid-1973.

While the Watergate case hit its highest pitch in late 1973,

I wrote a column which became partly wrong and partly correct.

My erroneous prediction was that the case "will hardly make the history books."

"More artfully concealed moves by earlier presidents have led the nation into war or affected the vote count on who became president, but those never managed to achieve the national publicity proportions of the Watergate case."

This statement remains accurate.

The massed media in Washington, particularly television, helped bring Nixon down. I say this without sympathy for Nixon's actions in response to Watergate, particularly his deception about knowledge of the burglary.

My principal complaint about the Watergate affair is its damage to public confidence in our system of politics and government at all levels. Those of us with first-hand information know politicians and elected officials aren't supermen, except in rare instances. Most are rather ordinary people with ordinary morality and ethics, and often influenced by venal forces seeking to use public office for private gain.

The point to remember about public officials is that they generally are "representative" of citizens who have both good and bad traits. Officeholders may even be a cut above the public average, but far short of perfection.

While the impact of Watergate was rising and falling in Washington, Texans remained relatively unruffled.

Former President Johnson died of a heart attack January 22, 1973, leaving a void in the state's political leadership where he had been a dominant factor for more than a quarter-century.

His body lay in state in the Great Hall of the LBJ Library which he had seen built and filled with papers and mementoes of a political career started more than forty years before. The body was carried to Washington for memorial services, followed by burial at the Johnson family plot on the LBJ Ranch at Stonewall, beside his beloved Pedernales River.

During his four years as a retired president, Johnson largely managed to stay outside the main political arena in the state, although he once described Lieutenant Governor Ben Barnes as a

Texan with "the ability to become president" before Barnes lost the governor's race to Briscoe in 1972. [12]

Although friends, Briscoe and Johnson were never political allies.

The new governor attempted to pick up the pieces of a shattered Democratic party leadership in Texas after McGovern lost in 1972. Chairman Strauss presided over a national convention to restructure party rules. Most delegates, holdovers from the McGovern election, opposed the so-called "unit rule" where a majority could cast a delegation's entire vote for a single candidate. The alternative is a proportional system allowing a delegation's votes to be divided among candidates.

Until Watergate, the beaten-down Republicans seemed to be rising again after losing heavily in the aftermath of the Kennedy assassination.

In Texas, John Tower retained his Senate seat in the 1972 election, defeating Democrat Barefoot Sanders by a much larger margin than Briscoe managed against Republican Grover in the governor's race.

The fallout from Watergate damaged Texas Republican candidates less than in many other states. The party won four of Texas' twenty-four seats in the U.S. House of Representatives in 1972 and kept the same number two years later, although an incumbent Republican lost and another one was elected.

Republicans in the State Senate retained three seats (of thirty-one total) in 1974, but lost two of the party's seventeen representative seats (of one hundred fifty total).

By 1981, Republicans held eight seats in the Texas Senate and thirty-five in the House of Representatives. With incumbent Governor Clements heading the ticket in 1982, and strong candidates for other top state offices, party officials expected to make further progress toward balancing party representation in state government.

Moreover, the Republicans made headway during the 1970s and 1980s in electing candidates to local office. Some former Democrats switched parties, particularly in Dallas County, because of the rising Republican strength.

Voters in Dallas and Harris (Houston) counties set precedent in 1974 by electing Republican county judges. A few smaller counties chose Republican judges earlier.

FOUR-YEAR TERMS

For the first time in history, the state's top officials were elected to four-year terms in 1974, following adoption of a constitutional amendment.

Major statewide officials who had previously been elected for two-year terms won new terms of four years. All Democrats, they were Briscoe, governor; Hobby, lieutenant governor; Hill, attorney general; Bob Bullock, comptroller; Jesse James, treasurer; Bob Armstrong, land commissioner; and John C. White, commissioner of agriculture.

Before the four years ended, James died and was replaced by Warren G. Harding, former Dallas County treasurer. White resigned to become Democratic national committee chairman when Carter was elected president in 1976. Reagan V. Brown of the governor's staff was appointed commissioner of agriculture. Briscoe appointed both Harding and Brown, who were subsequently elected to the offices.

In the general election of 1974, Democrats won the above offices by about two to one over Republican and other opponents. Although Briscoe quit campaigning personally during the final weeks of the campaign to be with his seriously-ill mother, the governor defeated Republican Jim Granberry, a Lubbock dentist, by 1,016,334 to 514,725. The governor's mother died in a Uvalde hospital in early December.

The size of Briscoe's new margin silenced critics who had called him a "minority" governor because he failed to win a majority over all candidates in the close 1972 elections.

Ramsey Muniz, again the candidate of La Raza Unida, received fewer than half the number of votes he tallied two years earlier.

The 1974 election was the first in which Texans of eighteen through twenty years old were eligible to vote in state elections, and their participation appeared to make little difference in the outcome.

In the Democratic primary, Briscoe defeated Frances Farenthold by more than two to one, a much greater majority than in the previous runoff.

Efforts to legalize parimutuel betting on horse races, prohibited in Texas for more than a quarter-century, got another setback when both Democrats and Republicans voted against the proposition submitted on party primary ballots.

Although a Constitutional Revision Commission in 1973 worked long and hard drafting a new state charter, the effort finally came to naught.

In 1974, legislators sitting as a constitutional convention, rejected their own final product, one hundred eighteen to sixty-two. Price Daniel, Jr., Speaker of the Texas House of Representatives, served as president of the convention.

The suggested constitutional provisions later were grouped into eight constitutional amendments submitted to the voters in 1975, but these, too, lost overwhelmingly.

Governor Briscoe's outspoken opposition to the proposed new Constitution, mainly the idea of requiring annual legislative sessions, helped defeat the effort. The existing Constitution limits legislative sessions to one hundred forty days in odd-numbered years, and thirty days at times and for subjects chosen by the governor.

The proposed new Constitution contained recommendations which drew objection from many directions other than those opposing annual sessions.

Many disliked the recommended removal of appellate judges from elective politics, along lines of the so-called "Missouri Plan."

Missouri changed from the Texas-style direct election of such judges in the 1940s and several other states adopted modifications of the Missouri system. In Missouri, a nominating committee composed of a majority of laymen (non-lawyers) and a minority of lawyers recommends three persons for each vacancy on the appellate courts. The governor's choice becomes the judge. The judge's name goes on the ballot at the next election to see if the appointment is confirmed by voters. No opponent's name appears on the ballot. If the voters approve, the appointee gets a ten-year term, after which he must submit his name on the ballot again to see if voters still wish to retain his services.

In 1948, I spent two weeks in Missouri studying the Missouri Plan and talking to judges, lawyers, and laymen acquainted with its operation. Approval was overwhelming, and it continued to be.

In Texas, interests seeking to retain political influence in courts have successfully opposed the idea, often misrepresenting it as a "lifetime appointment" such as federal judges receive. Because of the requirement for periodic submission of each judge's name and record to the votes for approval and disapproval, Missouri's plan is far different from the federal judiciary, where a few autocratic judges created a very bad impression with decisions distasteful to most citizens, and from which the public has no recourse.

Another negative for many legislators and labor unions to the proposed new Constitution was a new "right to work" provision which would prohibit labor contracts requiring union membership. Texas passed a law to the same effect long ago, but a constitutional requirement would be stronger.

Briscoe's main objection was to annual legislative sessions. Experience proves, he said, that the more often lawmakers meet, the more money they spend. [13]

"My opinion of the Texas Constitution of 1876 has changed since I came here as a new state representative from Uvalde in 1949," the governor added. "Then, I had the preconceived notion that the state's constitution must be rewritten completely or there would be no way the state government could function in the years ahead.

". . . I left the legislature in 1957 convinced that writers of the 1876 Constitution did an exceptionally good job. The state has prospered and developed. I am convinced that Texas has a better opportunity for all of the people to seek and secure their destiny than any state in the union. Reasonable means are available to amend the existing Constitution when the legislature sees the necessity and the people agree. This has been done 233 times (as of 1979)." [14]

Governor Briscoe voiced his objections to replacing the state constitution again in 1975 when it was submitted as eight propositions to the voters, and soundly rejected.

On the eve of the 1975 election, I wrote a column questioning Briscoe's opinion that Texas has an "exceptionally good" constitution.

". . . Neither do we think it is the chamber of horrors that its detractors contend," I added. "It has a lot of excess baggage but the main working parts are serving the people well." [15]

Even the United States Constitution, a concise document which some consider of almost divine inspiration, has come under increasing criticism, and it is much older than the state Constitution. By the 1980s a movement was under way to call a national constitutional convention, to require a balanced federal budget. Critics feared such a convention also might act to restrict the civil rights judgments made by some federal courts notwithstanding overwhelming complaints from the elected Congress and what appeared to be a majority of the public.

POLITICAL TEMPERATURES COOL IN 1975-1976

"The years 1975-1976 gave America a significant respite from the high political temperature of the previous several years. With Richard Nixon gone and the Vietnam war over, the two great issues that had convulsed the country for so long were gone. President Ford, with his low-key personality and moderate political stance, had a calming effect on the nation as well." [15]

The 1976 presidential contest was under way almost as soon as Ford became president, with California's personable former governor, Ronald Reagan, as Ford's chief contender for the Republican nomination. Many Democrats sought the nomination, and among the leaders were ex-Governors Wallace of Alabama and Carter of Georgia. Wallace was still badly crippled, confined to a wheel chair, from the attempted assassination, and Carter became the most active candidate. Among his final supporters and friends were Governor Briscoe and Democratic National Chairman Strauss of Texas, although Strauss refrained from expressing a choice before the party chose its nominee.

The 1974 election in the wake of Watergate brought large gains for the Democrats in Congress and governorships around the nation. In most cases, the Democrats held majorities of more than two to one, leaving the Republicans powerless to exercise even effective minority influence on the government. Moreover, many of the new congressmen were young liberals elected as a protest to Watergate and the Vietnam war.

At a National Governors' Conference in Seattle, we talked to Chairman Strauss about the Democrats "overdoing" success.

Strauss assured me that enough conservative Southern Democrats in Congress would side with the Republicans on critical issues to prevent any runaway liberal legislation.

In fact, 1975 found high unemployment (9.2 percent in May 1975) plus inflation in the United States and the nation facing an energy shortage that frightened Americans accustomed to unlimited cheap energy; first, oil and natural gas from the southwestern states and later from the Middle East before OPEC was organized to set higher prices.

In Texas, Governor Briscoe and Lieutenant Governor Hobby were inaugurated for new terms on a somewhat somber tone, although Briscoe declared himself to be more optimistic about the future of the state and nation than many others did, particularly in the industrialized "Frostbelt" states.

"There have been dire predictions that the greatest industrial and consumer nation on the face of the earth may soon sputter to a standstill, strangled by lack of energy resources and our own wasteful habits," said Briscoe in his inaugural address. [17]

"We are told that a nation founded on the work ethic will die as a hopeless welfare state. We are warned that immorality and permissiveness will bring us down as surely as the Roman Empire fell to the barbarians."

Briscoe disagreed with such pessimism, and he outlined a ten-point program for the new legislature to improve efficiency, fair elections, education, personal safety, health care, and environment.

The next day, appearing before the legislature, he repeated his credo taken from John N. Garner that government needs to do only two things:

260

"— safeguard the lives and property of our people, and

"— insure that each of us has a chance to work out his destiny according to his talents."

"I further believe that the closer the level of decision making is to the people, the more capable government is of responding to the needs and wishes of the people." [18]

This is the so-called "New Federalism" which various state officials, presidents, and congresses have endorsed over the ensuing years, drawing objections from those who favor centralized government and generous welfare spending on the national level.

Six years later, when President Reagan proposed to return more than forty federal programs to the states, with a trust fund to help support them during a transition period, many governors and administrators for the programs took a critical stance.

Texas Governor Clements cautiously endorsed President Reagan's move.

After the legislature held its regular session in 1975, Governor Briscoe declared its main accomplishment had been to strengthen the Coordinating Board, Texas College and University System, and to meet the state government's rising cost without new taxes, as the previous legislature was able to do.

Briscoe predicted the Coordinating Board's new authority would permit it to "reduce duplication and waste in higher education" especially in construction and new courses.

After World War II repeated efforts had been made for statewide coordination of higher education to the end that all Texans wanting to enroll could do it without being required to travel long distances from home or spend large sums for higher education. With money poured into college and university construction from the Permanent University Fund endowment and from special property taxes to build at colleges not under the university endowment, Texas built the nation's largest and finest physical plants in the nation, even if its academic excellence often failed to keep pace.

Texas higher education grew in quality as well as quantity at such places as The University of Texas-Austin, Texas Tech, and Texas A&M. By the late 1970s some other institutions struggled to attract enough students to justify maintaining faculties at previous levels.

The drive for an effective Coordinating Board was handicapped from two important directions. First, the powerful University of Texas Board of Regents did not want supervision from the statewide agency, and effectively lobbied against the Board's recommendations. Further, legislators yielded frequently to demands from home-district constituents for local "universities," with the result that the Board's recommendations against expanding the system often were ignored by the legislature.

BORN-AGAIN JIMMY CARTER

For the first time since the War Between the States, the country in 1976 elected a Southerner, Jimmy Carter of Georgia, to be president.

It was an historic step in which voters favored an "outside" candidate who campaigned as a "born-again" Baptist of deep religious convictions and attacked the Washington bureaucracy.

While Carter as President failed to fulfill his hope of returning more political power to state and local governments, he did help pave the way for his successor, Ronald Reagan, to make real progress in that direction.

A blend of political and religious evangelism with many crosscurrents developed a controversial "Moral Majority" sponsoring candidates and campaign support to accomplish their aims in both parties in the last half of the 1970s.

Religion long has been important in politics, and certainly in Texas. Democrat Alfred Smith lost this state's electoral votes in 1928 largely because he was a Roman Catholic. John F. Kennedy won the state's backing in 1960 after he convinced Protestant leaders that to deny him the presidency on the basis of religious conviction would be un-Christian bigotry.

In 1976, Texas voters favored Carter for the Democratic nomination despite the fact that Governor Briscoe and other state party leaders favored Senator Lloyd Bentsen as a "favorite son" candidate. Reagan supporters in Texas likewise upset the Republican state leadership, who favored President Ford for an elective term. Texas Republicans elected delegates almost unanimously committed to Reagan, although he lost the presidential nomination to Ford in a very close convention vote.

Governor Briscoe, who led the Texas delegation to the Democratic National Convention in New York's Madison Square Garden, was comfortable with Carter as a candidate, even though he had supported Bentsen for the nomination even before Carter began his campaign in 1974. Land Commissioner Bob Armstrong headed Carter's Texas campaign before the primaries were held.

The Briscoes and Carters were friends from meetings while Carter was governor of Georgia during the first two years of Briscoe's administration in Texas.

The Democratic convention directed by National Chairman Strauss was one of the most harmonious the often-unruly party ever held. There was some behind-the-scenes fighting over a choice for vice president, which finally went to U.S. Senator Walter F. Mondale of Minnesota, a northern liberal whose presence on the ticket was designed to attract union labor and ethnic minority votes who were suspicious of Carter's Southern background.

Governor Briscoe and many other Texas delegates would have preferred a more moderate vice presidential choice, such as Senator John Glenn of Ohio, who first attracted attention as an astronaut in the nation's space program. But the Texans made little public fuss in the matter, and accepted both Mondale and a party platform that virtually promised the millenium to U.S. citizens.

Carter won the delegate majority before he ever reached the convention hall. During the long primaries season starting the previous January in Iowa, Carter turned aside the efforts of George Wallace, Congressman Morris Udall of Arizona, Senator Edmund Muskie of Maine, Senator Henry Jackson of Washington, and Governor Jerry Brown of California to win delegate majorities.

The Georgian proved to be an extremely effective campaigner, and politically adroit in handling diverse factions within the party.

PRESIDENT JIMMY CARTER campaigned at the Alamo in San Antonio November 1980 but lost his bid for a second term.
— *Dallas Morning News Photo by Phil Huber*

JIMMY CARTER campaigns in Texas for president, September 1976.
— *Dallas Morning News Photo by David Woo*

During one dull period of the proceedings, I visited Governor Briscoe in the Texas section of "the Garden" and asked if he had any reservations about the Democrats achieving full employment and a balanced budget as the platform promised.

In my opinion, the nation can never balance a budget and provide a government job for everybody who is unable to find work in the private sector.

Briscoe indicated he agreed with my view, but that platforms were mostly window-dressing with little serious expectation of being followed after the election.

An interesting sidelight of the Democratic convention was a speech by Louisiana's Governor Edwin Edwards, seconding the nomination of California Governor Jerry Brown for president. It was a futile effort, because Carter had the nomination locked up, but Edwards, who disliked Carter, made a perceptive point:

"— This Jerry Brown knows there is no free lunch, and that Americans must face up to reality," said Edwards. [18]

Brown was hailed as an apostle of "New Liberalism" which others later came to term "Neo-Conservatism" whose practitioners held more conservative fiscal views than their predecessors of the New Deal, Fair Deal, Great Society era. While it was largely overlooked because his tenure as president lasted less than three years, John Kennedy could have been classified with the emerging group of social liberals favoring conservatism in taxing and spending. The movement continued into the 1980s.

Many conservative Democrats as well as Republicans went into the Texas Republican primaries in 1976 to choose Reagan over Ford. Most of the party professionals favored Ford, both for his record and because they felt chances for an incumbent being elected were better than for an "outsider." Reagan had developed a national following, however, through numerous speeches and radio broadcasts. As a movie star, he also had great name identification.

President Ford had a respectable record in the nation's highest office, as well as in his long career as a congressman from Michigan. But he lacked political appeal and suffered from media criticism of his occasional verbal and physical gaffes, which actually were unimportant to his qualifications as president.

The final vote on nomination at the Kansas City national convention was Ford 1,187 and Reagan 1,070. Reagan declined the vice presidential slot, and Ford chose Senator Robert Dole of Kansas as his running mate. Vice President Rockefeller announced early that he did not want the position any longer.

Senator Dole had a direct manner that some people disliked, but he was one of my favorite politicians, largely because of his wit as well as his manner and views.

Dole appeared on a television panel show in Austin in which I participated during the campaign, and repeated an anecdote which I reported in a *Dallas News* article that reached the president. Mr. Ford wrote me that he too was amused at the joke, which he had never heard before.

According to Dole's story, a bear once walked into a saloon and astonished the bartender by ordering a beer, as the other customers gave the bear plenty of room.

The flustered bartender retreated to a back room where he advised the proprietor "there's a bear out there wanting to buy a beer."

"Well, sell him a beer and tell him it costs five dollars a glass," said the owner.

The bartender followed orders. Then the curious owner came out to talk to the bear.

"We don't get many bears in here — ," he began.

"Guess not," growled the bear, "charging five dollars for a beer."

Television played an increasingly important role in the 1976 presidential campaign, where Ford and Carter debated before three national audiences and Dole went on the air once with Mondale. The result may have given the election edge to the Democrats, because Carter apparently succeeded in depicting Ford as an inept president, and Dole came across rather abrasively.

This campaign also marked the first time public funds were used to help finance presidential races, with the spending limit $21.8 million of federal funds per candidate.

My feelings are mixed about public financing of political campaigns. Except in judicial races, I see little to recommend the system over the old method of getting money from private sources, if there is full disclosure of the sources and amount of contributions before the election.

Numerous attempts have been made to purify the election finance process, but none has been much more successful than dependence on basic honesty to prevent "buying" elections. Elections at all levels have become frightfully expensive, costing many millions of dollars to elect a governor or United States senator in any large state with a contested race.

Such expenditures appear necessary, however, if any contender unseats an incumbent officeholder who has free access to the public media, a staff, and leverage to obtain contributions from citizens with interests involved in government.

So big spending probably will continue.

The Democratic South elected Jimmy Carter president, aided by the traditional eastern urban vote. Despite his Southern heritage, Carter ran very well among black voters.

Ford ran best in the Midwest and West.

Carter received 297 electoral college votes to 240 for Ford. In the popular vote, Carter received 50.1 percent (40,830,763) to Ford's 48 percent (39,147,793). [20]

Carter did slightly better in Texas than nationally, with 51.1 percent of all the votes to Ford's 48 percent.

Fewer than one percent of the votes nationally went each to former Senator Eugene McCarthy, running as an Independent, and Roger MacBride, on the Libertarian ticket.

Democrats continued with a two-to-one majority in the new U.S. House of Representatives after the election, and held sixty-two of one hundred Senate seats. The totals in Congress changed very little despite numerous turnovers including eighteen new senators.

Democrats continued to hold a three-to-one margin of governorships.

The new Congress in 1977 selected Thomas P. (Tip) O'Neill, Jr., Democrat from Massachusetts, as Speaker, succeeding Carl Albert of Oklahoma, who retired. Representative Jim Wright of Fort Worth became House majority leader, second in power to Speaker O'Neill.

PRESIDENT JIMMY CARTER, June 1978.
— Dallas Morning News Photo by David Woo

With unemployment around eight percent, President Carter sponsored several income tax reductions, none of great size, and took steps to create more public service jobs.

In 1978, the president proposed a more generous tax reduction, mostly on gains from capital investments and certain business taxes, but Congress enacted rather token reductions and offset these by increasing taxes on workers to support the fast-growing Social Security and Medicare programs. An increase in the payroll tax deduction, however, was postponed until after the 1978 election.

President Carter also proposed an energy program which he called the ''Moral Equivalent of War'' (MEOW) to develop fuel sources and encourage conservation. Critics thought it so inadequate they applied a kittenish ''meow'' title.

268

THE POLITICAL CLIMATE CHANGES

By 1977, the political climate was changing both on the state and national level.

President Carter's difficulties in Washington stemmed from inability to satisfy the diverse constituency that had elected him. And while he boldly promised to change the bureaucracy to "get government off our backs," his efforts were largely thwarted. As it turned out, Carter became a one-term president.

In Austin, Governor Briscoe continued in firm control of state government as Texas and the whole Southern "Sunbelt" enjoyed unprecedented economic growth and prosperity, which also brought record tax collections for the state. The state's tax structure is geared largely to the economic climate, particularly energy and related fields but also sales volume.

The legislature's 140-day regular session produced a Briscoe-backed law to assure more money for the state highway system, which for many years had been supported exclusively on "highway user" taxes levied on motor fuel, driver license fees, and other vehicle-related taxes.

The result was a formula to guarantee funds for road maintenance from general revenue when "road user" taxes were insufficient. The general revenue appropriation for the first two years under the new law totaled $528 million.

Some critics claimed the governor and other supporters were "putting highways ahead of education" whose lobbyists were seeking greatly increased revenues.

A special session was required to pass a school finance bill.

"The issue never was whether we should have good highways or good schools," Briscoe said as his administration ended two years later. "The true issue is whether Texas state government is responsible and farsighted enough to maintain a system of quality education AND a system of quality public transportation —both vital to our standard of living and our future well-being." [21]

Briscoe added that his six years as governor had brought more support for public education than any previous period in the state's history. The average teacher's salary increased from $8,680 to $13,200 while Briscoe was governor. Under his succes-

269

sor, William P. Clements, the increase was accelerated both on the public school and higher education levels.

Noting that state spending of nearly $2.5 billion a year for public schools (almost as much is added by local taxes), Briscoe called for greater accountability to the taxpayers.

"With public schools being criticized increasingly because many graduates are unable to read, write, and figure competently, citizens are demanding greater accountability of how these vast sums are spent. Society may be asking too much of its public schools by way of social engineering.

"It is a good time to examine this situation and I am glad my successor (Clements) comes into office free of any obligations to increase spending without taking a hard look at educational results." [22]

This referred to the fact that the Political Action Committee of the Texas State Teachers Association had endorsed John L. Hill for governor in 1978.

The attorney general upset Briscoe in the Democratic primary with the active support of the powerful teachers' organization, but Hill's loss to Republican Clements in the November general election had a devastating effect on the organization's influence at the capitol.

The legislature in 1977 submitted and voters adopted the next year a Tax Relief Amendment to the Constitution, which Briscoe termed the most important of his administration. Voters in a statewide election gave it eighty-four percent support.

Included in the amendment were restrictions on taxing agricultural land as property according to "market value" which frequently was far greater than the land's value for productivity. It also gave certain exemptions on homes from ad valorem taxation, and prohibited taxes on "personal property" which had long been eligible for taxation but more often ignored by the tax collector.

The property tax has become increasingly discriminatory, and applied in Texas almost entirely to real estate. There are other forms of wealth, often yielding greater returns to the owners than does real property. One tax which has proved highly productive and fairly popular is the sales tax. Its popularity is at-

ANYHOW... THE **POINT** I WAS TRYING TO MAKE BEFORE I WAS SO **RUDELY** INTERRUPTED!...

FREE ENTERPRISE

PRESIDENT CARTER's dilemma over free enterprise vs the windfall tax on oil and gas. Taxes won.

— Reprinted from The Dallas Morning News

tested by the fact that voters in Texas cities almost universally gave permission to levy a city sales tax. Schools and other districts, including counties, have proponents urging sales taxes to supplement the ad valorem tax revenue.

Although many politicians disagree with the idea that sales taxes are more equitable than others, local elections on levying sales taxes by city governments indicate most voters prefer this tax to others.

Critics call sales taxes "regressive" since they fall equally on the rich and the poor, when they spend equally. Food and prescription drug items are excluded from the tax in Texas. If sales taxes unfairly burden low-income citizens, more so do taxes levied to support the Social Security-Medicare system of the federal government. They apply equally to all citizens, up to a prescribed amount of income, without any exception for those earning modest incomes.

Texas and states with rich natural resources to tax are more fortunate than others, most of which have state income taxes. However, Texas' oil and gas have been shared by the whole nation at low cost until recent years. When the state's mineral resources are gone, Texas' tax structure must undergo drastic changes to find new sources. Oil and gas production have been declining for years, although higher prices (on which state taxes are levied) have allowed revenues to rise. Oil, natural gas, and even underground water reservoirs can be depleted so Texans have been literally "mining" their wealth to share with others. A day of reckoning is somewhere ahead.

One bright spot is that billions of dollars in oil and gas revenues from state-owned lands are being set aside to endow education. Repeated efforts have been made — unwisely, I think — to spend the endowment income as it is received rather than spending only the earnings, rather than capital structure. The oil and gas owned by the state comes from more than two million acres set aside in West Texas before minerals were discovered to assist The University of Texas and Texas A&M University systems.

All public schools share mineral ownership of submerged lands, such as the state-owned portion of the Gulf of Mexico and riverbeds.

Governor Briscoe considered the major achievements of his administration to be the improvement of state services without raising taxes (made possible by increased income from existing taxes) and on maintaining a favorable business climate which brought prosperity to Texas as great as any place in the burgeoning Sunbelt.

As he prepared to leave the office fellow governors expressed their opinion of Briscoe as follows:

"Dolph Briscoe . . . is a champion of the free enterprise system, as well as a forceful advocate of energy development and production free from excessive governmental interference.

"Dolph is a quietly effective man of the land, who has earned our respect and appreciation . . .

"Therefore, the governors of the Southern Governors Conference formally record our esteem for the Honorable Dolph Briscoe, a forceful member of the SGC and a governor who created an economic climate which has made his state of Texas a model of progress for the South . . ." [23]

Briscoe and some other Southern governors who had supported Carter for president were often disappointed at his actions. The energy-state governors of Texas, Oklahoma, and Louisiana were particularly upset by Carter's failure to fulfill a campaign pledge to decontrol federal prices for oil and natural gas. Carter finally did approve limited oil price decontrol, but natural gas price restrictions were to be retained until 1985, costly to producers, royalty owners, and taxing agencies of energy-producing states.

Briscoe was favored to win another four-year term in 1978, which would have made him Texas' longest-serving governor.

But Attorney General Hill outmaneuvered Briscoe and won the Democratic primary, receiving 932,345 of the 1,812,896 votes cast. Briscoe's total was 753,309, while former Governor Preston Smith ran third with 92,202. Remaining votes went to two other candidates.

Hill, an articulate attorney, received the backing of the political action arm of the Texas State Teachers' Association, the first time the organization had taken such action in a governor's race.

Briscoe was plagued with problems of the incumbency, such as scandals in the Office of Migrant Affairs, a federal-aid program administered through the governor's office.

Briscoe backers and most conservative Democrats were understandably disappointed, and there were predictions that the Uvalde rancher-banker might be the last conservative Democrat in the Texas governor's chair.

Hill made the mistake of underestimating his Republican opponent, Clements, in the general election campaign. A wealthy, self-made oil drilling contractor, Clements scored a stunning upset.

Thus Hill continued in the tradition of most other Texas attorneys general of the previous forty years — losing campaigns for other, more prestigious offices.

Since Allred, only Price Daniel, Sr. managed to go from the attorney generalship to higher office — first the United States Senate and next the governorship. Even Daniel had great difficulty becoming governor. Before he retired from public office in 1980, the senior Daniel was elected state representative, Speaker of the House, attorney general, U.S. senator and finally Texas Supreme Court justice.

HOW REPUBLICANS felt about Clements winning the Governor's race in 1978.   — *From The Dallas Times-Herald*

Will Wilson of Austin once commented that serving as a law enforcement official proved to be his biggest handicap in running for governor or U.S. senator, both races which he lost. Wilson served as district attorney of Dallas County, justice of the Texas Supreme Court, and attorney general.

An example Wilson cited was his success in "cleaning up" Galveston's organized gambling and related unlawful activities as attorney general.

Those put out of business never forgave the law enforcer, and the other citizens seldom seemed to appreciate his actions.

Briscoe appointees fared better than he did in the 1978 election. Secretary of State Mark White was elected attorney general, defeating Price Daniel, Jr. in the Democratic primary and Republican James Baker in the general election. Daniel Junior later was killed in a dispute with his second wife. Baker later became one of President Reagan's top aides in the White House.

Warren G. Harding was elected state treasurer, Reagan V.

Brown, commissioner of agriculture, Mack Wallace and John H. Poerner to the Railroad Commission — all originally appointed by Briscoe. Several Briscoe appointees to appellate courts also were elected by the voters.

RISING REPUBLICANS — CLEMENTS AND TOWER

The first time I saw Bill Clements was at a campaign appearance in Austin's Driskill Hotel, with a small group present.

Weeks later, I was congratulating him at the capitol on defeating Ray Hutchison and Clarence Thompson for the Republican nomination for governor. Hutchison was extremely able and personable, a leader in the Texas House of Representatives and former State Republican chairman.

But Clements beat Hutchison more than three to one.

I walked out of the capitol press conference with Clements, and joked: "If you keep this up, you may get elected president of the United States."

"What's wrong with that?" he shot back.

Later in a private interview, he convinced me of his reasons for insisting he could defeat John Hill, when the polls showed Clements faced an almost impossible task.

Clements had his own polls, reflecting a vast independent and conservative Democratic undecided vote which might join the Republican minority as had occurred several times in past national election.

Further, Clements calculated that a shift of five percent in the totals could have elected Republicans nominated over the last three Democratic governors — Jack Cox against John Connally in 1962, Paul Eggers against Preston Smith in 1970, and Henry C. Grover against Briscoe in 1972.

Clements outlined how he planned to beat Hill. He launched an expensive advertising campaign to acquaint Texas voters with his name, spent a month campaigning in rural areas where conservative Democrats supported Briscoe against Hill, and put together a highly-effective organization to pinpoint areas of support and get voters to the polls by use of sophisticated telephone banks.

GOVERNOR AND MRS. William P. Clements, Jr. with an honor guard of Texas A&M's Ross Volunteers at his inauguration in 1979.

While Governor Briscoe and his wife declined to join the Clements campaign, their children and many erstwhile Briscoe backers publicly endorsed the Republican.

Hill continued to exude confidence in his ultimate victory, including tentative preparations for an administration as governor.

Clements won by 1,183,828 to 1,116,919 to become the first Republican governor of Texas since Edmund J. Davis, a military-backed Reconstruction governor left the office January 15, 1874.

John Tower, Republican, was reelected to the U.S. Senate with 1,151,376 votes, a 12,127-vote margin over former Congressman Robert Krueger of New Braunfels.

On June 15, 1981, Tower celebrated his twentieth year as senator, succeeding Lyndon Johnson. Only three other senators have served as long from Texas. If Tower seeks and wins reelection in 1984 he could become the longest-serving senator in history, a remarkable feat for the man who became the first Republican since Reconstruction to be elected senator from Texas. A conservative, Tower also became one of the highest-ranking senators in terms of seniority.

". . . As Tower's election in 1961 marked a breakthrough in Texas' solid one-party system, the choice of Clements as governor in 1978 opened the way for much faster expansion of the Republican party in the state.

"Depending on their vantage point, Texans view the election of William Perry Clements, Jr., their first Republican governor of the indoor-plumbing age, as everything from the harbinger of a two-party state to a disaster," wrote Jon Ford, who later became Clements' press secretary.[24]

"The 61-year-old Clements, founder and head of a $750 million worldwide oil drilling firm, Dallas-based SEDCO Inc., won the office with the aid of a smoothly-packaged, high-cost campaign."

One campaign promise which Clements fulfilled was to be a "tough-as-nails" governor, keeping a close eye on the budget and attempting to reduce the state payroll by 25,000 people. While he enjoyed some success in both of these goals during his first term, Clements quickly exhibited a willingness to work with leaders of the Democrat-controlled legislature and to make appointments to state boards and court vacancies without strict regard for party affiliations.

Clements recognized that Republicans were a minority party in Texas, and that his success as governor depended on his ability to continue attracting support from conservatives of all political backgrounds.

Clements proved himself to be a quick learner. Although he lacked experience in state government, he avoided major mistakes. He applied the skills learned as chief executive of his large corporation and as deputy secretary of the United States Department of Defense in the Nixon and Ford years. Clements knew his way around Washington as well as Texas.

Further, he applied the skills of a salesman, which he was in selling oil drilling services. As one who has difficulty putting

RONALD REAGAN, later elected president, and former President Gerald Ford at a September 1978 rally for William P. Clements, Jr., who became Texas' first Republican governor in more than a century.
— *Dallas Morning News Staff Photo*

names to faces, I was frequently amazed at Clements' memory.

In press conferences. he could first-name reporters on short acquaintance and often recall the answer he had given weeks before to a similar question.

While Clements' blunt manner and arms-length dealing with the media failed to convert many into Clements admirers, they did respect the way he handled his affairs and willingness to make himself available for questioning, far more than his predecessor had done.

Clements proved to be a master at fielding hostile questions, and would reply frankly "I don't know" when he didn't have facts at hand to make a proper response.

Also, Clements came into elective office with a distinction few politicians can claim: He owed practically nothing to special interests for his election, including business. Most lobbying interests had put their money on candidates who lost in the governor's race. Most of Clements' seven million dollar campaign cash came from his own finances. After the election, contributions from others repaid his expense.

". . . Clements proved what he had been telling everybody — that he could win by diligent effort and 'not running out of money in the fourth quarter' as previous Republican candidates always did," I wrote.

"November 7, 1978 will be remembered as a new Thanksgiving Day for Texas Republicans. The victory in the governor's race was the major event, of course. But John Tower won reelection to six more years in the U.S. Senate . . . the party doubled its representation in the U.S. House of Representatives, from two to four members (Democrats still held twenty seats)." [25]

Further, the Republicans retained four seats in the Texas Senate (among thirty-one) and gained three state representatives, making twenty-two of the one hundred fifty total membership.

The shift to a two-party state continued in the 1980s. By 1982, before the year's elections, Texas Republicans held five seats in the U.S. House of Representatives, eight of thirty-one seats in the Texas Senate, and thirty-eight of one hundred fifty state representatives. Party officials expected to gain both in Congress, the legislature, and local offices in the 1982 election.

Dallas is Texas' Republican stronghold, followed by Houston. Democrats retained superiority over most of East Texas outside the cities and in the Mexican-American areas of South Texas, including San Antonio. Two-thirds of the party's voting strength was in the Dallas-Fort Worth and Houston-Southeast Texas metroplex areas.

A pair of national political columnists, surveying the party's gains in Texas, added:

". . . In most Southern states the Republicans have done nothing comparable to what they have accomplished in Texas in building their party from the bottom up. When there have been successes in electing a governor or senator, they have been most often personal triumphs that didn't change courthouse politics or Democratic leanings of the vast majority of Southern voters." [26]

Texas appears to be increasingly "Western" rather than "Southern" in its political outlook. For years, as populations grew in the West, so has Republican strength as evidenced by Ronald Reagan's election as president in 1980.

Rural East Texas retains the vestiges of the old Democratic South, but the remainder of the state has become more increasingly independent or Republican.

In 1982, Republicans offered more than 500 candidates for elective office in Texas. While this represented a noteworthy increase in numbers from the past, Republicans remained a distinctly minority party.

As of 1977, Texas elected 24,129 people to 3,833 public offices, boards, and commissions. [27]

Frequently officeholders lack party labels. City officials and school boards, water boards, and special district boards usually run without any political party identification or support.

Clements credited his success, and the party's, in part to the disenchantment of citizens with President Carter and the Democratic Congress and bureaucracy in Washington.

In both his inaugural address and his first speech to the legislature, Clements emphasized his ambition to keep government closer to the people and to keep a tight rein on growth of government in size and authority.

"He came into office promising to run state government like his own well-oiled corporation and assuring constituents that he would 'persist and prevail'," wrote one Austin-based reporter. [28]

"After five months, William P. Clements, Jr. hasn't always prevailed. But he has persisted — apparently to the satisfaction of the public. Radiating an intense, can-do personality and assertive, unpredictable leadership, the cocky former roughneck is garnering popularity as the state's first strong governor since John Connally left office a decade ago.

"Despite his credentials as a wealthy, conservative Republican, the sixty-two-year-old former Dallas drilling contractor has exerted a populist, Trumanesque image through his give-'em-hell statements, unexpected vetoes, and bruising confrontations. He has taken on teachers, preachers, lawyers, lenders, truckers, the federal government and the Democratic-dominated government, to name a few.

"He has made the most of his constitutionally-weak executive powers by using managerial know-how to improve and reorganize the bureaucratic framework of the governor's office.''

Glenn Ivy of the privately-financed Texas Research League complimented the new governor: ''On administration, he looks like one of the strongest people we've ever had in that office. He knows the tools of management and all the gobbledegook of running a business. We've never had an administrator in this office before and this guy is one.''

V. Lance Tarrance, Clements' poll-taker, added: ''Bill Clements is being perceived as a man who is willing to stand up and fight. He's meeting the standard tests of being a good strong governor.''

When that was written following the first legislative session with Clements as governor, the public recognized that ''what they see is what they get'' — a straightforward, no-nonsense, self-made successful business man in the governor's office. It was an image from which Clements never varied, even though some citizens — particularly those of different political belief — criticized his bluntness.

Clements surrounded himself with able people in the capitol. His first secretary of state was George W. Strake, Jr., forty-three, a Houston oil man. David Dean, thirty-one, who left Governor Briscoe's staff to campaign for Clements against Hill, became legal counsel. Tobin Armstrong, Jr., general manager of a large South Texas ranch and husband of Anne Armstrong, former U.S. ambassador to Great Britain, became a special assistant to help Clements choose persons for the 4,200 appointive offices to be filled by the governor in four years.

Armstrong and several other top-level assistants served without pay, except expenses.

Clements was described as Jeffersonian by *The Dallas Morning News*.

''In his inaugural address, Clements succinctly set forth his political philosophy,'' *The News* editorialized. [29]

'' 'Condensed to its most basic form (the new governor was quoted) my philosophy is this: The proper function of government is not to guarantee prosperity for its citizens; but, rather, it is to guarantee them the opportunity to achieve prosperity'.''

"It was Thomas Jefferson's view that the government governs best when it governs least," the editorial continued, "when it lets citizens alone to pursue their own affairs, free of paternalistic interference.

"The whole tendency of 20th-century government has been to repudiate Jeffersonian tenets. Into its capacious arms, government has scooped one responsibility after another, until there are almost literally no provinces of life which government does not touch . . .

"So large and powerful has government grown in the past forty-five years (the start of the New Deal is a good landmark from which to measure), that it has become an overbearing partner in the affairs of man. Government takes and spends about two dollars of every five we earn. It hamstrings the workings of the free market place. It tells us whom we may hire and how we shall make the things we create for sale . . .

"Government as the guarantor of prosperity is an idea that came to maturity during the New Deal and has afflicted us ever since."

Clements accomplished part of what he set as his goals during his first four years in office. While he did help restrain state spending, he failed in his effort to establish an Initiative and Referendum system whereby citizens could petition for elections on proposals without requiring legislative action. Clements made adoption of Initiative and Referendum part of his second-term platform. Opponents include both business lobby groups, union labor spokesmen, and many legislators all of whom felt they would surrender political influence if the program went into effect.

The governor's first budget proposal was one billion dollars below the legislature's, and he vetoed more than $250 million from the first biennial appropriation bill sent to him. The vetoed funds included construction for public universities and other state agencies.

He made only minor reductions in a twenty-seven billion dollar budget voted two years later for the 1982-1983 biennium. But Clements called a special legislative session in May 1982 to submit a constitutional amendment to abolish a thirty-five-year-

WILLIAM P. CLEMENTS, JR. of Dallas, elected governor in 1978, and his wife Rita.

— *Dallas Morning News Photo*

old property tax dedicated for building construction in higher education outside the endowed system of The University of Texas and Texas A&M. The legislature earlier tried to stop the tax levy by law, which was deemed to be insufficient. Clements said property taxpayers would save one billion dollars in back taxes if the property tax was repealed. Clements proposed to substitute $100 million a year of general revenue for the property tax income.

Clements predicted correctly that Ronald Reagan would carry Texas in the 1980 presidential election and he worked hard to help achieve that goal, ruffling Democratic feathers along the way with derogatory comments about the incumbent President Jimmy Carter.

After savoring the party's big national victory, Clements also enjoyed considerable success with his 1981 legislative program.

He proposed forty-four new laws and thirty-four of these were passed in a form acceptable to the governor. Clements considered his biggest legislative victory was passage of a bill to legalize wiretapping of telephones in certain criminal investigations, particularly drug traffic and gambling. Efforts of previous governors to pass such a law, favored by enforcement officers, had been thwarted in the legislature.

Clements' first term had several distinctions. In 1979 at Austin, he hosted the first Republican Governors Conference ever held in the state.

The Executive Mansion underwent a multimillion dollar renovation under supervision of Rita Clements, the governor's wife. Funds were contributed from private sources.

Rita Clements was what the Republican governor termed "my secret weapon" in his political success. Before his election as governor, Mrs. Clements had higher identity in state and national Republican affairs than he did. She had been an active worker in Republican campaigns and served on the party's national committee.

The active participation of wives in the governorship is commonplace. In various ways, wives of governors usually exercise strong influence in an administration.

The Dolph Briscoes were almost inseparable. The first governor I ever knew, Miriam A. Ferguson, allowed her husband, a former governor, to participate openly in conducting the office during her two terms.

Janey Briscoe and Rita Clements are but two examples. Mrs. Price Daniel (Jean), a descendant of Sam Houston, added greatly to her husband's political appeal. So did Nellie Connally to husband John. Mrs. Allan Shivers (Marialice) had less political visibility but graced both the lieutenant governor's apartment and the Governor's Mansion at many social events, as did Mrs. Preston Smith. Mrs. James V. Allred did likewise at the Mansion.

Governor Coke Stevenson's first wife died shortly after they moved into the mansion and his official hostess was his daughter-in-law, Mrs. Coke Stevenson, Jr.

Mrs. Beauford H. Jester seemed to care little for political life, but served as hostess on occasion.

The W. Lee O'Daniels differed from other couples occupying the Mansion. They had little previous contact with state political circles, or the capital social scene, and they were more reclusive than most governors and wives. They gave some large parties and invited the public to attend, which it did in large numbers.

REAGAN WINS THE PRESIDENCY

Two years after Bill Clements put a Republican brand on the governor's office, the nation witnessed just as stunning a change when Ronald Reagan defeated Jimmy Carter's bid for a second term as president.

Reagan, who first achieved public notice as a motion picture actor, won the Republican nomination in 1980 with relative ease, after a narrow loss to President Ford in 1976.

As a two-term governor of California, Reagan had proved that he was much more than "just a movie actor" as his detractors tried to depict him. Reagan had admired Franklin Roosevelt forty-eight years earlier when Roosevelt became president, but he quickly lost faith in the New Deal and what followed. He emerged during the 1960s and 1970s as the nation's best-known spokesman for curbing the powers and cost of government and cultivation of prosperity based on private investment and free enterprise.

The last Republican to contest Reagan in the 1980 primaries was George Bush of Texas, who was chosen to be Reagan's vice president. Reagan was sixty-nine years old when elected, and Bush fifty-six. The two had very different backgrounds and somewhat diverse philosophies.

Reagan grew up poor in Illinois, and worked his way through Eureka College, a small denominational school, during

PRESIDENT REAGAN (center) discusses official business with Vice President George Bush (far left) and U.S. Senator John Tower, R-Texas, (far right) and congressional leaders.

— *Official White House Photo*

the terrible depression of the early 1930s. Bush was an Ivy Leaguer from Yale, the son of a distinguished, wealthy U.S. senator from Connecticut.

Reagan tried out for the movies while serving as a sports radio broadcaster, and became one of Hollywood's best-known actors. Bush moved to Texas after serving as a U.S. Navy pilot and entered the oil and gas business, later moving to Houston where he was elected to Congress. Bush also served as U.S. ambassador to the United Nations, an envoy to China, National Republican Chairman, and head of the Central Intelligence Agency.

While Reagan was a novice in national government, Bush knew the ropes well in Washington.

Polls showed the race between Reagan and Carter to be quite close, right up until election day.

Reagan and Bush surprised the forecasters by winning 50.7

percent of the total vote and 489 votes in the Electoral College. Carter's vote totaled 41 percent and the outgoing president won only forty-nine electoral votes. Third place went to Congressman John B. Anderson of Illinois, running as an Independent and pitching his campaign to liberal voters. Anderson received 6.6 percent of the popular vote and no electoral votes.

The popular vote totaled 43,901,812 for Reagan, 35,483,820 for Carter, and 5,719,722 for Anderson.[30]

With Governor Clements, John Connally (who had dropped out of the Republican presidential race), and others leading a surge to enlist all conservative and independent voters, the Republican ticket did better in Texas than across the nation.

Reagan-Bush had 55.3 percent of the popular vote, tallying 2,510,705; Carter-Mondale 41.4 percent totaling 1,881,147, with Anderson receiving an insignificant 2.5 percent.

While Republicans gained the presidency, won a majority in the U.S. Senate, and increased the public offices held in Texas and the South, their success fell short of returning to the party's dominance in national politics evidenced during most of the period from 1861 until 1933.

Robert Eckhardt, a veteran liberal Democrat congressman from Harris County, was upset by a Republican newcomer Jack Fields.

But Democrats retained all the seats on the Texas Railroad Commission, often described as the nation's most powerful regulatory agency because of its authority over the oil and gas industry. They also unseated Governor Clements' appointee, Republican Will Garwood, on the Texas Supreme Court.

A highly-respected jurist and lawyer, well-heeled financially, and endorsed by most lawyers and judges, Garwood nevertheless lost to Justice C. L. Ray of the Texarkana Court of Civil Appeals. The outcome was considered by most observers to be a result of straight-voting by Democrats across the state for offices below the presidency. Few voters knew anything about either Garwood or Ray, and the election increased demands for a merit system of selecting judges for appellate courts.

All members of the Texas Supreme Court and Court of Criminal Appeals are Democrats. Seldom does anyone even

VICE PRESIDENT-TO-BE AND Mrs. George Bush (left) with former Governor and Mrs. John Connally in 1979.

— *Dallas Morning News Photo*

bother to file a Republican, because of the futility of such action.

The Associated Press rated the 1980 election as the year's major news event, followed by a diplomatic crisis caused by Iranians holding fifty-two Americans, mostly diplomatic service people, hostage. Third place in the important news category was the decline of the U.S. economy resulting from soaring inflation and interest rates accompanied by rising unemployment. [31]

President Carter attributed his defeat to the frustration of the American voters over affairs in general, rather than dislike of him personally. Probably that is correct.

The outgoing president was a decent man of respectable goals and intentions. But he never really gained the confidence of the mainstream of national party Democrats, whose views were closer to those of Senator Edward (Ted) Kennedy of Massachusetts and Vice President Mondale.

Carter won election in 1976 largely because he convinced voters he could help straighten out what he called "the mess in Washington." He lost the office in 1980 because he failed to make much progress in that direction, and Reagan persuaded the middle-ground voters he could bring "a new beginning."

Carter's legacy included the appointment of many more women, blacks, and Hispanics to office than his predecessors had done, and his most loyal support in 1980 came from ethnic groups.

During his four years, President Carter appointed 1,195 persons to full-time offices. His choices included twelve percent women, twelve percent blacks, and four percent Hispanics. Blacks make up about ten percent of total population, Hispanics five percent, and women in the work force about forty percent. [32]

Forty-seven women, forty-eight blacks and eighteen Hispanics were appointed to federal courts of 313 total chosen. While a new law permitted Carter to appoint more federal judges than any president in history, there was no appointment to the Supreme Court during his term.

Soon after Reagan took office, a resignation enabled the new president to appoint Sandra Day O'Connor of Arizona as the first woman United States Supreme Court Justice in history.

In Texas, the largest increase in population and political influence has come among Mexican-Americans, variously called Hispanics, Latin-Americans, and Chicanos.

They represent about twenty percent of Texas' 14.2 million population (1980 census). The exact numbers are difficult to ascertain because many Mexicans are illegally in the United States and avoid the census-takers. Also, this group is identified mainly by Spanish-origin names, an inexact measure. Mexican-ancestry Texas legislators, for example, sometimes have Anglo-origin names. In any event, this group is the fastest-growing segment in Texas, up an estimated 500,000 or thirty-three percent during the 1970s. [33]

When I first observed the legislature, there were no black

members and few identifiable Mexican-Americans. Women served as legislators as early as the 1920s, but they were few in number.

In 1933, Miss Margie E. Neal of Carthage (single women were designated as "Miss" in those days) served in the State Senate. Mrs. Sarah T. Hughes of Dallas, later a state and federal judge, was the lone woman state representative.

A number of blacks served in the legislature during Reconstruction and for a few years afterward. None was elected between 1895 and 1967, largely the result of a "white man's primary" system in which the Democratic party controlled by whites nominated the candidates who always won.

In 1967, voters of Harris County elected Barbara Jordan to become the first black senator of the century and they chose Curtis N. Graves as a state representative. A third black member was Representative Joseph E. Lockridge of Dallas.

Miss Jordan quickly distinguished herself in the Senate and later was elected to Congress, from which she retired to teach at the Lyndon Baines Johnson School of Public Affairs at The University of Texas-Austin.

No other black was elected to the Senate by 1980, but that year Texas voters chose thirteen blacks as state representatives, a somewhat smaller proportion than blacks among the state's whole population.

Based on surnames, three Mexican-Americans represented Texas constituencies in the Congress meeting in 1982. Three others served in the State Senate and eleven were state representatives.

The Reagan victory in 1980 represented in part a movement in population from the industrial states of the Northeast, where Democrats had built a power base starting with the 1930s.

The 1980s therefore created an opportunity for Republicans to regain some of the political influence they had lost fifty years earlier. The 1980 census reflected population losses of ten to fifty percent in thirty congressional districts, all of them represented in Congress by Democrats. [34]

Twenty-one congressional districts with the largest population gains during the 1970s are west of the Mississippi River. Of the nine fastest-growing "Eastern" congressional districts, seven are located in Florida and the other two in Georgia and Tennessee.

Based on allocations resulting from the 1980 census, seventeen additional seats in the U.S. House of Representatives are in the South and West, and an equal number lost by northeastern states. Texas gained three seats, for a total of twenty-seven. The biggest loss was five seats in New York; the largest gain, four seats for Florida.

Seven districts erased by declining population were represented by black Democrats, following a move by many Negroes from the troubled central cities to better life in the suburbs and even the South, which many blacks left during the 1930s and 1940s for northern and western states.

The fastest-growing racial group, particularly in Texas, is the Mexican-American. These voters remained loyal to the Democratic party but there were signs of defections to the Republicans by the early 1980s.

Voters continued to "vote their pocketbooks" and Democratic leaders, blaming President Reagan for an economic recession in 1982, predicted the party would recover lost political ground.

As with Franklin D. Roosevelt in his first term, President Reagan soon learned that problems which took years to develop — such as inflation — could not be solved quickly or without such painful consequences as rising unemployment.

President Reagan remained resolute in his determination to reduce taxes and increase the nation's defense forces, a difficult task. The revenue squeeze came mostly in social programs which had grown enormously expensive since World War II.

Dr. Charls E. Walker, a Texan and noted economist, cited the Reagan election as proof that the "great unwashed American middle class" rather than special interests such as business or organized labor still control the country's political destiny. [35]

Dr. Walker defined the "middle class" as families of $15,000 to $50,000 annual income. He predicted it would take five years to reverse the so-called "misery index," a phrase coined by Jimmy Carter in the 1976 campaign to reflect the combined negative effect of inflation and unemployment.

When President Carter left the office, Dr. Walker said, the two factors totaled twenty-one percent compared to 12.5 percent in 1976. Most of the economic "misery" resulted from an inflation rate of approximately fifteen percent in 1980.

By 1982, the inflation rate had declined sharply but unemployment rose from below eight percent to above nine percent. Job layoffs, particularly in transportation and construction, and continued high interest rates hurt the country. Economists put much of the blame on the federal government's demand for money to refinance its trillion-dollar deficit, paying more than private industry could afford to attract investors.

Shortly before taking office, President-elect Reagan wrote:

"Today the United States stands virtually alone among the industrialized nations in the adversary nature of the relationship between its government and the business-industrial sector.

"While this may have had its roots in the market crash of 1929 and the loss of public faith in the private sector that followed, the adversary relationship between the federal government and the business world reached its greatest intensity in the late 1960s and the early 1970s, the years of Vietnam and Watergate. Public opinion polls during those years showed steady declines in public confidence in business.

"Although the notion that government inherently possesses greater wisdom and greater good than private business is impossible to prove, it was nevertheless widely held through much of the last two decades. Only in recent years has there been widespread realization that well-intended government programs can and do fail of their own cumbersomeness; that laws and regulations put into place to solve one problem may create another even worse. And it is only in recent years that the public has come to understand that government's appetite for money and its propensity to spend more than it takes in is the root cause of our chronic inflation.

"During much of the '60s and '70s Washington attracted many bright young men and women who saw the federal government as the ultimate tool for solving all social problems. They mistrusted the states and cities to do the job, and they had deep distrust of the motives of business and industry.

"The resulting web of laws and regulations, coupled with tax policies which inhibited capital formation (by business and industry), contributed significantly to the erosion of U.S. productivity.

"... As a result, U.S. competitiveness in world markets has declined and inflation and unemployment have become not only our major economic problems but great social problems as well ..."[36]

Reagan stated the problem accurately, but his early years as president proved that the solution is neither easy nor simplistic. The president has displayed considerable political skill in trying to accomplish his goals of reducing inflation, maintaining employment, stimulating the private economy, and rebuilding the nation's military strength to discourage expansion of Communism by the Soviet Union.

The president demonstrated that "good politics is the art of compromise" in his effort to implement his goals in Congress. But the budget deficit continued and the transition back toward less government and more private enterprise remained a rocky road.

As did FDR, President Reagan communicated his views directly to the public, over the heads of Congress and the media, by frequent appearances on television and radio.

Democracy is an inefficient system of government, often awkward, but its success is unmatched once the public understands clearly the issues and the problems. I think it will continue to work for the best interests of its citizens as it has for more than 200 years, the longest-lasting democracy in the history of the world.

[1] *Politics in America,* Congressional Quarterly, Inc., page 126
[2] *Dallas News,* October 12, 1972
[3] *Op.cit.* November 9, 1972
[4] Governor's Report, The Briscoe Years 1973-1979, page 1
[5] *Dallas News,* June 9, 1973
[6] *Op.cit.* June 10, 1973
[7] *Ibid.*
[8] *The Briscoe Years* 1973-1979, page 6
[9] *Dallas News,* July 20, 1973
[10] *Politics in America, Op.cit.,* page 46
[11] *Ibid.*
[12] *Dallas News,* January 28, 1973

[13] *The Briscoe Years, Op.cit.,* page 18

[14] *Op.cit.,* page 19

[15] *Dallas News,* October 24, 1975

[16] *Politics in America, Op.cit.,* page 51

[17] *Dallas News,* January 21, 1975

[18] Briscoe's State of the State Address, January 22, 1975

[19] *Dallas News,* July 22, 1976

[20] *Politics in America, Op.cit.,* page 127

[21] The Briscoe Years, *Op.cit.,* page 10

[22] *Ibid.,* page 63

[23] Adopted September 20, 1978, at Hilton Head, South Carolina

[24] *Austin American-Statesman,* November 12, 1978

[25] *Dallas News,* November 12, 1978

[26] Jack W. Germond and Jules Witcover in *The Dallas Morning News,* April 24, 1982

[27] 1977 Census of Governments, U.S. Chamber of Commerce

[28] Dave Montgomery, *Dallas Times Herald,* May 20, 1979

[29] *Dallas News,* January 21, 1979

[30] *Congressional Quarterly Almanac,* 1980, page 6-B

[31] *Austin American-Statesman,* December 26, 1980

[32] Wesley G. Pippert, United Press International, 1981

[33] *Lubbock Avalanche Journal,* December 18, 1979, Bill Greer quoting Ruben Bonilla, national president of the League of United Latin-American Citizens (LULAC).

[34] Edward Walsh, *Washington Post,* July 5, 1981

[35] Dr. Walker at The University of Texas-Austin, November 14, 1980

[36] Written by Reagan in the *Wall Street Journal,* January 9, 1981

THE MIDDLE EAST struggle occupied President Reagan.
— *DeOre cartoon reprinted from The Dallas Morning News*

THE SOVIET UNION wanted nuclear superiority.
— *DeOre cartoon reprinted from The Dallas Morning News*

METROPOLITAN HOUSTON ...Texas moves into the Twenty-First Century.

7

TEXAS 2000

As population, jobs, and income increased in Sunbelt states of the South and West, Texas prospered at a record rate. The state's economy and employment rate remained better than the national average into the 1980s.

Clouds appeared on the horizon for future years, as outlined by the Texas 2000 Commission appointed by Governor Clements to help set a course for the future. A staff directed by Dr. Victor Arnold worked with a commission of leaders from business, state government, the professions, and academic world.

The Commission report in March 1982 commented:

"The future of Texas will be influenced greatly by the rich legacy of the past, by changing conditions of the present, and by national and international factors — many of which are beyond the control of the State and its people. [1]

"Rather than yield the future to a course of events imposed from outside, we are confident that Texans will choose to rely on a great, longstanding asset: the determination to shape their own destinies . . .

"The pervasive, self-confident optimism and can-do attitude of Texans, the good fortune of a rich endowment of natural resources, and an expanding technological base provided by universities and the private sector together create the ideal conditions for sustained progress in the State . . . We have accepted population growth and changes in the Texas economy as driving forces that will, to a large degree, influence Texas' future."

The 1980 census showed 14.3 million people living in

Texas, a far faster growth rate than forecast in 1972 by the U.S. Census Bureau. [2]

Forecasts set the 1990 figure for Texas at 16.3 million. By the year 2000, the projected total is twenty-two million, making Texas probably the second-largest state behind California and surpassing New York.

The projected age structure of this population will require creation of 170,000 new jobs annually. [3]

During the 1980s, Texans' income averaging $9,513 per capita was slightly above the national average for the first time, but still lower than Alaska and some industrial states. The improvement both in actual income and comparison with most other states continued in 1981-82.

Maintaining this trend and creating the new jobs necessary for Texas' growing population will require solving these problems, the Texas 2000 Commission said:

"Present and foreseeable acute water shortages affecting urban life, agriculture, and industry. Water use (statewide) in the year 2000 is projected to be 21.6 million acre feet. This exceeds dependable supplies in that year by 2.5 million acre-feet — even with cutbacks in irrigation, and by 8.5 million acre-feet, if irrigation demand is met.

"A declining trend in Texas' oil and gas production, which has significant implications for state revenues as well as every sector of the Texas economy. Texas' energy production from present sources is projected to decline at an annual rate of 1.4 percent, despite the projected substantial increase in lignite production.

"A slowdown in the rate of increase of Texas' agricultural productivity and a lack of access to markets. The rate of increase in agricultural productivity was halved between 1973 and 1978. If the present trends are not reversed, agricultural production will decline in Texas (because of rising costs of production).

"Inadequacies in transportation in both urban and rural areas as we enter a period of rapidly increasing requirements. Vehicle traffic, for example, is expected to more than double in Texas between now and 2000. Highway, rail, and waterway maintenance and improvements are not keeping pace with increasing use and need.

"A lack of understanding of the value of Research and Development and an inadequate level of investment in R&D focused on the key areas of concern of the state. United States expenditures for R&D (private and public) are $216 per capita, but Texas expenditures are only $126 per capita.

"The uncertain outlook for state and local revenues will be determined largely by the degree of success in dealing with the five preceding topics.

"Important relations with Mexico that depend greatly on national rather than state policy. However, Texas can influence both national policy and initiate certain actions on its own."

To a large degree, all of the above require political solutions —that is, the solutions must have majority public support guided by reasonable government leadership.

The current and increasing water problem is an example. While the shortage has become statewide, except in rural East Texas, many urban voters continue to reject water development programs based on the mistaken idea the principal beneficiaries will be West Texas irrigation farmers. The city dweller who buys groceries, cotton, wool, or mohair fabrics should be as concerned about the deterioration of the agricultural economy as the producer.

The situation, too little recognized by most citizens, is becoming desperate. A solution is further complicated and politicized by the fact that developing water resources is an interstate problem. California built a system of reservoirs, canals, and pipelines to bring surplus water from northern California to populous, water-short southern California because it involved only water within the state.

Texas must transport water, probably from a source within the Mississippi River system, to get the water it needs. States with surplus water, which usually runs into the Gulf of Mexico, have displayed attitudes ranging from disinterest to outright hostility toward the idea of sharing water with Texas. But it is a problem to be solved.

First, Texans must agree to support a development program

and funds to pay for it. Costs can and should be repaid by charges to users in cities and rural areas.

Texans are learning, and must learn more, about getting better results from water resources. Farmers of the northwest Texas plains, among the most innovative in the world, are developing a method of increasing production from known underground reservoirs, not unlike the so-called ''secondary recovery'' programs used in many oil fields to minimize loss of liquid assets left below the surface.

Some farmers also are using ''drip'' irrigation to apply water directly on the plants rather than running it down furrows with considerable loss to evaporation.

Perhaps my background as a youth in the Dust Bowl of the 1930s prejudices my opinion, but over a half century of observ ing development of many water conservation and use programs convinces me that all, or nearly all, expenditures to make more water available are good investments, whether for a reservoir to serve cities or a farm pond for livestock, recreation, and flood control.

Texas future prosperity depends on water more than anything else.

Some years ago, Charles E. Wilson, former automobile company executive then secretary of defense in President Eisenhower's cabinet, dedicated a new reservoir near Corpus Christi with these words:

''Three developments are giving the South a bright future — water . . . insecticides . . . and air-conditioning . . .''

I reported the dedication and was struck by the wisdom of a non-Southerner's view.

During the 20th century, Texas has been blessed with abundant oil and gas resources. While these are diminishing, they are expected to continue as the state's and nation's principal fuel supply at least until the start of the next century.

Once oil and gas were quite cheap, a few dollars for a forty-two-gallon barrel of oil (even less than one dollar during the 1930s) and a few cents per thousand cubic feet for natural gas, a highly-esteemed fuel because of its cleanliness and still relatively low cost.

The Organization of Petroleum Exporting Countries (OPEC) in the 1970s forced world prices for oil to as high as forty dollars a barrel, although the price subsided to thirty to thirty-two dollars a barrel by 1982 because world production had increased and higher prices brought conservation. Motorists bought more efficient, smaller cars and some fuel oil users, especially industrial, returned to the use of cheaper coal.

While the future supply of oil and natural gas is limited, nobody knows even approximately the ultimate limits because of new technology and discoveries. Moreover, alternative fuels are being brought to market. Texas has a huge supply of lignite, a low-grade coal, extending near the earth's surface from near Texarkana to Laredo. Much lignite already is being used for generating electricity, replacing natural gas.

Likewise, coal is being delivered to Texas and other states for generating electricity and other purposes. The nation's coal supply is considered to be enough for centuries, although using coal is fraught with pollution and other problems.

State Comptroller Bob Bullock commented concerning the future of Texas oil:

"Recent drops in production and in estimated reserves indicate Texas is running out of oil, but there is still a vast amount underground. The amount depends on advances in recovery techniques, future market conditions . . . and luck." [4]

Between the first large Texas oil discovery at Spindletop near Beaumont in 1900 and 1981, Texas wells produced about forty-five billion barrels of oil. Bullock estimated the state can produce another forty billion barrels in the future, although the "proven" reserves are much less.

In recent years, many older oil fields have been rejuvenated by injecting water, gas, or other substances into the reservoir to flush oil to the surface. Most early Texas fields were shut down after producing fifteen to forty percent of the oil underground, because the remainder was too expensive to recover by existing technology. Technical improvements and much higher-priced oil are making recovery economically feasible in many cases during the 1980s.

TEXAS ECONOMIC planners contend the windfall profits tax levied by Congress in the Carter administration handicap the nation's program for energy independence.

— *DeOre cartoon reprinted from The Dallas Morning News*

Besides conventional oil, North America has large amounts of oil shale and oil tars which can be tapped when the price is high enough to justify the cost. An oil price decline in 1982 caused some of these experimental programs to be closed temporarily, however.

Despite the high price and undependability of foreign oil, the United States continued to import about forty percent of its supply in the 1980s with little slowdown in sight as long as the petroleum is available. The discovery of large supplies on Mexico's south Gulf of Mexico coast in the 1970s added greatly to the continent's supply but availability to Texas and the other states remained a matter of bargaining with the Mexicans.

Equipment and technology for deep-well drilling, even below 25,000 feet, and in submerged areas such as the Gulf of Mexico likewise greatly improve the outlook for future supplies, particularly of natural gas.

One fact seems certain: The day of cheap oil and gas is gone forever. Only federal government controls kept prices from rising inside the United States to the level charged by producers in other countries.

The federal government also levied a "windfall profits" tax on oil and gas in the 1980s, a multibillion tax which penalizes the producers and producing states for the benefit of consuming states, which are stronger politically.

Any decline in oil and gas production carries serious implications for government at all levels which depend heavily on revenues from this source.

In fiscal year 1981, Texas collected $2.2 billion in taxes on oil and gas production. Motor fuel taxes added $480 million during the year and sales taxes on motor vehicles another $511 million. Collectively these sources represented more than one-third of state revenue. [5]

Without taxes on oil and gas properties, many cities, counties and districts would be hard-hit financially.

Education has been a major beneficiary. In addition to tax income, two large endowment funds have been created by income on state land, mostly oil and gas bonus and royalty payments.

The Permanent School Fund's $3.34 billion is shared by all public schools, although its earnings represent but a small fraction of public education's total cost. [6] This fund owns mineral rights in the state-owned portion of the Gulf of Mexico, riverbeds, and lakes, plus some upland.

The Permanent University Fund totaling $1.68 billion is shared two-thirds by The University of Texas system and one-third by the Texas A&M system. Repeated efforts have been made to expand its coverage to other state universities. [7]

Texans should be aware that the era of such heavy dependence on oil and gas revenues to support government, especially education, is waning and that other sources must be found in the near future.

Further, state and local government dependence on federal funds likewise would be reversed under the Reagan administration's "New Federalism" program of returning more responsibility to state and local government.

Federal "aid" to state government in Texas during fiscal year 1981 totaled $2.88 billion — 21.4 percent of total state income of $13.42 billion in fiscal year 1981. [8] The federal funds helped the state pay for highways, education, welfare, and other programs.

Although such "aid" programs have become so imbedded in government that removing them would be difficult to impossible, steps taken by the Reagan administration should be encouraged. Raising money at one level and spending it at another level is bad government, in my opinion.

The system is particularly senseless in the 1980s with the federal government so deeply in debt and still running deficits. State and local governments generally are in better financial condition than the federal government, and keeping administration closer to home is desirable.

Texas and the nation have energy possibilities for the future in addition to oil, natural gas, and coal.

Political opposition and other problems have largely stalled commercial development of nuclear energy. Solar power can be adapted to some areas which have plenty of sunshine and relatively low energy requirements.

Windpower also has potential for generating electricity in rural areas and small communities remote from major electrical systems. The list of possible energy sources is constantly being extended to include everything from city garbage to nuclear power from seawater. Economics as well as technology so far has put restraints on wider development of these.

"Despite its eighty percent urban population, Texas is among the nation's leading agricultural states. Its $9.9 billion cash receipts for 1980 ranked third in the country. Texas Agricultural Experiment Station estimates that the total impact of these receipts was $33.7 billion. The export value of Texas agricultural products is approaching $2.2 billion — an amount that emphasizes the importance of the state's agricultural production to the national economy as well as locally." [9]

The Commission noted that the rapid increase in agricultural production and income during the 1970s, in the face of a shrinking farm population, resulted largely from improved farming and irrigation methods brought about through research.

Nevertheless, the state's and nation's agricultural economy in the early 1980s was ailing and many producers were forced out of business by heavy debt, high interest rates, increased expenses for energy, transportation, and equipment, and slumping market prices.

"Texas farmers and ranchers are enduring difficult times," the Commission wrote. "Some of the hardships are cyclical, some are the result of government policies, and some have been induced by resource constraints such as the escalating costs of energy and transportation and declining water supplies.

"In addition, trends indicate that the rate of increase of agricultural productivity is declining. This decline in the rate of growth is the sign that the limits of widely employed agricultural technologies is being reached."

Much of the problem is political, and will require political solution. Using food as a weapon of foreign policy, such as grain embargoes to Russia, is an example. Agricultural products are the largest contributors to the nation's exports in foreign trade, while the total balance is unfavorable because so much American money pays for OPEC oil.

Since farmers and ranchers now represent less than four percent of the nation's total population, they have difficulty getting heard in Washington, especially if it means raising prices to consumers. On the other hand, government price support policies have contributed to surpluses such as milk products. We would do well to distribute food free to the poor people of the world rather than letting it spoil while the government pays storage charges.

Farms are getting much larger, and the small family farmer is becoming just a memory. Most younger family members move to the city for better incomes and more comfortable living. Still, agriculture attracts many young, well-educated people who like the independence and other aspects of farm and ranch life. Corporate farming is increasing.

When the day comes that corporation-owned farms and co-operatives can control the supply and ultimately the retail price of their products, the nation's small number of remaining agricultural producers will likely be much more powerful than they are today. Economic health of the agriculture producer is a vital matter to consumers, who may temporarily enjoy lower prices which drive producers into bankruptcy.

There is a brighter side. Many small towns in Texas, especially within easy reach of cities, are growing after long periods of decline. New industries dot the countryside, bringing income and workers to formerly-depressed areas. Many employees are part-time farmers, who live on the farm and supplement their income from produce. This also furnishes a quality of life for families which is impossible in crowded cities. A few new industries operate on a four-day week, allowing more days for such part-time farm and livestock operators to work on the land.

"Transportation, both personal and commercial, is a vital element in Texas' economic development. Transportation is not only an essential support service for business and personal use, it is an important industry in its own right. A complete transportation system encompasses six major modes: air, highway, rail, pipeline, waterway, and mass transit . . . In some cases government supplies the service; in others it is responsible primarily for regulation, planning or financial authorization. [10]

"In Texas, highway, road, and street travel will continue to be the dominant mode. Texans traveled 8,026 vehicle miles per capita in 1980, compared with the national average of 6,715. The state budget reflects this emphasis on motor vehicle travel; over ninety-nine percent of the transportation appropriation goes to providing highway services."

By the year 2000, the Commission noted, the expansion of highway travel and freight hauling — plus the expected eight million increased population — will put a severe strain on the transportation system, which was beginning to show severe deterioration by the early 1980s.

The Commission suggested setting up a special governor's task force to develop a long-range plan for transportation improvement, with state assistance for research and development. The federal government's financial plight, and reduction of its aid to states and local communities, increases the urgency of expanded state participation.

Perhaps it is nostalgia, but I strongly favor the development of fast, high-quality rail passenger service between major cities and from suburbs into cities. Every large Texas city has some facilities, at least the right-of-way and usually some track, to move people into downtown areas in large numbers. This would relieve traffic jams on freeways and downtown sections and reduce the strain on automobile drivers and riders.

Other countries have successfully maintained and improved their rail systems, often with government aid. We should start by building the "Texas Triangle" project for high-speed modern trains to travel between Dallas-Fort Worth, Houston, and San Antonio-Austin. Problems will need to be overcome, such as modernized tracks. These are surmountable.

Most funds for this purpose comes from the federal government, a shaky source for the future as already stated.

"Innovation influences inflation, stimulates productivity, employment, and the ability of U.S. products to compete in both domestic and world markets . . . This statement applies directly to Texas."[11]

"Steady economic growth will be required to accommodate the projected increase in population and to sustain a high quality of life in Texas. Traditional growth sectors — agriculture, oil and gas, and petrochemicals — must be supplemented by an expanding, diversified industrial base to create needed jobs and economic activity. . . .

"(This) will depend on an ample supply of highly-qualified people. High technology is attracted to areas that have first-class technical competence and an adequate supply of educated, skilled people to take the jobs."

All this, of course, provides both a challenge and an opportunity to the state's educational structure, as well as government and industry.

THE GOVERNMENT AHEAD

Because of necessity, and because it is right, the federal government likely will be reduced in size and scope in the years ahead. Nothing dramatic is likely to occur in this direction, but the Reagan administration is embarked on a proper course to reverse the fifty-year-old trend toward turning everybody's problems over to Washington.

Many in Washington appear more than willing to turn loose of some programs which have created a fiscal monstrosity. Some such functions will be turned over to states and local governments. Some will be performed by churches and private organizations which are already active in charitable and educational fields.

In my opinion, churches and church leaders in recent decades have neglected their mission and responsibility by advocating and supporting a government takeover of functions which the church historically performed — such as help for the needy, the lonely, the depressed, and ailing people.

Had the churches and local governments fulfilled their responsibility, perhaps these duties would never have been taken over in such a wholesale manner by the federal government.

308

Public and private assistance still are needed in large quantity. The system needs balance, and there are hopeful signs of change in that direction.

So far as state government is concerned, this and other changes call for a nonpolitical study of its financial outlook, both long- and short-term.

Texas 2000 Commission projected that oil and gas revenues (from which the state in 1982 derived twenty-eight percent of its revenues) will "increase significantly through 1990." [12]

This evidently is based on anticipated continued rise in oil and natural gas prices, on which state severance taxes are based. In the late 1970s and early 1980s, production of both oil and gas in Texas declined although a leveling-off seemed in prospect.

"After 1990, these tax revenues will not increase as rapidly and may even decrease. Because the cost of government is not expected to decrease, some change in the tax structure eventually will be necessary." [13]

The Commission noted Texas is in better financial condition that most other states because of its historic dedication to fiscal responsibility and a strong natural resource tax base.

"Texas legislators must strive to hold spending to levels that will avoid painful reductions in expenditures or unconscionable tax burdens in the future." [14]

The study added that local governments may find in the future that existing property, sales, and user taxes "may not be productive enough to sustain local government throughout this century."

Education is state-local government's greatest expense and the cost will continue to rise in cost.

"It consumes fifty percent of the total state budget and is the single greatest local expense," the Commission noted.

Although finances are central to government operation and must be addressed responsibly, other improvements can be made without any great burden on the treasury.

Generally, Texas governors have given their office business-like administration, despite the fact that a governor holds relatively little power. A governor's role is largely advisory in Texas, except for the power to veto legislation, make appointments to regulatory boards and commissions, and fill other vacancies, and call special legislative sessions seeking action on specific subjects.

I favor giving the governor more budgeting and auditing authority on state expenditures, but not any general expansion of power.

Texas has enjoyed good administration in most departments, thanks partly to the wisdom of early leaders in establishing governing boards whose members serve staggered terms usually for six years. Such boards choose and direct administrators over universities, highways, state police, prisons, health and welfare, and many regulatory agencies.

The Texas system, which has its critics, prevents a new governor from dismissing these governing board members when he takes office and appointing replacements immediately from his supporters.

In four years, a governor can appoint at least two-thirds of all state boards and these can accept his advice about the agencies if they desire. Any two-term governor can make all state board appointments.

Terms might be realigned to give an incoming governor the authority to make early appointments of at least a minority of each board. In some cases now, a governor must wait two years to make any appointments to important state agencies.

I am ambivalent in the matter of whether the state of Texas has too many elected top officials.

Past suggestions to appoint rather than elect the railroad commissioners, general land commissioner, state comptroller, state treasurer, commissioner of agriculture, and even the attorney general all have failed.

Arguments can be made both ways on whether these should continue to be elected, as seems likely. Most of these top officials need to be expertise in their fields, which they often lack when taking office.

Further, there is always the temptation to use one office as a "stepping stone" to another office. In 1982, for example, the attorney general, general land commissioner, and one member of the railroad commission all sought the Democratic nomination for governor. This generally brings justifiable criticism of using the first office to gain the second.

I strongly favor changing the state Constitution so the highest judicial officers can be selected on a merit basis. Experience proves, particularly in recent years, that many voters act without any knowledge of the candidates and often choose one with a familiar name.

More than thirty years ago, after studying the "Missouri Plan" in that state, I became convinced it is the best program for choosing appellate judges as well as trial judges in metropolitan areas where the voter is least likely to know much about candidates for judicial office.

In my opinion, founders of the "Missouri Plan" understood well the shortcomings both of electing judges directly and of lifetime appointments like those in the federal courts.

One often overlooked part of the Missouri Plan is its prohibition on participation in party politics, either by the nominating commissions or the judges. They are forbidden even to attend political dinners, much less accept contributions.

In the 1982 Democratic primary, a wealthy South Texas rancher-oilman who had been involved in extensive litigation and developed a dislike for certain judicial candidates and a preference for others, contributed hundreds of thousands of dollars to judicial candidates as well as huge sums on candidates for governor and attorney general.

A candidate for the Texas Supreme Court, to whom the rancher gave $200,000, lost his race but only because the candidate's dismal previous record was prominently exposed by the media. His opponent, a respected incumbent justice, had lost an earlier race to another person of very shaky credentials. In 1982, the incumbent justice decided he must run a name-calling campaign rather than lose again for failing to advertise his opponent's shortcomings.

The necessity for such a campaign in any race, particularly for the state's highest court, is disgusting, although no criticism is intended here for the winner.

In another 1982 race, the rancher contributed $100,000 to

a Supreme Court candidate who won the Democratic nomination. Surely this is an extravagant amount to accept from any donor in a state campaign, and especially for a Supreme Court justice who may later face an ethical issue if he helps decide litigation involving the contributor or his interests.

Further evidence of the Texas system's failure was the defeat of Carl Dally, a respected and experienced judge who had been appointed to the Texas Court of Criminal Appeals. He had to run in a political election to stay on the court. Judge Dally ran fourth in a four-man field. Candidates with better-sounding names all ran ahead of him in the Democratic primary.

"I think the system is bad and I think that's what beat me," Dally commented. [14]

Dally said he once considered changing his name to "Cactus Carl Dally" to attract voter attention.

"He says he lost to better names — not famous names, just more common names that attracted the eyes of voters who didn't know much about the race," reported Ken Herman of the Associated Press.

" 'About five years ago (friends) felt they were going to have to give me a different name. So several of them came up with 'Cactus Carl Dally.' They called me that for awhile, but it didn't work and I didn't too much like it,' " Dally was quoted.

Shades of Uvalde's "Cactus Jack" John Nance Garner of a half-century earlier, elected to a lifetime of public offices including Speaker of the House and vice president of the United States.

Earlier, capable Justice W. St. John Garwood took early retirement from the Texas Supreme Court rather than face the voters again. Garwood was unquestionably an able judge, but his close call in an earlier race against a little-known Austin lawyer named Jefferson Smith convinced the jurist that Garwood wasn't a name to attract voters. Later his son, Will, lost to another "better name" judge, although Will Garwood also had performed admirably as an appointee to the Supreme Court and conducted an extensive, well-financed campaign for election. Will Garwood was burdened also by running as a Republican against a Democrat. No Republican has been elected to Texas' highest courts in this century.

Former Chief Justice Robert Calvert of the Texas Supreme Court, a convert to the Missouri Plan-merit selection idea, once attributed his original election to the fact that his last name was the same as a popular brand of whiskey which was being extensively advertised.

Once judicial positions attracted the state's ablest attorneys. When I first reported on state government, I considered the Texas Supreme Court equal in quality to any in the nation. Perhaps this may still be true, but the difficulty of getting lawyers to leave high incomes in private practice, coupled with the uncertainties of expensive statewide campaigns to hold their offices makes the courts unattractive to the many capable attorneys.

Chief Justice Joe Greenhill of the Supreme Court, a highly-esteemed jurist, noted that in 1980 candidates for the Supreme Court alone spent "the staggering sum of approximately $2,122,485." [15]

"How many of you good lawyers would be willing to quit your practice to take the judiciary as a career knowing that you'd have to raise, and accept, that kind of money, for a salary which is a lot less than most of you earn?" Greenhill asked the State Bar of Texas convention.

"Some day we will come to some form of the Missouri-Plan, or merit selection, where persons of all financial strengths, or sex, or other background, will be selected and retained in judicial positions, on the basis of their merits."

Chief Justice Greenhill told the legislature the state judiciary needs to be given the "separate but equal" status intended by the Constitution rather than receive less attention than the Executive and Legislative branches.

Greenhill said Texas courts have been neglected financially and in other ways — to overcome delays, revise districts to balance caseloads, and above all attract qualified judges to act in a nonpartisan manner.

Neighborhood courts could be established to settle disputes between merchants and consumers as well as between individuals, involving small amounts of money or property. [16]

Texas also would do well to consider a program being tried in California, where litigants in civil cases can "hire a judge" from the ranks of retired judges to hear and decide their dispute rather than wait on the frequently-slow regular process.

Retired judges in Texas can be appointed for temporary service, and supplement their pension income. This is subject to assignment by the chief justice and local district presiding judges, from retired judges who are available.

Legislators today are better educated than those serving when I first started observing them during the 1930s, but they are not necessarily better, smarter, more honest, or more capable than those of yesteryear. In both times, legislators were fairly representative of their constituencies. Formerly most came from rural areas. Today, lawmaking is influenced much more by urban representatives serving more specialized and sometimes more selfish interests.

Election as a senator or representative from a rural area is a position of considerable honor and respect, and the member is much more likely to know his constituents.

Most legislators are honest and well-meaning, within the limits of the pressures upon them. Always there have been a minority of legislators "on the take" — usually only a few. Experienced lobbyists, who do not engage in any payoffs, say bribery is a very ineffective as well as an illegal, dangerous, and dishonest method of trying to influence lawmaking.

"Anybody who will solicit or take money for his vote is quite likely the type who would sell out to both sides," an old-time lobbyist told me once.

In my experience, any lobbyist who comes to Austin with a black bag full of money to buy votes is very probably an amateur who misunderstands the lawmaking process and is likely to foredoom any chance of success in legislation if not actually be prosecuted as a criminal.

The experienced lobbyist operates in more subtle ways, through development of friendships with legislators and their staffs, as well as the media in past years.

Contributing to campaigns is a favorite way of winning friends among politicians; also taking them to lunch, on hunting trips, or other pleasures.

A recent practice which has gotten out of hand is the "office account" which could serve as a form of legal bribery. Many officeholders have such accounts, which they can use to pay for political but not personal expenses. The funds often run into thousands of dollars and are spent at the discretion of the official, who is supposed to report contributions publicly.

Several officials, however, have gotten into serious trouble over "office account" contributions. The practice needs to be stopped, or at least severely policed.

Taxpayers should be required to pay public officials comfortable salaries and reasonable expenses, including staffs. Texas legislators drawing $600 a month are underpaid, but their expense allowances are generous. I favor much higher salaries — the amount, up to $25,000-$35,000 a year, isn't important. But the restrictions on accepting financial gifts from outsiders should be severely restricted, and unspent "campaign" or "office account" funds returned to the donors or given to the state treasury.

There is little relationship, in my view, between an official's salary and his integrity. Dishonesty and "easy money" are as likely to attract a greedy rich person as a poor man. Lawmakers were paid five dollars a day while in session when I first came to Austin. The officers then were just as honest and qualified as today. An important consideration is that anyone who seeks public office primarily for the salary is improperly motivated anyway. Public service should be more than just an opportunity to make money. A holder of the public trust has a special obligation.

How well Texas fares in the years ahead depends as much on the quality of its education, richness of its minds and skills, as on its store of valuable natural resources.

More than one million Texans are employed in manufacturing. High technology industries have developed in the state during recent years, and the combination of energy, water, and other transportation, plus other elements, brought petrochemical dollars and jobs.

One danger is that education is failing to keep up with the demand for trained people.

"Low educational achievement of a high percentage of our population plagues the economy," said Stanley A. Arbingast, a professor of marketing at The University of Texas-Austin. [17]

"We have many illiterates—people who can't read or write English or Spanish or they may be illiterate in some other language. Few jobs are available in 1982 for persons who can't write a sentence or read directions."

We heard another University of Texas professor, an astronomer, describe the knowledge of science and mathematics among high school graduates reaching his classes as "deplorable."

Public schools during the 1960s and 1970s became institutions for social experimentation at the expense of basic education. The 1980s saw a welcome return by some school systems to more discipline (backed by a new law authorizing such action) and the decline of "social promotions" advancing students automatically by grades without requiring satisfactory performance.

Public education, particularly in cities, has become one of the state's and nation's critical problems. Good teachers are scarce and getting scarcer because better-paying, less stressful employment is often available to them on the outside. Fewer good students train to be teachers.

Texas and other states bordering Mexico, as well as others teaching large numbers of foreign-language students, face a special problem.

Hispanic leaders have obtained legislative authorization for bilingual education at all grades. Formerly Spanish-speaking students were taught separately in Texas only until proficient enough in English to attend classes in English. Illegal alien families are adding greatly to the number of Spanish-speaking children enrolled at public schools.

Spanish should be a compulsory subject for every English-speaking student in Texas, in my opinion, because of the state's bilingual culture, which is increasing as the proportion of Hispanics grows. But English is the official language of Texas and the United States, and it has become an international language for such purposes as air traffic controls.

316

The influx of illegal Mexicans results from the fact they will do manual labor for less money than many native Americans are willing to work. The growth of welfare programs has brought a corresponding reluctance of Americans to work for low wages, which are acceptable to many aliens seeking a better life here than they found at home.

Governor Clements favors documenting illegal workers and permitting them to continue working in the United States. Some labor leaders favor keeping illegals out of the country on the theory they depress wage scales. While that probably is true in some cases, aliens often take jobs that wouldn't be filled by others. Agriculture is an example. While much hand-work is still done in vegetable and fruit-growing, cotton farming has become almost completely mechanized since World War II, partly because labor became unavailable to work in the fields.

Texas educators and their governing boards are struggling to develop better methods of training students to become useful citizens, and able to fill the available jobs. They have a long way to go to meet the 170,000 future new jobs annually which the Texas 2000 Commission forecasts will be needed for the state's growing population.

Because government is linked closely to all we do, most of the solutions to problems in the years ahead will require political action. Without proper education, how can a voter evaluate whether nuclear energy should be developed, for example?

In this age of instant communications by satellite, space travel, and scientific marvels in every direction, it is hard for the political system to adjust. An informed democracy is our best hope for survival.

In the words of Robert Strauss of Dallas, an adviser to President Carter:

"Government is going to be with us all the days of our lives . . . We'd better make it work." [18]

[1] Texas 2000 Commission and Recommendations, March 1982
[2] *Dallas News,* Bernard L. Weinstein, January 31, 1982
[3] Texas 2000 Commission report, *Op.cit.,* page 6
[4] Bullock's Fiscal Notes, "Texas Oil: How Much Is Left?", November 1981

[5] *Ibid.*
[6] *Ibid.*
[7] Figures as of April 30, 1982, Texas General Land Office
[8] Figure as of May 18, 1982, University of Texas' Chancellor's Office.
[9] Texas 2000 Commission Report, page 21
[10] *Op.cit.,* page 25
[11] Texas 2000 Commission Report quoting a congressional study, page 29
[12] *Op.cit.,* page 33
[13] *Ibid.*
[14] *Houston Post,* May 16, 1982
[15] *Texas Bar Journal,* September 1981
[16] *Houston Chronicle,* Anne Marie Kilday, April 22, 1981
[17] Notes supplied the author by Arbingast
[18] From a commencement address to graduates of the University of Texas-Austin LBJ School of Public Affairs, May 22, 1982

INDEX

A

ADAMS, Tod R., 119
ADENAUER, Konrad, 151
AGNEW, Spiro (Ted), 220, 221, 239, 243, 244, 252
AIKIN, A. M., Jr., 75
ALBERT, Carl, 267
ALGER, Bruce, 120, 136, 147
ALLRED, James V. (Jimmy), 16, 19, 21-24, 27-30, 57, 58, 61, 136, 213, 273
  Mrs. James V., 285
ANDERSON, John B., 287
  Robert B., 88, 108
ARBINGAST, Stanley A., 316
ARMSTRONG, Anne (Mrs. Tobin), 281
  Bob, 256, 263
  Tobin, Jr., 281
ARNOLD, Victor, 297

B

BAKER, James, 274
BARNES, Ben, 181, 208, 209, 227, 229, 231, 232, 234, 237-239, 254, 255
BASKIN, Robert E., 217
BATES, Daisy, 133
BENTSEN, Lloyd M., Jr., 124, 228-231, 262, 263
BLACKMUN, Harry, 230
BLAKLEY, William A., 124, 135, 149, 150
BRISCOE, Dolph, Jr., 64, 70, 90, 91, 209, 213, 232-236, 238-240, 244, 246, 249-252, 255-263, 265, 269, 270, 272, 273, 275, 276, 281, 284
  Janey (Mrs. Dolph), 213, 233, 238, 244, 284
BRODER, David, 4, 5, 203

BROETER, Lorenz, 92
BROOKS, Jack, 234
BROWN, Edmund (Pat), 197
  Jerry, 197, 263, 265
  Paul, 92
  Reagan V., 256, 274, 275
BROWNELL, Herbert, Jr., 116, 129
BRYAN, William Jennings, 51
BULLOCK, Bob, 256, 301
BURLESON, Omar, 184
BUSH, George, 3, 157, 178, 194, 200, 230, 253, 285-288
  Mrs. George, 288

C

CAHOON, Frank, 194
CALVERT, Robert S., 107, 193
  Robert W., 79-83, 251, 313
CAMACHO, Manuel Avila, 70
CANAAN, Gershon, 171
  Mrs. Gershon, 171
CARR, Waggoner, 150, 180, 191-193, 209, 233, 237
CARROLL, Harry, 92
CARSWELL, G. Harrold, 230
CARTER, Jimmy, 3, 5, 95, 246, 249, 250, 253, 256, 259, 262-269, 272, 273, 280, 284-289, 291, 317
CASTRO, Fidel, 152
CHRISTIAN, George, 157, 173, 195
CHURCHILL, Winson, 55
CISNEROS, Henry G., 118
CLAPP, Kenneth, 251
CLARK, Edward C., 21
  Tom C., 97, 101
CLEMENTS, Rita (Mrs. William P.), 283, 284
  William Perry, Jr., 3, 41, 76, 155, 200, 213, 255, 261, 270, 273-285, 287, 297, 317
CLIBURN, Van, 170, 171

COHEN, Toby, 225
COLLINS, Hal, 48
CONDRON, R.P., 46
CONNALLY, John Bowden, 39, 82,
    153-158, 161-165, 173, 175-177,
    179-183, 188, 189, 191-195,
    199-207, 209, 211, 213, 216, 217,
    221, 227, 229-232, 242, 244, 245,
    247, 275, 280, 284, 287, 288
    Nellie (Mrs. John B.), 162, 284,
    288
    Tom, 101, 102, 104, 161, 162
COX, Jack, 155, 275
CRICHTON, Jack, 177, 180
CRONKITE, Walter, 61, 62
CURRIE, Ralph W., 95

D

DALLY, Carl, 312
DANIEL, Jean (Mrs. Price, Sr.), 284
    Price, Jr., 257, 274
    Price, Sr., 38, 78, 90, 98, 102,
    103, 105, 122-124, 127, 135,
    136, 139, 149, 153-157, 199,
    213, 273
DAVIES, Ronald N., 133
DAVIS, Cyclone, 46
    E.M., 20
    Edmund J., 276
DEAN, David, 281
DEWEY, Thomas E.,, 82-84, 98
DIBRELL, T. Kellis, 81
DIEM, Ngo Dinh, 185
DIES, Martin E., 52, 53, 124
DODD, Thomas J., 202, 203
DOLE, Robert, 266
DOUGLAS, Helen Gahagan, 99
DUGGER, Ronnie, 154
DUNAGAN, Otis T., 125, 126
DUNCAN, Dawson, 154
DUPLAN, Luis, 71

E

ECKHARDT, Robert, 287
EDGAR, J.W., 88
EDWARDS, Edwin, 265
EGAN, James, 74
    William A., 249
EGGERS, Paul W., 205, 209, 275
EISENHOWER, Dwight D., 67, 79,
    83, 85, 88, 94, 98, 101-105, 108,
    109, 116, 120, 121, 124, 129,
    133, 143, 151, 300
ERHARD, Ludwig, 169-171
ESTES, Billie Sol, 160, 179
EUBANK, Paul, 67

F

FARENTHOLD, Frances (Sissy), 238,
    239, 257
FAUBUS, Orval E., 132
FAY, Albert, 239
FERGUSON, James E. (Jim), 1, 7, 8,
    11, 15-17, 19, 21, 284
    Miriam A. (Mrs. James E.), 1, 7-
    9, 12, 15-19, 21, 22, 36, 80,
    284,
FIELDS, Jack, 287
FORD, Gerald R., 178, 252, 253,
    259, 262, 265-267, 277, 278, 285
    Jon, 277
FOREMAN, Ed, 155
FORMBY, Marshall, 153
FORTAS, Abe, 230
FRANTZ, Joe B., 134
FULBRIGHT, J. William, 223

G

GARDNER, James, 81
GARNER, John Nance (Cactus Jack),
    2, 3, 11-13, 24-26, 34, 43-46, 49,
    50, 247, 260, 312

GARWOOD, W. St. John, 158, 287, 312, 319
GERMANY, E.B., 48
GILES, Bascom, 78, 121, 221
GILLIAM, Kathlyn, 113, 114
GILMER, Claud H., 74, 88, 93, 104
GLENN, John, 263
GOLDWATER, Barry, 177-180, 192, 197
GONZALEZ, Henry B., 136
GRAMM, Phil, 4
GRANBERRY, Jim, 256
GRAVES, Curtis N., 290
GREENE, A.C., 178
GREENHILL, Joe, 136, 313
GROVER, Henry C. (Hank), 194, 239, 244, 246, 255, 275

H

HALEY, J. Evetts, 123, 124, 178
HANCE, Kent, 4
HARDING, Warren G., 256, 274
HARSCH, Joseph C., 6
HART, Weldon, 95
HAYNSWORTH, Clement F., Jr., 230
HEAP, Marguerite (see Marguerite Stevenson)
HERMAN, Ken, 312
HILL, John L., 3, 209, 237, 256, 270, 273, 275, 276, 281
HINES, Harry, 46
HOBBY, Oveta Culp, 67
    William P., Jr., 246, 256, 260
HOGG, James Stephen, 19, 73
HOLLOWAY, Harry A., 153
HOOVER, Dennis, 319
    Herbert, 9, 15, 26, 201
HORNSBY, John, 20
HOUSTON, Andrew Jackson, 52
    Sam, 52, 153, 284
HUGHES, Duncan, 68
    Maury, 21
    Sarah T., 136, 162, 164, 290

HUMPHREY, Hubert Horatio, 134, 143, 175, 178, 200, 205, 216, 217, 220-222
HUNTER, Tom F., 17, 20, 21, 24, 32
HUTCHESON, Thad, 124
HUTCHISON, Ray, 275

I

IVY, Glenn, 281

J

JACKSON, Henry, 244, 263
JAMES, Jesse, 193, 256
JAWORSKI, Leon, 252, 319
JEFFERSON, Thomas, 282
JESTER, Beauford H., 72-74, 78, 85-87, 92, 120, 213
    Mrs. Beauford H., 285
JETTON, Walter, 164
JOHNSON, Lady Bird (Mrs. Lyndon B.), 144, 164, 171, 174, 226
    Lyndon Baines, 21, 27-29, 43, 45, 52-54, 65, 79-83, 92, 101, 121, 122, 134, 140, 141, 143-145, 147-149, 151, 153, 154, 156-158, 161-175, 177-180, 182-189, 192, 193, 195-197, 199-205, 214-216, 219-221, 223-226, 231, 246, 253-255, 276
JOINER, C.M. (Dad), 13
JONES, Luther, 92
    Marvin, 21
JORDAN, Barbara, 290

K

KEETON, W. Page, 75
KEFAUVER, Estes, 103, 122, 124
KELLEY, Rogers, 92
KENNEDY, Edward M. (Ted), 220, 289

Jacqueline (Mrs. John F.), 162, 164
John F., 136, 141, 143-149, 151, 152, 154, 155, 158, 161-170, 173, 175-177, 179, 185, 216, 222, 224, 246, 253, 255, 262, 265
Robert, 204, 216
KILGORE, Joe, 179
KINCH, Sam, Sr., 92, 109
KING, Martin Luther, 214, 215
KROCK, Arthur, 149
KRUEGER, Robert, 150, 276

L

LANDON, Alf, 179
LANDRUM, Lynn, 51
LAYNE, Bobby, 205
LEWIS, John L., 13
LINCOLN, Abraham, 22
LINDSAY, John, 215
LOCKE, Eugene, 209
LOCKRIDGE, Joseph E., 290
LODGE, Henry Cabot, 147, 148, 151
LONG, Stuart, 92

Mc

McCARTHY, Eugene J., 203, 204, 216, 217, 220, 221, 267
Joe, 99
McCRAW, William, 32
McDONALD, C.C., 16, 21
J.E., 95
McGHEE, George, 171
McGOVERN, George S., 220, 221, 239, 241, 244-247, 255
McKAY, S.S., 53
McKETTA, John J., 180
McKNIGHT, C.A. (Pete), 115
McNAMARA, Robert S., 203, 204

M

MACARTHUR, Douglas, 98, 99
MACBRIDE, Roger, 267
MAHON, George, 21, 22
MALOUF, Abraham, 194
MANN, Gerald C., 20, 52, 53
MARCH, Caso, 92, 93, 95
MARSHALL, George C., 70, 96
Thurgood, 126
MARTIN, Crawford, 191, 193, 237
MASEM, Paul, 117, 118
MASSEY, Tom, 251
MEREDITH, James, 219
MILLER, William E., 177, 178
MITCHELL, Stephen A., 105
MONDALE, Walter F., 263, 266, 287, 289
MOODY, Dan, 7, 8, 58
MOREHEAD, E.J., 11
Lucian, 11
MORELAND, Patrick, 29
MORRISON, deLesseps, 118
MORROW, Wright, 85
MOYERS, Bill D., 173, 195, 204
MULLEN, Bob, 140, 141
MUNIZ, Ramsey, 239, 244, 256
MURPHY, Audie, 67
MUSKIE, Edmund S., 220, 221, 263
MUTSCHER, Gus F., 227, 236, 237

N

NALLE, Ouida, 19
NAPOLEON, 3
NEAL, Margie E., 290
NEFF, Pat M., 8
NIMITZ, Chester W., 67
NIXON, Richard M. 99, 103, 124, 143, 147, 148, 151, 175, 178, 187, 200, 216, 220-224, 229-231, 239, 241-246, 252-254, 259, 277
NOLTE, Eugene, Jr., 72

O

O'CONNOR, Sandra Day 4, 289
O'CONOR, Robert, 114
O'DANIEL, Molly (Mrs. Jack E. Wrather, Jr.), 54, 213
   Wilbert Lee (Pappy), 17, 23, 28-42, 45, 46, 48, 52-57, 62, 64, 65, 124, 136, 213, 285
   Mrs. Wilbert Lee, 285
O'DONNELL, Peter, Jr., 192
OLIVER, I.W., 165
O'NEILL, Thomas P. (Tip), Jr., 267
OSWALD, Lee Harvye, 162, 163, 175, 176, 199
OVERTON, William R., 117

P

PAINTER, T.S., 75
PARKER, Alton B., 49
PARR, George, 81, 92, 93
PEDDY, George E.B., 82
PERRY, Ervin S., 180
PERSHING, Harley, 154
POERNER, John H., 251, 275
POOL, Joe, 136, 194
PORTER, Jack, 65, 82, 83
POWELL, Adam Clayton, 202
PRICE, Bob, 194
PRYOR, Cactus, 171
PURCELL, Graham, 194

R

RAINEY, Homer Price, 72
RAMSEY, Ben, 227
RAY, C.L., 287
RAYBURN, Sam, 101, 104, 122, 134, 145, 223
REAGAN, Nancy (Mrs. Ronald), 199
   Ronald, 3-7, 49-51, 149, 156, 157, 166, 178, 185, 197-201, 216, 224, 225, 253, 259, 261-263, 265, 266, 274, 278, 280, 284-287, 289-293, 304, 308
REAMS, Sam, 92
REAVLEY, Tom, 127
REED, W.O., 20, 37
REEDY, George, 148, 173
ROCKEFELLER, Nelson A., 70, 143, 216, 253, 266
   Winthrop, 223
ROGERS, Will, 8
ROMNEY, George W., 216
ROOSEVELT, Elliott, 45, 48, 49
   Franklin D., 1-6, 7, 9, 11-13, 15, 19, 21, 22, 24-30, 34, 43-47, 49, 50, 52, 53, 55, 58, 70, 71, 83, 101, 120, 130, 151, 177, 179, 187, 225, 246, 253, 285, 291, 293
   Theodore, 49
ROSS, Nellie Tayloe, 19
ROSTOW, Walter W., 195
RUBY, Jack, 163
RUDDER, J. Earl, 121
RUSSELL, Richard, 145

S

SADLER, Jerry, 46, 127, 193
SALINGER, Pierre, 170, 171, 173
SANDERS, H. Barefoot, 114, 136, 150, 246, 255
SAVAGE, Wallace, 120
SCHOCH, E.P., 56
SCOGGINS, Chuck, 194
SCOTT, Willie, 67
SEALY, Tom, 104
SELLERS, Grover, 72
SHAPP, Milton A., 249
SHEARER, Gordon K., 62
SHEPPARD, Morris, 42, 52
SHEPPERD, John Ben, 126
SHIVERS, Allan, 85, 87, 90-95, 103, 104, 108-110, 119-124, 127, 128, 135, 150, 179, 213, 231
   Marialice (Mrs. Allan), 90, 284
SHRIVER, R. Sargent, 204, 239, 241, 244

SMALL, Clint C., 21
SMITH, Alfred, 15, 28, 262
    Jefferson, 312
    Kelly Michelle, 207
    Preston, 90, 191, 193, 205-213,
        221, 226, 227, 229, 231-234,
        236, 238, 273, 275
    Mrs. Preston, 208, 212, 285
SMOOT, Dan, 109
SPARKMAN, John, 103, 104
STEGER, William M., 147
STENHOLM, Charles, 4, 184
STERLING, Ross, 7, 80
STEVENSON, Adlai E., 79, 98, 101,
    103, 104, 121, 122, 124
    Coke R., 9, 37, 52, 54, 60-66, 69-
        71, 79, 81-83, 96, 178, 203,
        213
    Fay (Mrs Coke R. #1), 54, 55, 83,
        285
    Marguerite (Mrs. Coke R. #2), 83
    Coke R., Jr., 83
    Mrs. Coke R., Jr., 285
STILL, Rae Files, 86-88
STRAKE, George W., Jr., 281
STRAUSS, Robert, 247, 255, 259, 260,
    263, 317
SWEATT, Heman Marion , 75, 77,
    126
SYMINGTON, Stuart, 143

T
TAFT, Robert A., 103
TARRANCE, V. Lance, 281
TARWATER, A.B., 9
TAYLOR, James E., 75, 88
THOMAS, Albert, 162
THOMPSON, Clarence, 275
    Ernest O., 32, 34, 45, 68
    Kyle, 154
THORNBERRY, Homer, 80
THURMOND, J. Strom, 43, 83
TIMMONS, Bascom N., 26, 44, 49
TORREY, Paul D., 139
TOWER, John G., 147, 149, 150, 191-

195, 198, 246, 255, 276, 277,
    279, 286
TOWERY, Kenneth, 194, 195
TRAVIS, Edmunds, 64
TRUMAN, Harry S, 29, 71, 80, 83-85,
    96-98, 101, 104, 222, 223
TUNNELL, Byron, 164, 165, 181, 193

U
UDALL, Morris, 263

V
VON BRAUN, Wernher, 170

W
WAGGONER, ____, 16
WALDER, John W., 117
WALKER, Charls E., 291
    Edwin A., 131, 132, 153
WALLACE, George C., 200, 216, 220,
    222, 223, 244, 245, 259, 263
    Henry A., 34
    Mack, 275
WARREN, Earl, 111, 176
WEEKS, O. Douglas, 151
WHITE, John C., 95, 105, 193, 256
    Mark, 274
WILLKIE, Wendell, 49
WILSON, Charles E., 300
    Will, 126, 153, 231, 274
WINFIELD, H.L., 54
WITT, Edgar A., 8, 21
WOODS, L.A., 88
WOODUL, Walter F., 29
WRATHER, Jack E., Jr., 54
    Mrs. Jack E., Jr. (see Molly
        O'Daniel)
WRIGHT, Jim, 267

Y
YARBOROUGH, Don, 153, 154, 177,
    209, 233
    Ralph W., 103, 119-122, 124, 134,
    135, 150, 154, 161, 178, 179, 192,
    209, 217, 229-231, 246